Flash Application Design Solutions
The Flash Usability Handbook

Ka Wai Cheung
Craig Bryant

friendsof

DESIGNER TO DESIGNER™

an Apress® company

Flash Application Design Solutions: The Flash Usability Handbook

ISBN-13 (pbk): 978-1-59059-594-7

ISBN-10 (pbk): 1-59059-594-7

Printed and bound in the United States of America 9 8 7 6 5 4 3 2 1

Distributed to the book trade worldwide by Springer-Verlag New York, Inc., 233 Spring Street, 6th Floor, New York, NY 10013. Phone 1-800-SPRINGER, fax 201-348-4505, e-mail orders-ny@springer-sbm.com, or visit www.springeronline.com.

For information on translations, please contact Apress directly at 2560 Ninth Street, Suite 219, Berkeley, CA 94710. Phone 510-549-5930, fax 510-549-5939, e-mail info@apress.com, or visit www.apress.com.

The source code for this book is freely available to readers at www.friendsofed.com in the Downloads section.

Credits

Lead Editor
Chris Mills

Assistant Production Director
Kari Brooks-Copony

Technical Reviewer
Paul Spitzer

Production Editor
Ellie Fountain

Editorial Board
Steve Anglin, Dan Appleman, Ewan Buckingham, Gary Cornell, Jason Gilmore, Jonathan Hassell, James Huddleston, Chris Mills, Matthew Moodie, Dominic Shakeshaft, Jim Sumser, Matt Wade

Compositor
Dina Quan

Proofreader
Dan Shaw

Associate Publisher
Grace Wong

Indexer
Lucie Haskins

Project Manager
Beth Christmas

Artist
April Milne

Copy Edit Manager
Nicole LeClerc

Cover Designer
Kurt Krames

Copy Editors
Nicole LeClerc and Marilyn Smith

Manufacturing Director
Tom Debolski

CONTENTS AT A GLANCE

PART THREE: PUTTING THE PIECES TOGETHER

CONTENTS

PART TWO: THE USABILITY SOLUTIONS

CONTENTS

ABOUT THE AUTHORS

Ka Wai Cheung has been creating web applications ever since he was a child (he was still a child at 19). He currently leads the user interaction design of Gritwire (www.gritwire.com), a Flash-based RSS reader and social network for daily Internet users.

Ka Wai has written for several online publications and resource sites, including Digital Web Magazine (www.digital-web.com), ActionScript.org (www.actionscript.org), and HOW design online (www.howdesign.com). He writes about topics from web standards to usability design to software development theory, but his main passion is Flash application development. He logs his past web projects and writings on his site, Project99 (www.project99.tv).

Ka Wai majored in Math, Computer Science, and Integrated Science at Northwestern University, where he first toyed with Flash by tweening a wingding character across his 640-pixel wide screen.

When not working on the Web, Ka Wai enjoys playing guitar, eating foods from all four corners of the world, and watching his beloved Chicago sports teams occasionally win.

Craig Bryant is a full-time Flash engineer who has been advocating the use of Flash in delivering rich Internet applications to top-ranked online communications agencies around the world for the past five years. Currently, Craig is a Senior Art Director at Arc Worldwide in Chicago.

Craig's devotion to Flash has driven his creative intrigue, while providing him with a technical expertise and perspective that only a Flash developer can attain.

Like many other Flash developers, Craig's background is not strictly programming-oriented. He has a degree in musical composition from Berklee College of Music in Boston.

When he isn't racking his brain in Flash, Craig is seeking out great music, catching up on twentieth-century American fiction, or awaiting a deep-dish pizza being delivered to his doorstep.

ABOUT THE TECHNICAL REVIEWER

Paul Spitzer is a software engineer living in Berkeley, California. Paul's Flash experience began in 1998 with Flash 3, and his primary focus has been user interface engineering in Flash/ActionScript. He has also worked with a variety of other technologies, including C#/.NET, WinFX, Java, and ColdFusion, to name a few. In his current job at San Francisco–based Fluid, Inc., Paul works closely with information architects, usability experts, and visual and interactive designers to realize state-of-the-art user experiences.

ACKNOWLEDGMENTS

I have learned an unbelievable amount about Flash, book writing, and the benefits of sleep over the past several months. First, I'd like to acknowledge my bed for being there for me through thick and thin. Sorry for neglecting you for so long; you'll be seeing a lot more of me now. As far as humans go . . .

First, Craig Bryant, this book's coauthor, for working on this book while juggling an already demanding schedule, and writing a ton of code.

Chris Mills, our editor, for giving us this great opportunity to write and for his overall wisdom and sage advice throughout the entire process.

Paul Spitzer, our technical reviewer, for policing our code, coming up with innovative refactorings and wise suggestions, and teaching me a new trick or two about Flash. Not all of his great suggestions made it into the final publication, but they should find their way into the source code updates for this book at the friends of ED website.

Nicole LeClerc and Marilyn Smith, our copy editors, for making everything we wrote make sense; Beth Christmas, our project manager, for keeping the house in order and her incredible amount of patience; Dina Quan, our compositor, for laying out these book pages so wonderfully.

Adam Hoffman, my former boss and senior architect at Hubbard One, for giving me a new appreciation and understanding of object-oriented programming and usability over the past three years and who I still rely on for some much-needed expertise.

Ian Carswell, COO of Dizpersion Technologies, whose creative mind and never-say-never attitude have taken me to places in Flash I never thought existed.

Kevin Sidell, founder of Dream Marketing Communications, for literally hundreds of web projects that have allowed me to exercise my design skill set over the past seven years.

Geoff Stearns for allowing us to showcase and discuss his creation, FlashObject, in Chapter 13.

Ka Wai Cheung

ACKNOWLEDGMENTS

First and foremost, thanks to Ka Wai Cheung for doing what it takes to make this a fantastic book and not just a bunch of rowdy-looking code samples. Your dedication and drive are the reason this book exists.

Thanks to the fine folks at Apress and friends of ED for the great opportunity and the patience throughout, as well as doing a great service to the design and development community.

Gratitude to my wife, Heike, for kicking me out of bed and chaining me to my desk. OK, it wasn't that extreme, but you keep me on my toes.

Todd Levy and Matt Macqueen, thanks much for the support you've provided—"uncharted" territory is always easier to navigate with help from guys like you.

Last but not least, a giant shout out to both Macromedia and the Flash development community for the ongoing commitment to Flash and the wealth of knowledge and support they have helped disseminate to the thousands of developers out there. Without you, we'd still be trapped in a <table> somewhere.

Craig Bryant

INTRODUCTION

Have you ever noticed how complicated all the instrument panels looked in those futuristic movies and TV shows from years past? The fact that Captain Kirk could operate the myriad buttons, lights, and widgets on the Starship Enterprise was a feat in itself. Sure, the producers of *Star Trek* probably weren't thinking a great deal about how usable the instruments should appear on-screen. Instead, they created a depiction of what this monster we call technology must look like in the future: a mess of complicated processes understandable only to a select, brilliant few. See Figure 1 for another example.

Figure 1. The classic 1980s TV series *Knight Rider* featured a talking car named Kitt that could think on its own. But how would you operate a car with a dashboard as confusing as Kitt's?

Unfortunately, it's not just at the movies or from prime-time TV where we get the impression that technology is difficult to use. From radio clocks, to stovetops (see Figure 2), to computers, to the Internet, you'll find plenty of examples of poorly designed interfaces masking otherwise great engineering. Take a multi-disc DVD player, hook it up to a TV with multiple video ports, and try to navigate through to the favorite scene of your movie with an all-in-one TV/DVD/VCR remote. If you can get through it all without a few mental stumbles along the way, and without the aid of the instruction booklet, maybe you can help the rest of us!

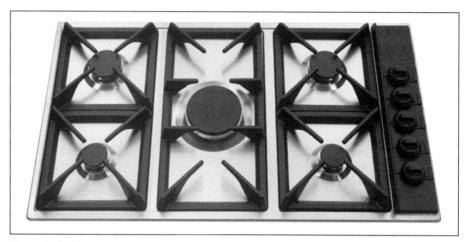

Figure 2. The classic stovetop usability problem: which knobs turn on which burners?

Over the past decade, we've encountered the same kinds of frustrations with the Internet. Superfluous Flash intros, slowly loading sites, obtrusive JavaScript alert boxes, complex navigation, excessively long pages, broken links, unexpected pop-up ads, and unintuitive forms are just a few of the usability problems we've seen in the brief history of the Web. As web designers and developers (if you're reading this book, you more than likely fall somewhere within or near this category), we know that technology works best when we can interact with it like it's our best friend rather than our worst enemy. In general, we've coined this concept under the term *usability*. But what exactly does usability mean? Is it something more than just a sophisticated term for easy to use?

Defining Flash usability

Because this is a book on developing usable web applications with Flash, we're going to define usability as follows:

> *Usability measures how intuitive, efficient, and pleasurable the experience of using a Flash application is, as well as how effective the application is in achieving a user's end goals.*

Let's take a closer look at what this means:

- **Usability should be intuitive.** The more obvious you can make the features of your web application, the better. Users should be thinking less about how to *use* your application and concentrating more on how to *benefit* from your application. The most intuitive interface is one that the user isn't even aware of—an "invisible interface." The interface is so fluid that the user and the application become one.

- **Usability should be efficient.** The user should be able to get from point A to point B as efficiently as possible. Every interaction you have with your software should be directed toward the goal you are trying to achieve. As developers, we need to hide all of the processes that occur behind the scenes as much as possible. Users should be presented with only what they need to know, not everything that is actually occurring at a particular moment.

- **Usability should be pleasurable.** The design of your application should be pleasing and engaging. This means understanding good design principles, as well as knowing how to handle user input in an elegant way.

- **Usability must be effective in achieving a user's end goals.** In the end, if your application is intuitive, efficient, and pleasurable, but doesn't get the user to complete the task at hand, you've failed. While keeping in mind the three previous points, ultimately, you need to make sure that the darned thing actually does submit a customer order, print a patient's medical records, or whatever it was originally designed to do!

So, is that it? Well, yes and no. For the purposes of our book, we wanted to keep the discussion of usability *itself* as concise as possible. Instead, we're going to devote the majority of our pages (Part Two) to showing you how we solve specific usability problems with Flash. Think of this book as an analysis of usability case studies, rather than an A-to-Z primer on usability. After digging into these pages, you should feel comfortable with how to solve specific usability issues and how to approach new ones down the road. In Part Three, we'll focus on how to plan for usability in the design process and present a final application that integrates all the solutions.

At the same time, we don't want to dismiss the more theoretical study of usability. A host of great books, websites, and people are dedicated to this ever-evolving subject and many equally important related topics, such as user research, goal-oriented design, and task analysis. We've provided an appendix to this book to point you to other resources if you'd like to dig further into usability theory.

Building for usability

Usability engineering is not just about good interface design. While the visual appeal of a web application is important, the underlying structure and programming can equally contribute to "good usability." Usability doesn't just begin and end with the user. A usable website that's built poorly won't survive the kinds of revisions and feature additions that are inherent to all living web applications. It's akin to a magnificent-looking house that's being eaten through by termites. Eventually, it will fall apart and have to be redone. This is the part that is left out of most books about usability.

In the solutions presented in this book, we won't just talk about creating Flash applications with user-friendly design. We'll also introduce different techniques for designing your code, letting you better integrate the discussed solutions into your own Flash projects. After all, the easier it is to make your applications more usable, the more likely you'll strive to achieve it!

Who is this book for?

We hope you've gotten the idea that this is not your prototypical usability book. As we mentioned, we're not going to dig that deeply into theory. Likewise, this book isn't your usual "how-to" Flash book. We're not going to start from the ground up. We will lay out each usability solution in detail, but assume you already have a good familiarity with Flash. These solutions are geared toward Flash developers who are comfortable with the Flash development environment. You should know what buttons and movie clips are, and the differences between, say, frame-based actions and object-based actions.

To get the most out of this book, you should have a basic knowledge of ActionScript 2.0 (AS2) and a solid understanding of object-oriented programming (OOP). The solutions in this book will rely heavily on using AS2 classes, and we will look at some key concepts in OOP to implement these solutions. If you are relatively new to Flash or aren't familiar with AS2, that's still OK! There will be plenty of take-aways from each chapter that don't necessarily have to do with the development process. We recommend that you read this book alongside any good AS2 programming book (see this book's appendix). Rather than wrapping them up into rigid components, we've made our solutions fully exposed to you and available for download in their entirety from this book's page at www.friendsofed.com (just search for this book in the menu on the front page, and then go from there). We want you to be able to take what we've done and enhance it in your own projects!

This book is the ultimate synthesis of a usability discussion and programming guide. We'll talk about how Flash can best enhance the usability of your applications. We'll also give you our perspective on the best way to develop these solutions, from designing the interface all the way down to how to structure your ActionScript code.

So, while this book is geared toward more experienced Flashers who are well acquainted with AS2, these solutions offer something for Flash developers at any level looking to improve the usability of their projects.

A note about our approach

Before we get started, we'd like to stress one very important point to you. As anyone who has developed applications in a programming language knows, programming is an iterative process. There are always multiple ways of approaching a solution to a problem. The solutions in this book are no different.

None of the coding solutions in this book should be taken "as is." We highly encourage you to download our source code; examine our examples; and find ways to improve on them to make them more scalable, reusable, and maintainable. In fact, we're fully aware there are more optimal implementations of the solutions we've provided in this book. However, in some cases, we've held back from a "better" approach to a problem because we introduce a concept inherent to the better approach in a later chapter. In other instances, we've held back in order to simplify the method for discussion purposes. Our goal is that, after reading the book, you'll be equipped with a few different kinds of strategies you can take in ActionScript programming as it relates to usability.

Be sure to check the page for this book on the friends of ED website (www.friendsofed.com)—we will post revisions of our code examples as we (or maybe you) find ways of improving them!

PART ONE **INTRODUCING FLASH USABILITY**

1 FLASH: THEN, NOW, LATER

Foundation Flash 8
Foundation MX Express
Foundation MX Studio
Foundation MX Upgrade Essentials
Foundation MX Video
Foundation XML for Flash
New Masters of Flash
The Flash Usability Guide

Flash Books

Timeline   Scene 1

- 📄 title
- 📄 info text field
- 📄 range text fields
- 📄 drag handle clips
- 📄 slider range bar

Address 1*

Address 2

City*

State   AL ▾

Zip Code*

Work Phone*

To get a better understanding of where Macromedia Flash stands today, it's important to look at its beginnings. Only after examining why many Flash-based web applications suffered from poor usability design in the past can we apply the lessons learned from those mistakes. It's up to us, the designers and developers, to figure out how to get around these issues and use the powerful flexibility of Flash to aid—rather than obstruct—our users.

In this chapter, we explore Flash's history and lay out some of the advantages it has over traditional web media. We then discuss the role it should play in the web community as a truly powerful tool for usability. We'll accomplish this by covering the following topics:

- The brief, turbulent history of Flash
- How the Flash environment changed with MX 2004 and ActionScript 2.0
- Flash's advantages (and disadvantages) compared to HTML with Flash
- Flash versus Ajax, a competing technology
- Breaking the Flash usability stigma
- The increasing importance of usability on the Web

The brief, turbulent history of Flash

Today, Macromedia Flash is a robust piece of software, with its own application framework and object-oriented programming (OOP) language. With Flash's remoting and XML parsing capabilities, creating truly dynamic, sophisticated software in Flash is a reality. But it wasn't always this way.

When it began as FutureSplash Animator, Flash was just an animation tool with modest drawing capabilities. When Macromedia bought FutureSplash in 1996 and built upon its authoring tool and plug-in, the web design revolution broke loose in both good and bad ways.

Many interactive designers began exploiting the early versions of Flash, creating magnificent, dynamic websites that juxtaposed the otherwise mundane landscape of the Web. Beauty and aesthetics can take you only so far, though. Companies in the mid-to-late 1990s clamored for their own lengthy Flash intros until they started realizing that users were turning away from all this glitz and glamour. For users, the initial excitement of seeing a new kind of technology hit the Web quickly dissipated. Long intro animations, fancy page transitions, and complex navigation metaphors kept users from seeking the basic information they wanted from their web experience. The added showiness of web design meant users had to wait longer, search harder, and become more vigilant. As soon as how things *looked* became more important than how things *worked*, many users' patience began to wear thin.

Flash has since become synonymous with "flashy, engaging sites" that lack true usability. However, it's an unfair assumption, as it has little to do with what kinds of applications Flash's tools can produce and everything to do with how Flash developers decided to use

1

these tools. When Macromedia hired Jakob Nielsen (one of the world's most well-known web usability experts), it became clear that the company wanted Flash to garner the same attention for building usable web applications as it had for merely creating fancy interfaces.

Shortly thereafter, Flash software noticeably became more like HTML. As you probably know, Flash text fields can render basic HTML tags like <b>, <i>, <img>, <a>, and others. With the release of Flash MX, a set of form components appeared on the scene that mimics the behavior of many traditional HTML form widgets (e.g., select boxes, text areas, and radio buttons). It seems as if the Flash development team figured that in order to compete with the mainstream popularity of HTML, they had to produce components that look and feel like HTML with the special enhancements that Flash can offer.

> *A complete list of supported HTML tags in Flash can be found at* http://livedocs.macromedia.com/flash/mx2004/main_7_2/ wwhelp/wwhimpl/common/html/wwhelp.htm?context= Flash_MX_2004&file=00001040.html.

While the team had the right idea, we'd like to stress that just because Flash can "act" like HTML, that doesn't mean it has to. Flash offers an out-of-the-box select component, but we shouldn't immediately resort to using it any time we want users to select from a group of items. There may be more intuitive, pleasurable, and ultimately usable ways of solving this problem, as you'll see in our Chapter 6 example.

Flash MX 2004 and the release of ActionScript 2.0

Our perception of Flash has evolved from its early days as strictly a design tool that can create amazing visual effects, to an all-purpose web-authoring tool equally capable of building sophisticated software and crafting stunning visuals. Flash is now synonymous with the development of rich Internet applications (RIAs; more on this a bit later in the chapter), and since the release of Flash MX 2004, Flash developers have been introduced to a new underlying programming language: **ActionScript 2.0** (**AS2** for short).

Sure, by Flash 5, many of the interactive capabilities of the software that we use today were already at our disposal. Many beautifully done pieces of Flash on the Web date back a few years. Even a few versions ago, we had about the same control over Flash's built-in objects as we do now. However, the transition from ActionScript to AS2 (and specifically, the transition to a full-fledged OOP language) was what vaulted Flash into a platform that could compete with—and outperform—traditional HTML-based applications, both from an interface and functional design perspective (as described in the upcoming section, "The advantages (and disadvantages) of Flash over HTML").

New features introduced by ActionScript 2.0

AS2 lets you script code outside of the Flash environment in ActionScript files (text files marked with the .as extension). Though you could do this in ActionScript 1.0 by placing code into external files using the #include compiler directive, with AS2, you also have the ability to build code with some fundamental object-oriented techniques such as the following:

- Object-oriented architectural structures such as packages and classes
- Object typing
- Class protection (public and private keywords)
- Object-oriented constructs such as interfaces and inheritance

The inclusion of these new features allows you to reuse behavior, maintain your code more easily, and scale up functionality far more rapidly than before. These new features also help assist other developers understand the intent of your code.

Usability benefits of ActionScript 2.0

As the saying goes, there's more than one way to skin a cat. In programming, you have many ways to produce the same end-user functionality. AS2 offers you far more elegant ways of developing your code to achieve the same result than ever before. In addition, it eliminates the old, hard-to-manage techniques that Flash developers employed in the past, like creating movie clips offstage as storage depots for ActionScript code, or using timeline frames to manage states.

Because of these new advantages, you can now start thinking about developing usability solutions that you can easily adapt to new applications. The more modular you make your code, the less time you'll have to spend in the future building out the same kinds of functionality over and over again! Instead, you can spend more time tweaking the behavior or design to accomplish your usability goals. This book will provide a basic open code base for you to use, modify, and enhance in your Flash usability development endeavors.

The advantages (and disadvantages) of Flash over HTML

You should know that we don't mean to condone Flash as the be-all, end-all platform for every usable web application. Every kind of web project brings with it a new set of questions regarding how it's best delivered to an audience. Sometimes, Flash isn't the answer. There are times when a combination of Flash and traditional HTML/CSS/JavaScript provides the optimal solution. There are other times when Flash may not be part of the answer at all.

For example, pure Flash may not be the best route if your audience is primarily using older browser versions or lower-bandwidth connections. The good news is that the penetration of Flash Player is tremendous. Recent statistics have shown that almost 98 percent of Internet-enabled desktops have a version of Flash Player installed.[1] This level of market penetration is greater than that of many other commonly used programs such as Adobe Acrobat Reader, Java, and Windows Media Player. Also, as computer users continue to migrate toward high-speed Internet connections, bandwidth issues will become less and less significant over time.

Flash also may not be the best medium if your web application needs to be scannable to search engines. If your site's content must be easily found by search engines, you may want to think about using traditional HTML programming for your site (or, perhaps, providing an HTML version of a Flash site that can then redirect itself to the Flash version).

Of course, this is a book advocating Flash usability, so we should point out that a great many traditional Flash usability issues can be resolved with a little creativity. For instance, we'll show you how to enable your browser's Back button for Flash sites (in Chapter 12), as well as how to create effective full-browser-width liquid layouts in Flash (in Chapter 13).

Ultimately, we would like to convince you that there are certain inherent advantages Flash brings to the table over traditional HTML design, regardless of the kind of project you're working on. As we discuss in this section, these advantages include Flash's flexibility, its excellent cross-browser and cross-platform compliance, its asynchronous processing and state management capabilities, and its various design features that help developers achieve elegant visual effects. Moreover, with each version of Flash that appears on the scene, the advantages of HTML diminish even further.

Flexibility

Of course, you know about Flash's flexibility by now. Flash has always been the delinquent, trouble-seeking child of the web development family, unbound from the web constraints imposed on HTML. But while Flash's almost boundless design flexibility can allow for annoyingly long-loading intros, obtrusive ad blasters, and confusing site layout, it can also enable us to build tools and widgets in more beautiful and elegant ways than traditional HTML programmers could ever hope for.

In HTML, there's really only a finite set of tools at your disposal. If you want to build in any sort of interactivity, you typically create a <form /> block with form elements that we've all used repeatedly by now: text fields, radio buttons, drop-down lists, and check boxes. Any kind of usability design we create with HTML interactivity usually translates to decorating these form elements, but how you interact with them remains largely the same.

In Flash, you're presented with a blank canvas. Want to build an online store? You don't necessarily need to have drop-downs to select the quantities of an item you want. Instead, you can decide that a slide meter will do a more efficient job. Or, you might allow a user to drag and drop items into a basket area in your store. These choices, along with the drop-down design, are all possible options in Flash, while not all are necessarily feasible in HTML.

---

[1] See www.macromedia.com/software/flash/survey.

This isn't to say that you can't build some pretty clever and beautiful applications in HTML. In fact, you could probably build an on-the-fly calculator using JavaScript events and something similar to a slide meter using HTML and JavaScript or a third-party source. However, such an element isn't going to be nearly as easy and reusable as it would be if you built it in Flash. Flash is simply a better tool for building innovative solutions that aren't going to be bound to the traditional constructs HTML brings with it.

Cross-browser and cross-platform compliance

Design once and you're done! Flash has the distinct advantage of not having to rely on how a browser interprets its code to render. HTML and CSS are certainly making progress in developing a series of web standards that most browsers are adopting, but there are still many years of work ahead before all major browsers fully adhere to strict XHTML/CSS standards.

From a development perspective, browser dependence can wreak havoc on your design goals and timelines. You have to consider not only what your target browsers are, but also how your application should look and feel on browsers that don't fully support your code. Also, it forces you to waste time considering whether a particular bug is really a bug on your end or an incorrect interpretation of your code on the browser's end. If you've had experience with browser compatibility issues, you're probably familiar with **code forking**, or building multiple sets of code to achieve the same desired functionality and appearance on different browsers.

With Flash, you have the luxury of knowing that the resulting application will function and look just about the same on all browsers and operating platforms, as long as users have the latest Flash plug-in installed. In this way, Flash is a lifesaver when it comes to having to comply with users' many different browser types and versions.

Asynchronous processing and state management

HTML applications are typically synchronous processes. When you fill out an HTML form, it's only when you click the Submit button that all your information is sent. Moreover, while the form submits, there's little else you can do but twiddle your thumbs and wait for the screen to refresh. When you want to complete a task in an HTML application, you're generally led through a linear workflow process that adheres to whatever the underlying data model is. As users, we spend a significant portion of time *waiting* for things to happen—time that could be better spent doing other things.

AS2 has the unique ability to manage the state of the application on the client. This allows you even greater flexibility when it comes to creating seamless Flash applications. While JavaScript can be used to manage an application's state to some degree, it's certainly not a common practice. It's far more efficient to handle application state on the server side, and code maintainability becomes a bigger issue the more you intertwine JavaScript with HTML.

Flash offers a far more robust set of tools that allow for asynchronous activity. If you ask Flash to, say, give you information on three new products in a store's inventory, Flash can spit back the information as the items are processed. In HTML, your options are to either wait for all three processes to return or ask for one piece of information at a time.

Things are rapidly changing, however. The benefits of asynchronous processing in Flash are now being ported over to the HTML world. For example, you may be familiar with emerging web technologies such as Asynchronous JavaScript and XML (Ajax), which can produce rich, seamless web applications similar to those created in Flash. (We'll talk more about Ajax shortly.)

Robust design capabilities

By now, we've all become accustomed to the typical effects interlaced within most mainstream Flash applications. We can make objects fade out and fade in. We can make items grow, shrink, bounce, speed up, slow down, drag, hover, stick, slide—you get the idea.

Just as you can use effects to create captivating visual presentations in Flash, you can also use them to enhance the user-friendliness of your applications. Good usability design is often a matter of deciding when these effects are appropriate and how best to create them. Subtle, elegant visual changes to a button rollover can be pleasing to the eye. The way in which a text window responds as you scroll through it can be made to look jerky, or smooth and forgiving. With Flash, you have a laundry list of available effects that you can implement to provide that extra "wow" factor and seamless design when a user interacts with your applications.

Flash can achieve these elegant effects better than HTML-based technologies because, first and foremost, Flash is a design and animation tool. It's very easy to increase frame rates to give Flash movies a smoother look and feel. It's also easy to change the way objects move or transition from one visual state to another in ActionScript because Flash objects inherently contain those properties.

There isn't a really good parallel to Flash design in the HTML world. A combination of HTML, JavaScript, and CSS can partially get us there. But these languages aren't suited for creating elegant tweening techniques. We can create some elegant visual designs with CSS, but concepts like tweening and animation aren't a native component to these languages.

Flash 8 now comes with an even more robust framework to enhance the visual appeal of your projects. Here are just a few key improvements:

- Bitmap filters let you add effects to your objects that once were achievable only by importing images created in a graphics program like Adobe Photoshop. Filters like drop shadows, glows, blurs, and bevels are available at the click of a button!

- Text rendering capabilities far superior to those in any previous release of Flash. Flash 8 provides customizations for anti-aliased text so that it appears much sharper and is optimized for animation and readability.

- The Custom Easing feature, which makes it much simpler to tween objects in Flash in more complex mathematical ways than ever before. You can adjust tweens with a graphical interface rather than relying on complex math calculations.

Flash vs. Ajax

As previously mentioned, new Internet technologies have emerged recently that compete with Flash on the points we've just described. Many web applications these days (Google Maps, Google Suggest, and Flickr, to name a few) are employing one of these new technologies, Ajax, to give them a seamless, rich, software-like feel.

Ajax is not a new language, but a name given to a programming technique that combines DHTML, JavaScript, XML, CSS, and other web languages. Its main distinction from traditional HTML is its capability to make server requests without having to reload the page it sits on. Ajax applications have a rich look and responsiveness somewhat similar to Flash-based web applications.

Does the emergence of new technologies such as Ajax signal the end of Flash? Quite the contrary. If anything, they give us more evidence that rich web applications are here to stay. Ajax may be competing for its share of the Web with Flash, but there are still many advantages to using Flash. For example, from a features perspective, Flash can integrate audio and video content directly into its plug-in. It also has far more robust sets of out-of-the-box user interface components than Ajax does (after all, Ajax is still working off the HTML Document Object Model).

Remember as well that Ajax is a combination of different web languages. From a development perspective, building an Ajax component takes a bit of HTML, JavaScript, and CSS, which means you can again run into browser compatibility issues. Also, Ajax uses the XMLHttpRequest object to do its asynchronous "magic," and is thus at the mercy of browsers' willingness to support this object in the future. The *advancement* of Ajax application development is very much dependent on how future browsers support all the new enhancements offered among these different languages.

By contrast, in Flash you need only concern yourself with one language, ActionScript, which is fully supported by its very own plug-in, Flash Player. And, in terms of development, you can more neatly reuse your AS2 code if you build it properly in external files. With the Ajax method, you're left with the need to write spaghetti code, intermingling JavaScript calls inside of HTML tags that may, in turn, reference CSS class names.

So, consider the explosion of Ajax as a good thing for Flash. It's further proof that Flash-like applications are worthwhile and becoming increasingly mainstream. By exploiting the advantages of Flash over Ajax, you can make powerful, usable tools that will have staying power on the Web.

Breaking the Flash usability stigma

Web usability has carried with it a stigma of being, well, downright boring. Peruse various blogs and online articles and you'll notice a distinct line drawn between those who condone and those who condemn the "usability guru." Much of this ambivalence among those in the web community comes from the generally conservative attitude that many of the foremost usability experts have projected.

There seems to be a constant push and pull between usability experts, who want to maintain certain arcane web conventions (keeping, say, text links in their traditional blue color), and web designers, who want to break the boundaries of interface design. In the end, for usability to be both innovative and truly "usable," we need to find common ground between the two extreme factions of the usability issue. Sure, usability can and should follow a set of basic design principles. But it also must embrace those of us trying to invent innovative, *better* ways of allowing users to interact with the web applications we build. Take the following two statements, for example:

- Text links should be easy to see and appear as though users should click them.
- Text links should be blue and underlined.

The first statement refers to how users should perceive a text link. The second refers to what a text link should look like. As a general rule, we should create and follow principles like the first. Rather than describe the solution, we should instead identify how users will interact with a successful solution. In this way, we aren't forcing an exact design standard, but a desired result. We can then begin thinking innovatively about solving usability problems, rather than always following some standard, set-in-stone design convention. Ultimately, it's the users who need to benefit the most from usability, and they will benefit the most if they understand both what the existing conventions are and where we can improve upon them.

For the solutions we discuss in this book, we'll give you our opinions on what optimal Flash solution best resolves a usability issue. We'd like to stress that these are *opinions*. You may have a taste that differs from ours, and that's OK. The beauty of it is, you should be able to take the foundations we present in this book and adjust their behaviors in ways that will best fit your own projects. Better yet, you'll be compelled to come up with completely new ways of solving the same problems!

Why Flash usability is important

The need for more usable Flash applications is arguably more important now than at any previous point in the brief history of the Web. As much as usability has developed a stigma for being too convention oriented, there certainly are some good reasons for it. With billions of web pages floating around the Internet today, it's nice to standardize a web user's experience as much as possible. It's indeed helpful that nearly all websites follow some basic layout conventions (e.g., navigation area, stylized links, etc.). On an interactive level, it's also beneficial that the widgets we interact with all behave similarly from one site to another. Yet, as we mentioned, the tools available in the non-Flash world are fairly limiting. The kinds of tasks we can accomplish on the Web require more intuitive interfaces. Flash is the perfect medium to start enhancing usability.

Let's take a look at the current trends in web development and where this is all headed to get a sense of the increasing importance of Flash usability.

Current trends in web development

The functionality of the Web is getting ever more complex. At the time of this writing, it has been ten years since Yahoo was incorporated. Back then, the idea of having a directory that categorized some of the more popular sites on the Web was novel and innovative. Fast-forward to a decade later, and now we're buying airline tickets, doing our taxes, and making love connections online. The stakes for usability are far higher now than they were in the mid-1990s. Yet, sadly, the tools at our disposal aren't evolving at the same rate as the functional complexity of these applications.

Also, as the complexity of what we do on the Web grows, certain things are becoming more ubiquitous. The distribution of content, media, and underlying technical processes is getting easier and faster every day. Take, for instance, the growing popularity of RSS and blogs. Suddenly, we're seeing a trend toward content aggregation and consolidation of information. Rather than having to go to ten sites to read about topics we're interested in, we can download an RSS aggregator to bring the content to us in a central place.

These factors lead to yet another trend we're seeing in web development: the push toward **rich Internet applications (RIAs)**. RIAs aren't just another vague marketing catchphrase. They're applications on the Web with the look and feel of typical desktop software. Unlike the abrupt start/stop feel of a normal HTML application, RIAs are seamless and almost instantly responsive.

Figures 1-1 and 1-2 show examples of some RIAs built in Flash. Figure 1-1 shows an RSS reader that aggregates and categorizes multiple content sites into one sleek interface; Figure 1-2 shows an example of a shopping cart. (Note that the online store in Figure 1-2 uses drag-and-drop functionality to put items into the shopping cart, which results in a much more natural feel than having to select a quantity from a drop-down list and click Submit each time you want to add an item to your cart.)

Figure 1-1. A Flash-based RSS reader

Figure 1-2. The shopping cart in Macromedia's sample online store

Future developments

With the growth in popularity of podcasting and photo blogging, we're starting to see other types of media aggregate in much the same way as traditional RSS. The Web very well could evolve from a vast expanse of information that may overwhelm beginners to a few central applications that excel in giving users the kind of information they want, when they want it.

In the near future, we may not be surfing the billions of available web pages that inherently needed the constraining web conventions we see today. Instead, we might use a handful of web applications that will get us what we want in a faster, easier, more intuitive way. Developing these applications with the nearly boundless design flexibility of Flash will enable the usability on the Internet to catch up with functionality. While there may be a few learning curves for users early on, the benefits in the long run will far outweigh whatever growing pains (if any) occur in the beginning.

And as we've mentioned, the growing popularity of Ajax (as well as Flash) just goes to show that building rich applications on the Web is the next phase of web development. In order to really let users profit from the amazing innovations in web technology, we must start using Flash in ways that make accomplishing all these tasks better, simpler, and faster. It all starts with building for good usability.

Summary

In this chapter, we provided an overview of Flash's history and where it stands currently in the web development world. We also identified some trends in web development and how they relate to usability concerns. So, now that you have a good idea about the direction we think the Web is heading, it's time to roll up your sleeves and start building usable application features!

In the next chapter, you'll ensure your environment is set up properly before you start to dig into the usability solutions featured in the next part of the book.

2 SETTING UP YOUR FLASH ENVIRONMENT

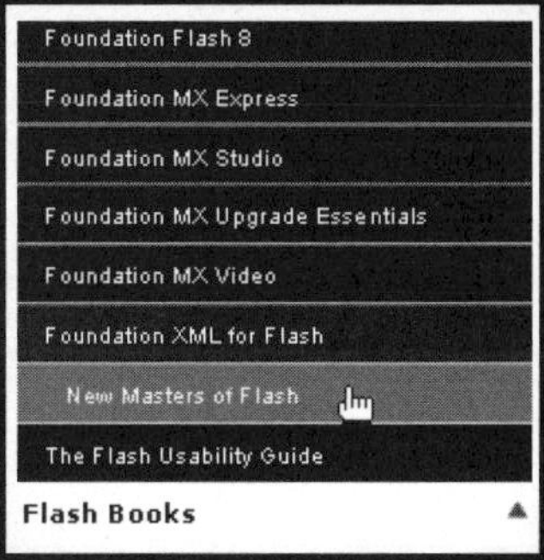

Foundation Flash 8

Foundation MX Express

Foundation MX Studio

Foundation MX Upgrade Essentials

Foundation MX Video

Foundation XML for Flash

New Masters of Flash

The Flash Usability Guide

Flash Books

Timeline   Scene 1

title

info text field

range text fields

drag handle clips

slider range bar

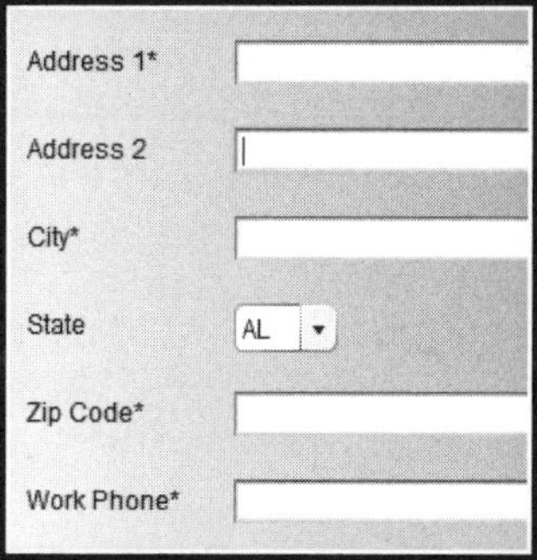

Address 1*

Address 2

City*

State   AL

Zip Code*

Work Phone*

Because the Flash environment is such a flexible development platform, you can structure your Flash projects in several ways. Ultimately, the way you organize your Flash projects is a matter of personal style. The real key to maintaining your current and future Flash projects successfully is *consistency*.

Before we dig into our solutions, we want to briefly explain how we've set up our code and directory structures for all the solutions in this book. It's important that you read this section first if you're planning to follow along with creating the projects and examples in the chapters that follow. Here's what we'll cover in this chapter:

- How to set up the source directory structure
- How to create a classpath
- How to apply a Flash library structure

All the solutions presented here are downloadable from the friends of ED website at www.friendsofed.com. You'll find each of our chapter solutions in ZIP files named according to the convention `ChapterX_Final.zip`, where the X stands for the chapter number associated with the solution. When you download each ZIP file, all you need to do is extract the files contained within the ZIP into a directory on your hard drive. The files should automatically be placed in the source directory structure we've set up while developing these solutions.

Setting up the source directory structure

We've organized our source code and assets in a similar way for each chapter. First, all the source files are placed in a `/source` directory. Within the `/source` directory are up to four subdirectories, as shown in Table 2-1.

Table 2-1. Source subdirectories

Subdirectory	Description
/classes	Contains all the ActionScript files associated to a particular solution
/fla	Contains the FLA files associated to the solution
/swf	Contains the final compiled SWF files and, in some cases, associated HTML files
/images	Contains bitmaps that are particular to the solution, if any are needed

For each solution, we'll place all of our ActionScript files into the /source/classes folder without any further subdirectory structure underneath. This is due to the fact that each solutions chapter covers a fairly specific usability topic, and sub-categorizing the classes for these solutions is unnecessary. For more complex solutions, we suggest compartmentalizing your code into specific subdirectories (called **packages** in the object-oriented programming world). In Part Three, when we build our final usability solution, we'll use packages and explain the hows and whys then!

> *While we usually won't have any directory structure beyond the subdirectories just mentioned, when you build complete web solutions in Flash, you'll want to be a bit stricter about your directory structure. In Part 3 we discuss this in greater depth.*

Creating a classpath

All the ActionScript files in our solutions chapters lie in the /classes directory. If you're already familiar with the AS2 scripting environment, you're probably also familiar with setting up a classpath for a Flash movie. In a nutshell, a **classpath** is a list of directories on your hard drive that help the Flash compiler know where to look for classes you're referencing in code (be it in your Flash movie or in another ActionScript file).

By default, the root directory that your FLA file resides in is part of the classpath. Therefore, if you save an ActionScript file named MyClass.as in the same directory as your FLA file, you can reference it simply by MyClass in your code. If you've created a directory structure inside of your root folder called /com/util and placed your MyClass.as file in there, you can reference it by com.util.MyClass. The com.util portion of this reference call is commonly referred to as the **class package**.

In our solutions examples, because we've placed all classes inside the /source/classes directory and we've placed all of our FLA files inside the /source/fla directory, we can directly reference classes living in the /classes directory from the FLA by adding ../classes to the classpath. The compiler will then know to look under the /source/classes path to find class files that we reference in code.

To create the classpath, go to Edit ➤ Preferences. From the Preferences window, click the ActionScript tab, and then click ActionScript 2.0 Settings. The ActionScript Settings window will pop up, where you can add default classpaths to your Flash movie (see Figure 2-1). Click the + button and add ../classes as a new classpath.

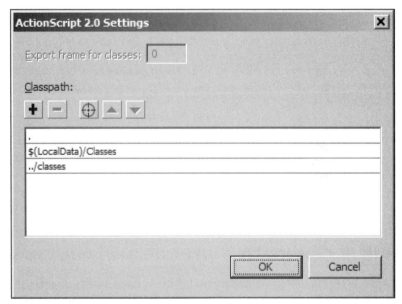

Figure 2-1. The ActionScript settings default classpath setup with ../classes added

Our solutions assume that you've added ../classes as part of the classpath for each FLA you're working on. If you get errors from the compilation that external ActionScript classes can't be found, check that you've added the classpath correctly.

Applying a Flash library structure

Just as we have a pretty basic structuring system for our source files, we also have a fairly simple directory structure for all the symbols contained within a Flash file's library. In general, the libraries for the solutions in this book have three folders: Buttons, Graphics, and MovieClips. This structure works well for small Flash projects where there aren't more than a few dozen assets that we'll be working with. For more robust projects, this may not work as well. Too many objects inside of a library folder can become difficult to manage.

For more complex solutions, we may group buttons, graphics, and movie clip folders into a parent folder to distinguish between distinct parts of a Flash movie. As an example, we create two parent folders called Selection System and Scrolling List in Chapter 4, each with the requisite Buttons, Graphics, and MovieClips folders located inside them.

Summary

That's about all there is to know about how we've tailored the Flash environment for our solutions examples. Of course, there may be specific configuration issues within each chapter example that you'll need to know about, and we'll address those as they arise. Now that you're armed with a general knowledge of how to structure your Flash environment for these solutions, let's start the adventure!

In Part 2, we'll discuss 11 different usability topics that we encounter in most every web application in use today. We'll talk about what potential red flags might be raised and explain how a given concept has been traditionally implemented in HTML. Then, we'll discuss and design a Flash implementation with an eye toward usability.

PART TWO **THE USABILITY SOLUTIONS**

3 A BASIC SELECTION SYSTEM

| Foundation Flash 8 |
| Foundation MX Express |
| Foundation MX Studio |
| Foundation MX Upgrade Essentials |
| Foundation MX Video |
| Foundation XML for Flash |
| New Masters of Flash |
| The Flash Usability Guide |
| **Flash Books** |

Timeline	⇦	🎬 Scene 1
🎬 title
🎬 info text field
🎬 range text fields
🎬 drag handle clips
🎬 slider range bar

Address 1*	
Address 2		
City*	
State	AL ▾
Zip Code*	
Work Phone*	

What would you consider to be the most fundamental building block of all web applications? Arguably, it is the **selection system**, by which we mean any set of similar items from which a user must choose. You can find selection systems anywhere on the Web. Whether a user is browsing your site via a row of navigation elements, picking from a list of items in an online store, or selecting configuration options from a drop-down menu, you (the designer/developer) must design these interface elements to handle the basic mouse interactions that will drive your application's functionality.

Forgetting to make these basic interactions *simple and clear* could lead to a bad user experience and, even worse, could cost you or your client some business. Imagine trying to find the entrance to a store whose door is indistinguishable from the brick wall that makes up the building façade. Perhaps you'll go next door where you can find the doorknob!

> *Good usability dictates that forcing the user to search for a navigation element or failing to reflect any sort of selection or interaction options is a major design flaw.*

In this chapter, you'll learn how to design a *framework* that allows you to easily integrate a usable selection system into every project that requires one.

Here's what we'll cover in this chapter:

- Selection systems in HTML versus those in Flash
- How to create a reusable Flash selection system framework
- How to build a basic book selection system

We've started off the solutions part of this book with this chapter because, as you'll see, many of the usability solutions to follow will reuse the code presented here. Think of this chapter as an appetizer before the main course of usability topics that we'll address over the next 11 chapters.

Selection systems in HTML vs. Flash

Before we dive into building our Flash selection system solution, let's quickly discuss the kinds of selection systems typically encountered in HTML. This will give you an idea of the key points to consider and how to use Flash to better accomplish the same tasks.

HTML offers you a couple of ways to create selection and rollover effects. The first and foremost, of course, is using the <a> anchor tag to create a hyperlink. A browser's built-in functionality offers a basic default status (usually underlined), a hover status, and a visited status (usually a different color from the default status).

The capabilities of CSS add a lot more options to a designer's bag of tricks. You can create very realistic-looking buttons through a few CSS calls and stylize text items in some elegant ways. You can easily add to and modify the hover and visited states of a hyperlink.

Another technique you've probably encountered for displaying a selection system is the use of image swaps in JavaScript when hovering over an item with your mouse. This solution usually requires the browser to load additional images from the server to reflect such selections. The additional need to intertwine JavaScript calls into HTML code and create arrays of image paths for these items makes this technique pretty painful to maintain.

> *One of the early design triumphs of the Web was the ability to create links that appeared to "glow" when rolled over by using the handy trick of swapping a "glowing" image for a nonglowing one using JavaScript.*

But with Flash, not only can you build a solution that's much cleaner to implement, but also you can easily jazz up the visual appeal of these items. With some very simple lines of code, you can, say, make items fade in and out, or "pop" when you roll over them. It's just a matter of deciding what looks best and enhances the user's experience!

We think we hear you whispering, "Hey Craig and Ka Wai, what's the difference between what we're going to build versus just simply adding a repeating number of button items to the Flash stage?" Good question. Remember, you're actually going to create a *framework* to make it easy to modify, add, or remove any number of items in your selection system. The distinct advantages of building this framework are that you can

- **Build the design and behavior for each individual item in the selection system once and reuse them at your leisure**. If new items are needed, just modify a simple array to add the data needed for those items. In HTML, if you use the image-swapping technique, you have to go back to your favorite graphics program to create the image swaps and implement those back into your website.

- **Configure the layout and positioning of the items in one centralized method**. There's no need to hassle with reconstructing HTML in case the layout of your items has to change. Of course, that also means there's no need to worry about how your items will look in different browsers as well! The framework manages the positions of the items in relation to each other.

- **Customize states that are not included with the default Flash button**. Unlike regular out-of-the-box Flash buttons, the selection system presented in this chapter also implements a selected state (for the item currently selected) and a visited state for each item.

- **Focus your work on enhancing usability**. The framework takes care of a lot of the overhead associated with building out a selection system each time, so you can instead focus your development time solely on making your items easy to use!

Introducing the Flash selection system

Follow along by downloading the `Chapter3_Final.zip` file from this book's download page (www.friendsofed.com) and exporting the files within the ZIP file into a directory on your machine. Open the `Chapter3_Final.swf` file within the /source/swf/ subdirectory to see the final product.

You should see a simple but elegant selection menu of some great friends of ED book titles. For this very basic example, the system displays an image of a book when you click a button from within the menu. Notice how every item you roll over reacts by pushing its text out slightly. Now, click one of those buttons, roll off the menu, and you'll see that its state has been changed to a selected state, while the cover image for the book appears on the right. Lastly, click another button, and you'll see that the previously selected clip becomes unselected, and the new clip is selected. In the meantime, the previously selected item fades slightly, indicating that it has been visited previously (see Figure 3-1).

Figure 3-1. A simple selection system of book titles

Simple, but effective. If you're like us, you probably implement this sort of basic functionality in many projects that you create, so to save some time in future projects, as well as learn something about usability and interface design, let's make it so that you never have to code this logic again. Instead, you'll spend your time on the niceties that make Flash such a cool tool, such as motion design and interaction. Before we go over the code and showing you how it works, let's map out what's going on behind the scenes.

Blueprinting the selection system solution

First, each individual item in the selection system must be able to change its appearance based on specific events. As we mentioned earlier, the "buttons" in our selection system will have states that the default Flash button objects don't have—namely, "currently selected" and "visited" states. It makes a lot of sense for us to make these items `MovieClip` objects rather than `Button` objects to allow for the added flexibility.

In addition, because we're building a framework, we need to build these items in a fairly abstract way so that they're robust enough to apply to many different applications. To accomplish all of this, we'll create a base class called UIButton that will store the methods and properties of our generic button item. More on this in a bit.

Next, we're going to need another movie clip to house all of our buttons and selection logic. Think of this as a container for any number of UIButton items that can also answer questions pertaining to the whole system, such as

- Which button is currently selected?
- How many buttons are there in the selection system?
- Where should a button be positioned?

We'll then need to create another ActionScript 2.0 (AS2) base class for this selection system clip called the SelectionSystem class. The code in this class will be in charge of attaching instances of the movie clip associated to the UIButton class as well as keeping track of the state of the selection system (to answer the questions just posed). It will also have the ability to "talk" to the buttons; in other words, it can command a button to change to its selected state or return to its unselected state based on which button was clicked.

These two classes, UIButton and SelectionSystem, make up the base reusable framework for our selection system. In our example, we're working with a specific kind of selection system—namely, a menu of book titles that displays book cover images when clicked. To implement the specific functionalities of this simple book-viewing application, we'll extend the two base classes with custom classes named BookItemButton and BookSelectionSystem.

Extending a class into another class (declared in a class directive, such as class SubClass extends SuperClass*) allows you to inherit all the properties and functionality from one class (*SuperClass*) into another class (*SubClass*). It also gives you the ability to override the functionality of the superclass (meaning you can change how a particular method is defined) as well as add in additional functionality.*

You should consider extending classes only when the subclass truly is a type of the superclass. Coding blunders are often made when programmers extend a class into another class that really isn't a type of the superclass. In our solution, this requirement is clearly met; each book item button is truly a particular kind of UI button, and the book selection system as a whole is truly a particular kind of selection system.

These classes, in turn, will be linked to a book button item movie clip (MC BookItemButton) and an empty container movie clip (MC BookSelectionSystem) on the stage.

Figure 3-2 displays the architecture for the selection system framework, including how we extend the base classes to customize the functionality we need for this chapter's example.

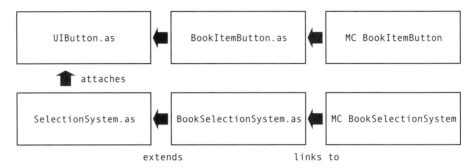

Figure 3-2. A schematic diagram of the selection system's framework, extension classes, and movie clips

So, now that you have a better idea of the task ahead, let's break it down into individual parts, starting with the pair of base classes.

Examining the base classes for the selection system

As mentioned earlier, the two base classes we've built are called UIButton.as and SelectionSystem.as, and should be located in the /source/classes/ folder within the directory you extracted the chapter ZIP file into. Let's look at each class in more detail.

The UIButton base class

Open up UIButton.as from the /source/classes/ folder. The responsibilities of this class include selecting and unselecting itself visually when the selection system tells it to, as well as providing a structure for defining mouse events (rollOver, rollOut, release, etc.).

Note that each one of these UIButton clips is assigned a numeric ID. This value is passed to the selection system when the button is clicked, so it can keep track of which button in the selection system is selected.

Here's a rundown of the key properties and methods within the base UIButton class:

- private var itemData:Object: This is a generic object property that stores the title of the button (as itemData.title) and whatever other data the button needs to do its job. For example, in this chapter's solution, the itemData object stores both the title of the button and an image path to the associated cover image. When you extend the UIButton class, you can use this object to grab whatever data you need for the various methods you'll be writing. You'll see this in action later in the chapter.

- `public function init(_selectionSystem:SelectionSystem, _id:Number, _itemData:Object):Void:` This is a public method called by the selection system after attaching the button to the stage. It takes three parameters: a reference to the selection system, a numeric ID assigned by the selection system, and a generic object that will be assigned to the preceding itemData property.

- `private function handlePress():Void, private function handleRollOver(): Void, private function handleRollOut():Void:` These private methods define what should happen to the button when the mouse clicks, rolls over, or rolls off of the button item. In this class, you don't actually define anything within these methods. They need to be overridden in the class that extends UIButton, since what happens should be specific to the application you're working on.

- `private function handleRelease():Void:` This private method is called when a user completes a click of the button. It then calls a method in the parent selection system called setSelection(), which stores the ID of the selected button, ensures it "selects itself" and the previously selected item "unselects itself," and then calls a method that will do whatever is intended to be done by clicking the button.

- `public function setSelected():Void, public function setUnselected():Void:` These public methods are called directly by the selection system, telling the clip to select or unselect. In our base class, the setSelected() method disables all mouse events tied to the button, and the setUnselected() method enables the same mouse events. When extending the UIButton class, you can tack on additional code to modify the appearance of the button when it's selected or unselected.

The UIButton class in its entirety follows. Bear in mind that this class is a base class for your applications and doesn't need to be customized when used (instead, you'll just be extending it). Please consult the code comments for further explanation of each method and property within the class.

```
import SelectionSystem;

class UIButton extends MovieClip
{
  // Stores a reference to a SelectionSystem instance
  private var selectionSystem:Object;

  // Numeric ID passed in by SelectionSystem when attached
  private var id:Number;

  // Title holder clip (holds a text field)
  private var title_mc:MovieClip;

  // Background clip
  private var bg_mc:MovieClip;

  // Keeps track of the selection status of this clip
  private var selected:Boolean;
```

```actionscript
  // Holds any custom visual information (such as title)
  private var itemData:Object;

  // Stores the history of this item
  private var visited:Boolean;

  // Constructor
  public function UIButton()
  {
  }

  /*
    Set up our reference, ID, and item data,
    and then take care of the clip's UI.
  */
  public function init(_selectionSystem:SelectionSystem, _id:Number,
➥    itemData:Object):Void
  {
    _focusrect = false;
    selectionSystem = _selectionSystem;
    itemData = _itemData;
    id = _id;
    setTitle(itemData.title);
    setPosition();
    initMouseEvents();
  }

  /*
    Select this clip. It will stay visually selected
    because the mouse is rolled over it.
  */
  public function setSelected():Void
  {
    selected = visited = true;
    killMouseEvents();
  }

  // Unselect this clip
  public function setUnselected():Void
  {
    selected = false;
    initMouseEvents();
  }

  // Set the title of this button clip
  private function setTitle(_val:String):Void
  {
    title_mc.title_txt.text = _val;
  }
```

```
private function setPosition():Void
{
  // Override this method
}

/*
  Tell selectionSystem about the click
  and pass this clip's ID with it.
*/
private function handleRelease():Void
{
  selectionSystem.setSelection(id);
}

private function handlePress():Void { // Override }
private function handleRollOver():Void { //override }
private function handleRollOut():Void { //override }

/*
  Capture all of our mouse events and pass them
  to the internal handler methods.
*/
private function initMouseEvents() : Void
{
  useHandCursor = true;
  onRollOver = handleRollOver;
  onRollOut = handleRollOut;
  onReleaseOutside = handleRollOut;
  onPress = handlePress;
  onRelease = handleRelease;
}

// Remove all mouse events while the clip is selected
private function killMouseEvents():Void
{
  useHandCursor = false;
  delete onRollOver;
  delete onRollOut;
  delete onReleaseOutside;
  delete this.onPress;
  delete this.onRelease;
}

// Public getter/setters
public function getId():Number
{
  return id;
}
```

3

```
public function setId(_val:Number):Void
{
  id = _val;
}
}
```

The SelectionSystem base class

Now open up `SelectionSystem.as` from the code download. This class's main responsibilities include maintaining the state of the selection system, as well as attaching the buttons to the stage and passing down their individual data through a generic object. Just as we did for UIButton, let's take a look at the key methods and properties that make up this base class:

- `private var systemData:Array`: This is an array of generic objects that each represent the itemData property for a button in the selection system. In a nutshell, the systemData array defines how many buttons should be created for the selection system (by the number of objects in the array) and each button's itemData property (by each object).

- `private var exportName:String`: This is a string that holds the identifier name for the button items that will attach to the selection system. The **identifier name** (sometimes referred to as the **linkage name**) is the name that references any given object in the Flash library and can be set by right-clicking the object in the library, selecting Linkage, and then keying in the name in the Identifier field in the resulting dialog box.

- `public function doInit(_systemData:Array, _exportName:String):Void`: This public method takes an array of generic objects and the identifier name for the button item, and assigns them to the systemData and exportName properties. It then calls a method to attach the buttons to the stage and sets each button's itemData property to the corresponding object in the systemData array.

- `private function attachButtonItems():Void`: This private method is in charge of attaching buttons to the stage and then calling each button item's init() method discussed previously.

- `public function setSelection(_id:Number):Void`: This is a public method called by a button when a user releases the mouse over the button (see the handleRelease() method in the earlier UIButton discussion). The button passes in its ID, and if the button isn't already selected, it unselects the currently selected button, selects this button, and then calls doAction(), as explained next.

- `private function doAction():Void`: This private method defines what actually happens when a particular button item is selected. Naturally, it changes with each different application of this framework, so we'll be overriding this method in the extending class. In our example, we'll load the appropriate cover image to the stage when an item is clicked. You will generally use the values stored within the button's itemData object to implement the action that occurs when a user selects a button.

The following code shows the SelectionSystem class in its entirety. Similar to the UIButton class, the SelectionSystem class requires no editing when you use it in your applications. Consult the class comments for further explanation.

```
class SelectionSystem extends MovieClip
{
  // Data array passed in at instantiation
  private var systemData:Array;

  // Linkage name of button clip
  private var exportName:String;

  // Store our current state as a number
  private var currentSelection:Number;

  // Store references to our items
  private var listItems:Array;

  // Constructor
  public function SelectionSystem()
  {
  }

  public function doInit(_systemData:Array, _exportName:String):Void
  {
    systemData = _systemData;
    exportName = _exportName;
    listItems = new Array();
    attachButtonItems();
  }

  /*
    Attach a button clip for each data item in our systemData array.
    Call init() on the new clip, passing it an ID and data item (for
    title, etc.).
  */
  private function attachButtonItems():Void
  {
    for(var i:Number = 0; i < systemData.length; i++)
    {
      var item:MovieClip = this.attachMovie(exportName,"Item_" + i,i);
      item.init(this, i, systemData[i]);
      listItems.push(item);
    }
  }

  /*
    Called by button items to switch selections.
    ID is passed from button item calling the method.
  */
  public function setSelection(_id:Number):Void
  {
    if(currentSelection!=_id)
```

```
    {
      listItems[currentSelection].setUnselected();
      currentSelection = _id;
      listItems[currentSelection].setSelected();
      doAction();
    }
  }

  /*
    Take some action in response to the new selection;
    this is overridden by extending class.
  */
  private function doAction():Void { //override }

  // Getter/setters
  public function getSystemData():Array
  {
    return systemData;
  }

  public function getCurrentSelection():Number
  {
    return currentSelection;
  }

  public function setCurrentSelection(_val:Number):Void
  {
    currentSelection = _val;
  }
}
```

Now that you've seen both of the base classes in full, you're probably wondering how to implement them into your applications, right? Let's do just that. We'll first create the MC BookItemButton and MC BookSelectionSystem movie clips, and then we'll write the initialization code in the movie. Finally, we'll complete the solution by extending UIButton and SelectionSystem in this chapter's example to the BookItemButton and BookSelectionSystem classes.

Using and customizing the selection system

As a refresher, Figure 3-3 shows how the end product should look.

As we'll do in all of our usability solutions, we'll first open up the FLA file for this chapter and walk through the various objects that you'll need to be aware of to make this solution run. Open the Chapter3_Final.fla file and then open the library (Window ➤ Library).

> As a general rule, we set all of our FLAs in this book
> to a frame rate of 31 frames per second (fps).

Figure 3-3. The resulting book selection system solution

Creating the book item button clip

Follow these steps to see how we create the book item button clip:

1. Within the movieclips folder in the library, right-click (*CTRL*-click on the Mac) the MC BookItem movie clip and select Linkage from the menu. Remember from Figure 3-2 that this movie clip will link to BookItemButton class, which extends the UIButton class just discussed.

2. In the Linkage Properties dialog box, you should see that we have typed MC BookItemButton into the Identifier field and BookItemButton into the AS 2.0 Class field. The value in the Identifier field means we can reference the clip when attaching it to the stage by MC BookItemButton, and the value in the AS 2.0 Class field means that the clip will bind to the functionality and properties as defined within the BookItemButton.as class file (you'll build this class in a bit). Also note that the Export for ActionScript and Export in First Frame check boxes are checked; you'll do this every time you link an AS2 class with a movie clip going forward.

3. Double-click the movie clip in the library to edit it.

4. On the bottom layer, labeled bg, we've created a basic rectangle on the stage with the dimensions 169 × 22. We've also used the Set Corner Radius tool located on the Tools panel to give the rectangle a corner radius of 3. The fill color of the rectangle has been set to #5A5C6D. We've positioned this at (0,0). This rectangle serves as the background to our book item button. We've also made it into its own movie clip, graph_buttonBackground, and given it an instance name of bg_mc in the Properties panel (Window ➤ Properties).

5. Above the bg layer is a title layer that will hold the title movie clip for the button. Our title movie clip, MC Title, holds a text field labeled title_txt that has been set to Arial, 10 pixels and a white color to boldly contrast with the darker background. All of this information is modifiable in the text field's Properties panel. Note that we've also offset the movie clip to (5,2) to give the title text some padding when you view it on top of the background layer. The instance name of the movie clip is title_mc.

OK, that's all for our book item button. Let's move on to create the movie clip for the book selection system. Since the selection system is just a container to hold these book item buttons, the movie clip will be empty.

Creating the book selection system movie clip

Follow these steps to see how we create the book selection system movie clip:

1. Within the movieclips folder in the library, right-click (*CTRL*-click on the Mac) the MC BookSelectionSystem movie clip and select Linkage from the menu. Remember from Figure 3-2 that this movie clip will link to the BookItemButton class, which extends the UIButton class discussed earlier.

2. In the Linkage Properties dialog box, you should see that we have typed MC BookSelectionSystem into the Identifier field and BookSelectionSystem into the AS 2.0 Class field. This means we can reference the clip when attaching it to the stage by MC BookSelectionSystem, and that the clip will inherit the functionality and properties as defined within the BookSelectionSystem.as class file (we'll build this class in a bit). Also note, once again, that the Export for ActionScript and Export in First Frame check boxes are checked.

3. Double-click the movie clip in the library to edit it. Notice that the movie clip is completely empty! You'll use the MC BookSelectionSystem movie clip as a *container* for your book items, so nothing actually needs to go in it off the bat.

The next thing we'll do here is create an instance of the selection system on the stage, hand it the data it needs, and get all the pieces attached to the stage correctly.

Adding the initialization code

Go back now to the _root timeline and view the frame actions on frame 1 of the actions layer. This is where you're going to plug in the code that will instantiate the book selection system.

This code first defines the data that will be passed to the attached book item buttons. Remember that the selection system expects an array of objects (systemData) that define the button visuals as well as any additional application-specific data. In the case of this simple book application, each button needs two pieces of information: the title of the book item and a path to the cover image of each book. The following array, named selectionData, includes just what's needed. The object's title is named title and its path to the cover image is named image. In more advanced applications, this array of data may be constructed dynamically via XML or Flash remoting, but for the sake of this example, hard-coding it into the movie will serve us just fine:

```
//Data for the book button items
var selectionData:Array = [
    {title:"XML for Flash",image:"../images/image_1.jpg"},
    {title:"Actionscript Animation",image:"../images/image_2.jpg"},
    {title:"Foundation Flash 8", image:"../images/image_3.jpg"},
    {title:"DOM Scripting", image:"../images/image_4.jpg"},
    {title:"Web Standards Solutions", image:"../images/image_5.jpg"},
```

```
        {title:"Podcast Solutions", image:"../images/image_6.jpg"},
        {title:"Foundation Flash MX 2004", image:"../images/image_7.jpg"}
    ];
```

After this, you attach a fresh instance of MC BookSelectionSystem to the stage to house the system using Flash's built-in attachMovie() movie clip method. Recall that the identifier name of this clip is MC BookSelectionSystem. Also give it an instance name of bookSelectionSystem_mc and position the selection system at (80,70) on the main stage:

```
    this.attachMovie("MC BookSelectionSystem", "bookSelectionSystem_mc", 1,
    ➡ {_y:70, _x:80});
```

The final step is to actually initialize the book selection system. Remember that the doInit() method in the base SelectionSystem class sets the wheels in motion by attaching the book items onto the stage, referencing the array of objects we pass in. The identifier name for each book item is MC BookItemButton, so the call to doInit() looks like this:

```
    bookSelectionSystem_mc.doInit(selectionData, "MC BookItemButton");
```

So there you have it. Our book item clip (MC BookItemButton) and book selection system clip (MC BookSelectionSystem) are complete, and we have the initialization code we need to create the selection system. Of course, there's the matter of creating the two classes that extend our base classes, right? Let's get those done right now!

Creating the BookItemButton class

Open the BookItemButton.as class file from the chapter download. At the top of this class, we import the UIButton class to be able to inherit its functionality. Next, we import two built-in Flash packages, mx.transitions.easing and mx.transitions.Tween. These packages contain simple-to-use methods for creating property tweens with your Flash objects. We use them fairly often in this and subsequent chapters, although you should certainly feel free to use whatever you're comfortable with.

```
    import UIButton;
    import mx.transitions.easing.*;
    import mx.transitions.Tween;
```

> For a comprehensive tutorial on using the Tween object, which we highly recommend you acquaint yourself with, visit www.actionscript.org/tutorials/advanced/ Tween-Easing_Classes_Documented/index.shtml.

Then we'll make our class definition. Note that this class inherits all of UIButton's functionality, and UIButton inherits all of MovieClip's functionality. This concept is termed **chain of inheritance** in OOP-speak and is a great way to string along functionality to make superpowered classes. We place this code next:

```
    class BookItemButton extends UIButton
    {
```

After this, we'll add a couple of new properties into the mix to aid in our presentation. Both properties are tween instances. One tween, bgTween, will handle changes to the _alpha property of the bg_mc background clip when the button is rolled over, rolled out, selected, or visited. The other tween, titleTween, will handle changes to the x-position of the title when the button is rolled over, rolled out, or visited. This code appears next:

```
private var bgTween:Tween;
private var titleTween:Tween;
```

Next, we'll write the constructor method for the class. In reality, you don't need to create the constructor if it's empty, but for completeness we always include it anyway.

```
public function BookItemButton()
{
}
```

Setting the position of each book item button After that, we'll write the method setPosition(), which overrides the method of the same name within the base UIButton class. Recall that setPosition() is in charge of placing the button in the correct spot on stage. For this example, we multiply the clip's id by _height + 10 and set that number as the clip's _y position. We tack on 10 pixels to give a bit of line height to each button so it stands out better visually. Here's the code to add next:

```
private function setPosition():Void
{
  _y = id * (_height + 10);
}
```

Implementing the rollover and rollout events Then we define the handleRollOver() and handleRollOut() methods, which will override the methods of the same name in the base UIButton class. We've chosen not to do anything special when a user clicks the button, so we simply won't override the handlePress() method.

In handleRollOver(), both Tween objects are used to give some aesthetic quality to the changes in property of our buttons. When a user rolls over a button, we tween the _alpha property of the background clip to 50 percent in a timeframe of .5 seconds. We also tween the _x property of the title clip to 15 pixels in a timeframe of .2 seconds (remember that in this solution, we set title_mc's x-position to 5 in the construction of the clip, so in reality, the title will shift 10 pixels to the right).

```
private function handleRollOver():Void
{
  bgTween = new Tween(bg_mc, "_alpha", Regular.easeOut,
➥ bg_mc._alpha, 50, .5, true);
  titleTween = new Tween(title_mc, "_x", Regular.easeOut,
➥ title_mc._x, 15, .2, true);
}
```

In handleRollOut(), both Tween objects are again used for aesthetics. When a user rolls off a button, we tween the _alpha property of the background clip back to 100 percent if the button hasn't been visited before. If it already has been visited, the background clip fades back to only 80 percent of its original opacity to give it a slightly faded look. The title clip will tween back to its original x-position of 5.

```
private function handleRollOut():Void
{
  if (visited)
  {
    var fadeVal:Number = 80;
  }
  else
  {
    var fadeVal:Number = 100;
  }

  bgTween = new Tween(bg_mc, "_alpha", Regular.easeOut,
➥ bg_mc._alpha, fadeVal, .5, true);
    titleTween = new Tween(title_mc, "_x", Regular.easeOut,
➥ title_mc._x, 5, .2, true);
}
```

The last method we override is setUnselected(). Recall that setUnselected() is called on the previously selected button by the selection system's setSelection() method when a user has clicked a different button. In the override, we just call the UIButton's setUnselected() method by using the super property inherent to all subclasses that inherit from another class. However, we also will call handleRollOut() so that the unselected button goes back to its original visual state. Our next bit of code looks like this:

```
public function setUnselected():Void
{
  super.setUnselected();
  handleRollOut();
}
}
```

That's all it takes! The following shows what your completed BookItemButton class should look like:

```
import UIButton;
import mx.transitions.easing.*;
import mx.transitions.Tween;

class BookItemButton extends UIButton
{
  private var bgTween:Tween;
  private var titleTween:Tween;
```

```
public function BookItemButton()
{
}

/*
  Calculate where we place this clip by
  multiplying its ID by its height.
*/
private function setPosition():Void
{
  _y = id * (_height + 10);
}

/*
  Fade bg_mc's alpha to 40 percent and
  ease title_mc 10 pixels to the right.
*/
private function handleRollOver():Void
{
  bgTween = new Tween(bg_mc, "_alpha", Regular.easeOut,
➥ bg_mc._alpha, 40, .5, true);
  titleTween = new Tween(title_mc, "_x", Regular.easeOut,
➥ title_mc._x, 15, .2, true);
}

/*
  If clip has been visited before, fade bg_mc's alpha to 80 percent;
  otherwise fade to 100, then ease title_mc 10 pixels to the left.
*/
private function handleRollOut():Void
{
  if(visited)
  {
    var fadeVal:Number = 80;
  }
  else
  {
    var fadeVal:Number = 100;
  }

  bgTween = new Tween(bg_mc, "_alpha", Regular.easeOut,
➥ bg_mc._alpha, fadeVal, .5, true);
  titleTween = new Tween(title_mc, "_x", Regular.easeOut,
➥ title_mc._x, 5, .2, true);
}
```

```
    /*
      Unselect this clip, and reflect visually by calling doRollOut().
    */
    public function setUnselected():Void
    {
      super.setUnselected();
      handleRollOut();
    }
  }
```

Creating the BookSelectionSystem class

Now let's finish off this application by examining the BookSelectionSystem class. Open up the BookSelectionSystem.as file in the chapter download. Notice that there's not a whole lot of code in this file. Most of the functionality we need for the book's selection system is already embedded into the base SelectionSystem class.

The first bit of code imports the base SelectionSystem class:

```
    import SelectionSystem;
```

Next, we create the class construct. Notice that this custom class extends the base SelectionSystem class.

```
    class BookSelectionSystem extends SelectionSystem
    {
```

After that, we'll write our constructor method. In this example, the constructor won't do anything. Again, it's not necessary to add, but we like to be thorough, so we'll include it next.

```
    public function BookSelectionSystem()
    {
    }
```

The only method we need to override from the base selection system class is doAction(). Recall that this method defines what should happen when a button is selected. In our case, we load the cover image into the application from this method, which comes from the generic UIButton object systemData.

Defining what happens when a button is clicked After the constructor method, we'll add the override method, which takes the image path passed in from the systemData array and places it inside an empty movie clip. We can access the correct image path of the selected item by grabbing the image property of the corresponding object within the systemData array (systemData[currentSelection].image). We then create an empty movie clip called image_mc and load the image into it. We've positioned the clip at (315,52), which is roughly centered to the right of the menu items.

```
  private function doAction():Void
  {
    _parent.createEmptyMovieClip("Image_mc", 100);
    _parent.Image_mc._x = 315;
    _parent.Image_mc._y = 52;
    _parent.Image_mc.loadMovie(systemData[currentSelection].image);
  }
}
```

That's all there is to it! The following shows what the completed BookSelectionSystem class should look like:

```
import SelectionSystem;

class BookSelectionSystem extends SelectionSystem
{
  public function BookSelectionSystem()
  {
  }

  private function doAction():Void
  {
    _parent.createEmptyMovieClip("image_mc", 100);
    _parent.image_mc._x = 315;
    _parent.image_mc._y = 52;
    _parent.image_mc.loadMovie(systemData[currentSelection].image);
  }
}
```

Wrapping up

So there you have it! We've created a very simple book selection system using our base selection system framework. Then, overriding a few mouse handler methods, we've made it a lot easier to see what buttons we've rolled over, rolled off, clicked, or visited previously. Hopefully, you found it easy to see how we can customize the visuals and the actions that happen when a user clicks a button by modifying a few methods from the base classes.

You'll see this particular selection system framework reused in many of the usability solutions to come, so if you need a refresher, Chapter 3 will always be here at your disposal!

Summary

With the basic selection system complete, you're ready to dive into some common web usability topics. As we said at the beginning of the chapter, the code presented here will resurface in many chapters to come. The next chapter utilizes this framework and shows an innovative way to create a Flash menu that circumvents some of the drawbacks of HTML-driven menus.

3

4 NAVIGATION MENUS

| Foundation Flash 8 |
| Foundation MX Express |
| Foundation MX Studio |
| Foundation MX Upgrade Essentials |
| Foundation MX Video |
| Foundation XML for Flash |
| New Masters of Flash |
| The Flash Usability Guide |
| **Flash Books** ▲ |

| Timeline ⇦ 🖺 Scene 1 🖾 |
| 🗐 title |
| 🗐 info text field |
| 🗐 range text fields |
| 🗐 drag handle clips |
| 🗐 slider range bar |

Address 1*	
Address 2	
City*	
State	AL ▾
Zip Code*	
Work Phone*	

In the previous chapter, you saw how to build a pair of base classes to create a functional, usable selection system. We enhanced the usability of the selection system by adding some aesthetics to the familiar rollover, rollout, and selection states that you see on most websites.

In this chapter, we're going to push the envelope much further. Now that our base classes are built and out of the way, we'll focus on extending the selection system by applying it to one of the most basic components of the Web: the navigation menu.

If you think about it, the selection system we built in Chapter 3 is ultimately just a list or menu of interactive items. Here, we'll explore what else we can do with the behavior of these menu items to enhance the user's experience. But first, we'll take a look at the different selection devices written in HTML and their limitations. Then we can figure out ways of improving the functionality of navigation in Flash. Here's what we'll cover in this chapter:

- The pros and cons of different styles of menus in HTML
- How to devise an optimized menu solution in Flash
- How to create expandable and collapsible menus
- How to program mouse-position-sensitive scrolling functionality

Exploring the HTML menu conundrum

In HTML, you see menus in three general flavors:

- A simple menu of hyperlinks down the side of a web page
- A selection box using the HTML <select /> and <option /> tags
- A customizable CSS/JavaScript-based drop-down list

Let's take a look at the pros and cons of each of these different selection devices.

The simple text menu

A simple text-driven menu, like the one shown in Figure 4-1, can work nicely in some contexts. However, a problem arises if the list contains too many items, because then you're forced to use the browser's scrollbar or your mouse wheel to view all of the choices. In the meantime, other bits of information on the website may disappear from view when you scroll down the page.

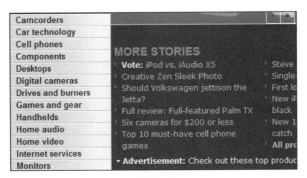

Figure 4-1. A simple static HTML text menu

4

Some usability experts argue that the optimal number of items to have in any list is seven. This theory derives from studies by famed psychologist George Miller, who determined that people tend to remember, at most, about seven (give or take two) items at any given time. However, some argue Miller's study on short-term memory doesn't necessarily correlate to how people view visual design. But both sides agree that reducing the number of destinations on your web application, to reduce the number of navigation items in your menu, makes navigation easier for the user.

In addition, static menus can consume a lot of your precious screen real estate. If you're building a web application for an audience using 800-pixel-wide screen resolutions, even a modest 100-pixel-width sidebar of static links eats up a significant portion of a user's screen width. Yet, at the same time, not making your sidebar wide enough will cause longer menu items to wrap onto a second line, which is also certainly not desirable.

You typically scan menus to figure out where you want to go to next. And, once you've figured out where you need to be, there's really no reason for the list to still be fully visible on your screen. It would be akin to having a restaurant menu shown to you even after you've ordered your meal. It makes more sense to see the menu again later, if you're interested in dessert or want to change your order. Otherwise, it just clutters up space on your table! Similarly, hiding a web menu and giving easy access to it only when it's needed gives you more screen real estate and less clutter. So, to improve on our menu construct, we should consider allowing users to decide when the list should appear or disappear.

The select box list

The HTML <select /> form component, like the one shown in Figure 4-2, conserves space because of its compact design. However, a disadvantage is that you must make potentially *three* mouse movements just to select an item: click the drop-down arrow to expand the list, drag the scrollbar (or use your scroll wheel) down the entire menu to see all your options, and finally click the desired option. It's certainly not the worst thing in the world, but it does become a bit onerous when you have multiple select boxes from which to choose. Think about it next time you're on a site that asks for your birth date and requires you to scroll down a list of 12 months, 31 days, and 100 years!

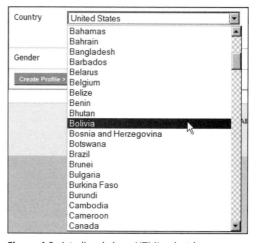

Figure 4-2. A tediously long HTML select box

Furthermore, because it is a user interface control, the possibilities for changing the select box's form or behavior are limited. Sure, you can stylize it with a different background color or text size with CSS. With JavaScript, you can even work in some pretty nifty functionality as well. But, inherently, a select box is still a select box. You're left with the same usability problems just described. CSS/JavaScript-based menus solve these problems by allowing you to better control how the component behaves and looks.

The customized drop-down menu

Now, we've come to the most flexible, and perhaps most usable, kind of HTML-based navigation display: the customized CSS and JavaScript-based drop-down menu. Because it's built mainly using a combination of JavaScript, HTML, and CSS, you have a host of ways to alter its form and behavior.

However, this type of menu does have a few limitations. Typically, the entire menu pops out on the screen when you request it to appear. As with a simple text menu, if the menu has many items, you'll be forced to scroll down the page. Some sites have tried to circumvent the issue by creating multitiered CSS/JavaScript navigation, as shown in Figure 4-3.

But this could end up hiding large areas of your site underneath your menu system, or even worse, have the menu extend past your browser's screen width (trust us, we've seen this happen).

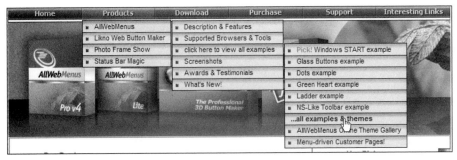

Figure 4-3. A CSS and JavaScript-based drop-down menu with multiple tiers

Also, as is often the case with CSS/JavaScript-based widgets, cross-browser compatibility issues will inevitably arise. Although the latest versions of most major browsers support most CSS/JavaScript objects and properties, you'll need to spend a significant portion of your development time testing your widgets on many kinds of browsers. This can be a frustrating and very unrewarding period of your development process.

None of these three traditional HTML solutions are necessarily bad. Some will suit a user just fine. However, each one presents usability issues that can frustrate the user. With that said, let's discuss how you can harness Flash to build a navigation menu solution that will give your users a better experience.

Devising an optimal Flash menu solution

As you've seen, the HTML selection devices have functionality issues that make them less than optimal. Here are three goals for a better solution:

- A menu should not take over a significant portion of your screen real estate. Since menus are mainly used to "get somewhere else" or "choose an option," you should have the ability of viewing the menu only when you wish.

- A menu should not force users to scroll down using the browser scrollbar because of the number of items. You want to limit the size of the menu to a specific size, regardless of the number of items in the list.

- A more user-friendly menu minimizes the number of mouse clicks necessary to find, and then select an item.

Considering these goals, let's take a look at an optimal Flash menu solution. To demonstrate, we've taken the same book selection system functionality from Chapter 3 and placed the items within the context of a navigation menu.

First, download the `Chapter4_Final.zip` file from this book's download page at www.friendsofed.com and export the files within the ZIP file into a directory on your machine. Then open the `Chapter4_Final.swf` file in the `/source/swf/` folder.

As shown in Figure 4-4, you should see three tabs at the top of the movie, labeled Flash Books, Photoshop Books, and Web Design Books. On the right of the tab is a small, red arrow pointing downward. This makes it fairly obvious that this tab is meant to be expanded and will consume the space underneath it when opened. After all, you see the same visual arrow cue as with the well-known `<select />` box!

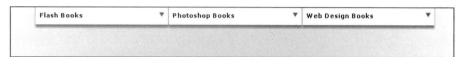

Figure 4-4. An optimized Flash menu component with three expandable tabs

By simply rolling over any area within a tab, the menu items swing out into the body of the screen. You don't need to click a small arrow button as you would with an HTML select box. Try this with the Flash Books tab. As shown in Figure 4-5, your mouse arrow now hovers directly over a list of friends of ED titles particular to Flash, and the little, red indicator arrow points upward, indicating that the menu can be collapsed.

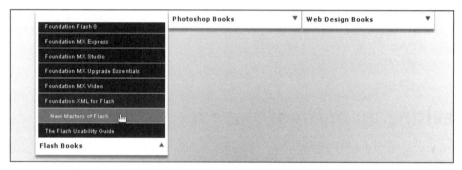

Figure 4-5. Rolling over a tab reveals its menu

Notice that the height of the expanded menus remains constant, regardless of how many items they contain. This means that you never need to worry about having lists of items that expand past the available height of the screen. How do you navigate through a long list of menu items then?

With the menu open, if you now move your mouse toward the bottom of the menu, the list begins scrolling up to reveal new items underneath. The speed at which the menu scrolls increases the closer to the bottom you get. If you then move your mouse back toward the top of the menu, the list will slowly stop scrolling, and then gradually scroll in reverse until it has reached the very beginning. Without having to drag a scrollbar or press an arrow button, the "movement-sensitive" menu gives users a more efficient and lucid mechanism for scanning through a list of menu items.

Furthermore, the menu collapses only when you no longer need to see it. When you either roll off the expanded menu or select a particular menu item, it slides back into the top of the screen, leaving a whole lot of extra real estate available!

If you think about it, all we've really done is taken the same general archetype of the HTML select list but made a few enhancements. Instead of needing to click the arrow, click and drag the menu scrollbar, and then click off the area to deactivate the list, we've reduced the number of clicks to just one—when you want to actually select something. All the other functionality is driven by how you move your mouse cursor over the menu.

This new kind of menu construct might be a little strange to people comfortable with more traditional HTML-based lists. But, after a while, you should be able to cruise around your menu in a much faster and more efficient way than with conventional HTML techniques.

> *Much inspiration for this mouse-position-based scrolling menu comes from the work done by Michelangelo Capraro and Duncan McAlester in their book Skip Intro: Macromedia Flash Usability and Interface Design, written back in 2002 for Flash MX. They refer to this sort of scrolling as a "gesture-driven" scroll and note that its appropriateness depends on your user base.*
>
> *In our experience implementing a gesture-driven scrolling mechanism in real-world applications, we've discovered that more advanced computer users (users who typically work with the Internet daily) found this kind of menu to be easy to use and rather intuitive. Once users saw how the menu moved when they rolled over it, they quickly got the idea of how the menu accelerates and decelerates based on mouse position.*
>
> *The takeaway here is to always think of the kinds of users who will be accessing your applications. Gesture-driven scrolling tends to work better for more savvy Internet users. If your user base will be mostly less advanced users, you may want to consider more traditional menus.*

We're now ready to discuss how to build this kind of functionality. Programming these elements takes a bit of effort, but the good news is that much of the work has already been completed from the previous chapter.

Building the Flash solution

As we mentioned earlier, the items within each of the menus in our optimized solution bear a striking resemblance to what we built in the previous chapter. In fact, we've simply ported over the same code base with a few minor adjustments to the items in this solution! So, the bulk of the work in this chapter involves the following:

- Creating the visual assets for the frame of the menu items
- Building the code to support the menu's expanding, collapsing, and mouse-position-based scrolling functionality
- Tweaking the setPosition() method in the book item button menus to position them directly underneath each other

Our plan of attack will be to design a movie clip with required components, and then build an ActionScript file that we'll link to this clip. First, let's create the menu frame.

Building the scrolling menu frame

Let's start by building the assets for the menu frame. Essentially, the entire menu frame is composed of the following distinct components (see Figure 4-6):

- **Holder clip:** This will be an empty movie clip that simply houses the book selection system we created in Chapter 3.
- **Panel clip:** We'll build in a panel behind the holder clip that will "frame" the holder movie clip. Because it frames our menu, it will also act as the active area that will cause the menu to collapse back to its default state when the mouse rolls off of it.
- **Tab area:** We'll also be creating a hotspot clip, an arrow clip, and a title text field that will make up the various pieces of the bottom tab for this menu.

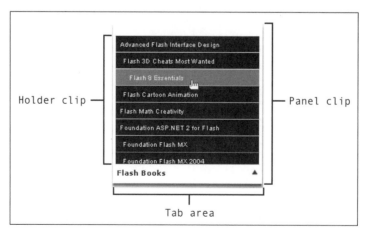

Figure 4-6. A general layout of the different sections of the menu clip

Begin by opening the Chapter4_Final.fla in the /source/fla/ folder of the code download for this chapter. Next, view the library for this clip (Window ➤ Library). You'll notice a folder called Scrolling Menu Frame in the library. We've placed all the assets that relate to the menu frame inside this folder. Double-click into the folder, and then double-click inside the movieclips folder. From there, double-click the MC ScrollingMenuFrame movie clip icon to edit it. This houses the frame for our menu.

Creating the panel clip

On the very bottom frame, labeled background panel, we've placed a solid, white rectangle (240 pixels wide × 250 pixels high) positioned at (0,0) to the registration point of the menu frame. This creates the border and edges of the entire menu frame. Notice that we've made this its own movie clip (named MC Panel in the library) and given it an instance name of bgPanel_mc.

To add some aesthetics to this panel, we've taken advantage of Flash 8's built-in filter tools to cast a drop shadow underneath the clip. To see how to add a drop shadow, click the bgPanel_mc clip and access its properties (Window ➤ Properties). Then click the Filters tab. Next, click the + icon on the upper left of the Filters panel and select the Drop Shadow option from the exposed menu. We've set the Blur X, Blur Y, and Distance values to 5, and toned down the strength of the shadow to 50% opacity. Also, we've set the angle to 90 degrees, which makes the shadow drop straight underneath the menu. Figure 4-7 shows these settings.

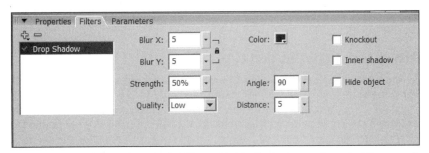

Figure 4-7. Settings for a drop shadow filter added to the background panel of the menu frame

Note that filters are only compatible with Flash 8 Player. If your project requires you to build for lower versions of Flash, you can achieve a similar drop shadow effect by doing the following:

1. Within the MC Panel clip, create a new layer below the current layer called shadow. Name the current layer as background.

2. Copy and paste the panel background from the background layer onto the shadow layer.

3. Lock and hide the background layer.

4. Fill the panel in the shadow layer with a darker color (black would work well).

5. With the dark panel highlighted, select Modify ➤ Shape ➤ Soften Fill Edges. Use a distance of 20 pixels and 20 steps, setting the shadow to Inset, as shown in Figure 4-8.

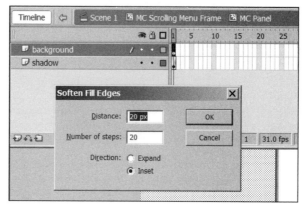

Figure 4-8. Implementing a drop shadow effect using the Soften Fill Edges dialog box for non–Flash 8 users

6. Adjust the shadow so it sits slightly below the white panel on top.

This will give you a comparable shadow effect to that of using the filters. A key difference is that in this case, the shadow becomes a part of the MC Panel clip, whereas when you apply the Flash 8–enabled drop shadow filter, it's created on the bgPanel_mc instance of the MC Panel clip.

Creating the menu holder clip

Above the background panel layer lies the menu holder layer, which contains the holder clip for our menu items. As we've mentioned, the holder clip is just an empty movie clip that we'll use to attach the book selection system to later on. We've given this a name of MC Holder in the library and an instance name of holder_mc. Also, we've positioned this at (5,20) to the registration point of the menu frame. As you'll see later, the overall width of our menu items happens to be 230 pixels. So, by placing the holder clip's x-position at 5 pixels inside the left edge of the 240-pixel-wide background panel, we'll create a 5-pixel border on both the right and left sides of the menu items.

Next, we've created a masking layer called mask above the menu holder. Since the menu holder's height is determined by how many items are in the menu, the mask will restrict what the user sees (and also fix the overall height of the entire menu). The mask is 230 pixels wide by 200 pixels high and is positioned at (5,20) so that it sits exactly over the position of the holder clip.

Creating the tab area assets

Above the masking layer, we've created a layer called hotspot. In this layer, a rectangular movie clip (MC Hot Spot) lies completely over the tab area and will serve as the active mouse-over area for the tab. The _alpha property of this clip is set to 0 so that it's invisible to users. We've given it an instance name of hotSpot_mc. This clip will be used in code later on to expand the list when the mouse cursor rolls over it.

Above the hotspot layer lies the title layer. You guessed it! This will simply hold the title of the menu so users will know exactly what they're going to see when they roll over the menu tab with their mouse cursor. In this layer, we've made a dynamic text field with an instance name of title_txt. We've set the font to 11-pixel Verdana.

One important thing to note is that we've also aliased the text and embedded the font outlines for the text field to display only uppercase and lowercase letters (you can do this by clicking the Embed button in your Properties panel for this clip). In the section "Putting the pieces together" later in this chapter, we'll explain why we've embedded the fonts.

Finally, above the title layer is a layer called arrow. In this layer, we've created a small, red arrow (named MC Arrow in the library and with an instance name of arrow_mc) that points downward. If you're building this on your own, make sure you set the registration point to the center of the clip and give it an instance name of arrow_mc. In our code, we'll rotate the arrow 180 degrees when the menu is expanded. Hence, we need the axis of rotation to be right in the center.

That's all there is to it! With all the parts of the MC ScrollingMenuFrame movie clip complete, let's begin wiring it to add in its interactive behaviors.

Bringing the menu to life with ActionScript

Because we're going to assign all the functionality and properties of the MC ScrollingMenuFrame clip externally via an ActionScript file, let's now see how to link this to the class file (even though we haven't written it yet). Right-click the MC ScrollingMenuFrame clip in your library and select Linkage. As shown in Figure 4-9, we have set the Identifier field to MC ScrollingMenuFrame and the AS 2.0 class field to ScrollingMenuFrame, and, as customary in all of our solutions, the Export for ActionScript and Export in first frame check boxes are checked.

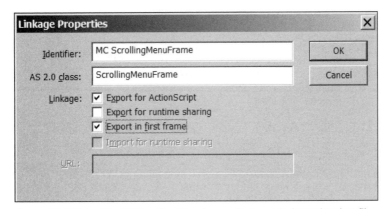

Figure 4-9. Linking the MC ScrollingMenuFrame clip to an ActionScript class file

Now, we just need to build an ActionScript file named ScrollingMenuFrame.as so that we can create all the cool functionality associated with our pretty menu frame.

Because we have linked MC ScrollingMenuFrame to a class named ScrollingMenuFrame, we'll need to name our new ActionScript file ScrollingMenuFrame.as. Your Scrolling➡ MenuFrame.as file should already be in the `/source/classes/` directory within this chapter example's folder. Feel free to start from scratch, or simply follow along as we dig through the code.

Starting the ScrollingMenuFrame class

We'll start the coding of this class by importing all the external classes needed to provide some of our functionality. Add the following code to the blank .as file, if you're building it yourself:

```
import mx.transitions.easing.*;
import mx.transitions.Tween;
```

We've included two mx.transitions namespaces that will provide us with an easy way to create some of the tweening motions used in this clip.

Next, we'll write the class signature. Notice that we're extending the MovieClip class, as this class is linked to the MC ScrollingMenuFrame movie clip.

```
class ScrollingMenuFrame extends MovieClip
{
```

Following this, add the properties of the ScrollingMenuFrame class that will be critical to the functionality of the clip.

```
Private var bgPanel_mc:MovieClip;
private var hotSpot_mc:MovieClip;
private var arrow_mc:MovieClip;
private var holder_mc:MovieClip;
private var title_txt:TextField;

private var initY:Number;
private var initHolderY:Number;
```

As you can see, our first set of properties all reference the movie clips and text field we made when we built this clip. We follow these with three private variables that we'll need to keep track of the various states of the clip itself.

We create the initY and initHolderY variables to set the initial values of the MC ScrollingMenuFrame clip's y-position and the holder_mc's y-position at runtime. The initY value gives us the initial y-position of the MC ScrollingMenuFrame clip, so we know the y-position the clip must tween back to when it collapses. The initHolderY value gives us the initial y-position of the holder clip. We'll use this later when we implement the scrolling functionality of the book selection system that will sit within the holder clip.

Setting the scrolling menu's runtime events

After these properties, we add in the constructor method for this class:

```
public function ScrollingMenuFrame()
{
  doInit();
}
```

When we first instantiate the MC ScrollingMenuFrame clip at runtime, we call a doInit() method that will handle all the initial settings needed for the clip. It will do the following:

- Set the initY and initHolderY values to the initial y-position of the clip and y-position of the holder_mc clip

- Invoke a method named setHotSpot(), which will define what happens when the mouse rolls over the hotspot_mc clip, based on whether the menu is currently expanded or collapsed. In its initial state, the menu will be in a collapsed state.

- Define the holder clip's onMouseDown() event handler, so that when you click a menu item within it, the menu will collapse.

In code, doInit() looks as follows. Add this code below the constructor function:

```
private function doInit():Void
{
  initY = _y;
  initHolderY = holder_mc._y;
  setHotSpot(false);
  holder_mc.onMouseDown = function()
  {
    if (this.hitTest(_root._xmouse, _root._ymouse, true))
    {
      _parent.disableMenu();
    }
  }
}
```

Notice that the holder clip's onMouseDown() function checks to see that the mouse arrow is over the surface of the holder clip using the built-in Flash hitTest() method. If it is, the menu frame will call a disableMenu() method that will collapse the entire menu frame. We'll build this in just a bit.

Next, we'll define the setHotSpot() method that's called in doInit(). We want to have the hotspot expand the menu if it's collapsed and a user rolls the mouse over it. But, when the menu is expanded, we want no action to take place when the mouse is rolled over that

4

same hotspot area. The following code takes care of this based on a Boolean variable passed to it. Add this next if you're building the solution from scratch:

```
private function setHotSpot (_isMenuEnabled:Boolean):Void
{
  if (_isMenuEnabled)
  {
    hotSpot_mc.onRollOver = undefined;
  }
  else
  {
    hotSpot_mc.onRollOver = function()
    {
      this._parent.enableMenu();
    }
  }
}
```

We can safely assume that the menu has not yet been opened when the clip is first initialized, so the doInit() method calls setHotSpot(false).

Enabling and disabling the menu

Notice two methods in the code that we have yet to define: enableMenu() and disableMenu(). These functions will not only control how the menu expands and contracts, but also will turn on and off different functionalities that should be active only when the menu is expanded. Following setHotSpot(), we include these next two methods. Let's take a look at enableMenu() first.

```
private function enableMenu():Void
{
  var listTween = new Tween(this, "_y", Regular.easeInOut, _y,
➥ initY + bgPanel_mc._height - hotSpot_mc._height, .5, true);
  var arrowTween = new Tween(arrow_mc, "_rotation",
➥ Regular.easeInOut, arrow_mc._rotation, 180, .5, true);

  initMouseWatch();
  initMenuScroll();
  setHotSpot(true);
}
```

In enableMenu(), we take advantage of the built-in mx.transitions package that we imported earlier to create two different tweens when the menu expands. First, we'll move the entire menu frame clip from its current y-position to the fully expanded position (given by initY + bgPanel_mc._height - hotSpot_mc._height). Later in this section, we'll place our three frame menus above the top edge of the stage so that just the tab area overlaps the stage area. So, the correct y-position of the entire menu, when expanded, follows from this equation. Here's where you also see the use of the menu's initY come into play.

Next, we'll do another tween on the red indicator arrow located on top of our tab. Remember how the arrow rotates upward when we expand the menu? That's taken care of in the next tween. We'll modify the _rotation attribute of the arrow clip to 180 degrees so that it points upward. This is why it was critical that the registration point of the arrow clip is actually in the dead center of the clip, because that is where the rotation axis will lie.

After this, we make two calls to methods that we'll build in a bit: initMouseWatch() and initMenuScroll(). In a nutshell, initMouseWatch() will sense the mouse cursor for when it rolls outside the menu frame so that we can then collapse the clip. The initMenuScroll() method will turn on the ability for gesture-driven mouse scrolling. To round out the method, we call setHotSpot(), passing in a value of true, indicating the menu is expanded, so that the hotspot will turn off its onRollOver() functionality.

After enableMenu(), we'll add the disableMenu() method. Notice it looks very similar, but we essentially do everything in reverse.

```
private function disableMenu():Void
{
  var listTween = new Tween(this, "_y", Regular.easeInOut, _y,
➥ initY, .5, true);
  var arrowTween = new Tween(arrow_mc, "_rotation",
➥ Regular.easeInOut, arrow_mc._rotation, 0, .5, true);

  killMouseWatch();
  killMenuScroll();

  var aClip:MovieClip = this;
  listTween.onMotionFinished = function() {
    aClip.setHotSpot(false);
  };
}
```

In disableMenu(), we tween back the entire menu frame to its original position of initY. Also, let's not forget the arrow, which will rotate back to its original starting position. Notice that only when the tweening of the menu's y-position has completely finished do we reenable the hotspot functionality on the tab area with the setHotSpot(false) call. If we reenabled the hotspot right away, the menu could roll up and make contact with the mouse arrow, which would force the menu back down again!

After this, we make two calls to methods that we'll build a bit later as well: killMouseWatch() and killMenuScroll(). If you're guessing that these two methods will disable the initMouseWatch() and initMenuScroll() methods, there's a good chance you're right.

Everything should make sense to you now, except four little method calls that we haven't explained yet: killMouseWatch(), initMouseWatch(), killMenuScroll(), and initMenu➥ Scroll(). OK, we apologize for throwing these at you now, but it's not that bad—we promise.

Implementing the mouse watch methods

Remember in our implementation that, although you must roll over the tabbed area (hotSpot_mc) to expand the MC ScrollingMenuFrame clip, you can roll anywhere off the menu to hide it. The initMouseWatch() method (invoked when the menu expands) will monitor our mouse cursor location. When it senses that we've rolled off the clip, it will call disableMenu() again, which will tell the clip to roll back and hide.

Our implementation will involve assigning the clip's built-in onMouseMove() event handler to a function that will call disableMenu() if our mouse cursor isn't over the clip. We'll use the hitTest() method, which returns true if the mouse cursor is over the clip, to test this for us. The instant that the mouse is not over the clip (when hitTest() returns false), it will call disableMenu() to collapse the menu. Here's the full initMouseWatch() method. Add this code next, if you're building this class from scratch:

```
private function initMouseWatch():Void
{
  this.onMouseMove = function()
  {
    if (!this.hitTest(_root._xmouse, _root._ymouse, true))
    {
      disableMenu();
    }
  }
}
```

Once we do roll our mouse cursor off the menu frame clip, it would be smart for us, and generally good practice, to unassign the onMouseMove() event, since we don't need it any-more. Hence, we call the killMouseWatch() method when the menu is disabled. The killMouseWatch() method, as you might expect, is fairly simple. Here's what goes next:

```
private function killMouseWatch():Void
{
  this.onMouseMove = undefined;
}
```

Implementing the menu scrolling methods

Now, we get to the fun part (for you mathematicians out there). Remember that we have both an initMenuScroll() and killMenuScroll() method called in enableMenu() and disableMenu(), respectively. Just as with our mouse watch methods, we'll initialize the scrolling of our selection system only when the mouse clip is expanded, and we'll remove the scrolling functionality when the clip is hidden. In initMenuScroll(), we initialize scrolling only if the holder clip is greater than the height of the mask (200 pixels). Add these methods to the code next:

```
private function initMenuScroll():Void
{
  this.onEnterFrame = function() {

    if (holder_mc._height >= 200)
    {
      doMenuScroll();
    }
  }
}
private function killMenuScroll():Void
{
  this.onEnterFrame = undefined;
}
```

4

Again, as we did with the menu sliding, we've abstracted the scrolling functionality in a new method, this time called doMenuScroll(). This is where a little bit of math comes in. As this method is a bit more involved than the other ones we've built in this chapter, let's step through the code in bits at a time before we come to our final method implementation. If you're building this code from scratch, we suggest that you read through the entire explanation first, and then copy in the final doMenuScroll() method implementation at the end of this section.

As you saw from using the menu clip, the scroll rate increases as your mouse cursor moves closer to the top and bottom edges of the masked area of the clip and slows down when your mouse cursor moves toward the center of the masked area of the clip. Figure 4-10 shows a schematic of where we'll define the top, bottom, and zero y-coordinates of the masked area, along with how the holder_mc clip scrolls behind the mask.

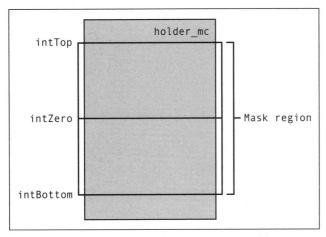

Figure 4-10. Schematic diagram of intTop, intZero, and intBottom positions defined by the masking layer

Thus, it makes sense that we start defining our doMenuScroll() method by setting the values of intTop, intZero, and intBottom appropriately:

```
private function doMenuScroll():Void
{
  var intTop:Number = initHolderY;
  var intBottom:Number = intTop + 200;
  var intZero:Number = (intBottom + intTop) / 2;
```

The intTop variable is easy; it's the same as the initHolderY value. The intBottom variable simply adds 200 (the pixel height of the mask) onto intTop, and intZero takes the very middle of both those numbers to find the center point.

We'll now need to consider how we'll translate this kind of movement into an equation that will give us the correct y-distance to scroll the menu given a mouse cursor's y-position relative to the selection system holder clip itself. Many equations will work—some better than others. A very simple but effective one is the equation y = x^2. Don't get confused with the x and y of this equation with x- and y-position parameters of a movie clip. Instead, treat y as the change in y-position of the holder_mc clip and x as the distance that the mouse cursor is from the very middle of the masked area (intZero).

As you can see from the graph of this equation shown in Figure 4-11, if we take the y-axis to be intZero (because this is where the distance from intZero equals 0), moving our mouse cursor away from the y-axis gradually increases the velocity of the holder clip. The nice thing about this equation is that it flattens out toward intZero. In other words, the acceleration of the holder clip when your cursor is somewhere close to the middle is much less than if your mouse cursor begins moving out.

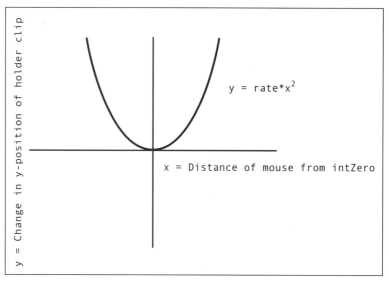

Figure 4-11. Graph of y = rate * x^2, the source equation for how the scrolling clip will behave

> *Try replacing this equation with a similar one, such as y = |x| or y = |x^3|. We've chosen to model our scroll after y = x^2, but that doesn't necessarily mean there aren't better options for your users.*

OK, here's where things might get a tad tricky. While on a high level, this equation suits our needs for how the holder clip should scroll, it currently lacks any bounds. We haven't put any restrictions on how large or small x should be. Let's do that now.

We'll restrict our values of x from –1 to 1. In other words, when your mouse cursor is at the exact same position as intBottom, the resulting value should be –1, and when it's at intTop, the resulting value should be 1. We can achieve this by simply dividing the distance between the mouse cursor and intZero (which we'll call intMousePos) with the distance between intBottom and intZero (if the mouse cursor is below intZero) or intTop and intZero (if the mouse cursor is above intZero). So, we can now define three new properties for doScroll() (notice we give the names intMaxUp and intMaxDown to the distance between the top and zero coordinates and bottom and zero coordinates, respectively). Here's the code to follow:

```
var intMousePos:Number = _ymouse - intZero;
var intMaxUp:Number = intTop - intZero;
var intMaxDown:Number = intBottom - intZero;
```

Figure 4-12 illustrates this.

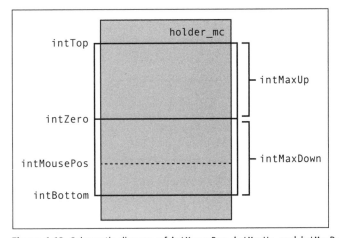

Figure 4-12. Schematic diagram of intMousePos, intMaxUp, and intMaxDown

Because our x values are restricted to the range −1 to 1, this also means our y-value (the square of x) can go only from 0 to 1. This allows us to introduce a rate factor to the equation so that we can assign a maximum change in height to the clip when we move our mouse cursor. The final equation then is simply $y = rate * x^2$. For this example, we've set the rate factor to 5 (meaning the fastest the clip will move is 5 pixels per each frame passed). So, the next line will set the rate:

```
var intRate:Number = 5;
```

Putting all the pieces together, we can now define the new y-position of the holder movie clip based on where the mouse cursor sits. When our mouse cursor is below the intZero y-coordinate, the holder clip should begin scrolling upwards to reveal the menu items that are past the bottom edge of the masking layer.

However, remember that when we reach the very bottom of the holder clip and no more items exist, we should not allow the holder clip to scroll up any farther. Hence, we'll compare two values every time we are recalculating our holder clip's _y value:

- The new value based on our math equation
- The _y of the holder clip when we are at the very bottom of the list

In the case of the first value, since our holder clip is scrolling up and the _y values get smaller when you go up, we'll subtract the distance of change calculated from our math equation from the current holder_mc._y.

In the case of the second value, we can define the bottom of the list as the initial bottom _y at runtime (intBottom) minus the _height of the holder clip. Each time these two are compared, we want to accept only the larger of the two values, since that correlates to the _y position that is "lower" on stage. Thus, our definition of how to scroll the clip when the mouse cursor is below intZero looks like this:

```
// If below the intZero, the clip should scroll upwards. . .
if (intMousePos > 0)
{
   holder_mc._y = Math.max(holder_mc._y - intRate * Math.pow(
➡ (intMousePos/intMaxDown),2), intBottom - holder_mc._height);
}
```

Very similarly, our definition for how the scrolling behaves when our mouse cursor is above intZero looks like this:

```
// If above the intZero, the clip should scroll downwards. . .
else if (intMousePos < 0)
{
   holder_mc._y = Math.min(holder_mc._y + intRate * Math.pow(
➡ (intMousePos/intMaxUp),2), intTop);
}
```

The only thing that's left is to add an _isHit Boolean to make sure that the scrolling happens only when the mouse is actually over the holder clip. Therefore, we'll wrap the scroll portion of our code with if (_isHit) { // Scroll code }. Our final doMenuScroll() method looks like this. Add this entire method next, if you're working from scratch:

```
private function doMenuScroll():Void
{
  var intTop:Number = initHolderY;
  var intBottom:Number = intTop + 200;
  var intZero:Number = (intBottom + intTop) / 2;
  var intMousePos:Number = _ymouse - intZero;
  var intMaxUp:Number = intTop - intZero;
  var intMaxDown:Number = intBottom - intZero;
  var intRate:Number = 5;

  var _isHit:Boolean = this.hitTest(_root._xmouse, _root._ymouse,
➥ true);

  if (_isHit)
  {
    // If below the 0, should go up. . .
    if (intMousePos > 0)
    {
      holder_mc._y = Math.max(holder_mc._y - intRate *
➥ Math.pow((intMousePos/intMaxDown),2), intBottom -
holder_mc._height);
    }
    // If above the 0, should go down. . .
    else if (intMousePos < 0)
    {
      holder_mc._y = Math.min(holder_mc._y + intRate *
➥ Math.pow((intMousePos/intMaxUp),2), intTop);
    }
  }
}
```

Building the menu loading method

To round off the entire ScrollingMenuFrame.as class, we need to have a function that will actually load the menu items into our holder clip. There wouldn't be much use for this entire movie clip otherwise!

We'll build a method called doLoad() that accepts an array of data (as explained in Chapter 3, this array holds the title of each menu item, along with any other assets it may need) and a title for the menu frame. The method will then attach an instance of the MC BookSelectionSystem clip we built in Chapter 3 to the holder clip and initialize the selection system. Also, it will assign the title to the title_txt text field that sits on the tab area of the menu frame. This function will be public, so we can then create the array of data in another location (such as the main timeline itself) and load the menu externally. Add this method next:

```
public function doLoad(_dataArray:Array, _title:String):Void
{
  holder_mc.attachMovie("MC BookSelectionSystem",
➡ "BookSelectionSystem_mc", 1000);
  holder_mc["BookSelectionSystem_mc"].doInit(_dataArray,
➡ "MC BookItemButton");
  title_txt.text = _title;
}
}
```

And that's it! We've just created all the functional logic we'll need to create the usable menu clip you saw earlier this chapter. If you need to see the whole class, just open the ScrollingMenuFrame.as file that comes with this chapter's download.

Adjusting the menus' appearance

We need to make just a few slight adjustments to get these menus to look like our solution example. When we ported over the book selection system code from Chapter 3, we also made a few changes to the BookItemButton.as file. Recall that this class provides specific functionality for each book item, including where it is positioned within the entire group of book item buttons (the setPosition() method). In Chapter 3, we modified each item to have a padding of 10 pixels between each item. In this example, we will pad each item with only a single pixel, which stacks the items one beneath the other, with only a single pixel's worth of spacing. So, in BookItemButton.as for this example, the setPosition() method looks like this:

```
private function setPosition():Void
{
  _y = id * (_height + 1);
}
```

Also, we've gotten rid of the rounded corners on the background clip for the book items and resized the rectangle to 230 pixels wide by 25 pixels high for this solution. If you want to see the changes, just click into the Selection System ➤ movieclips folder in the library for this solution and view the MC BookItemButton clip.

Putting the pieces together

Congratulations for getting this far in the build process! Your scrolling menu frame component is built and linked to the associated ActionScript file that we just stepped through. You now have all the pieces ready and just need to place them on the root timeline of your application. Let's now get these menus up and running!

Again, open Chapter4_Final.fla in the /source/fla/ folder from the chapter download. We'll step through the root timeline, shown in Figure 4-13, to show you how to create those menus you saw in the beginning of this chapter.

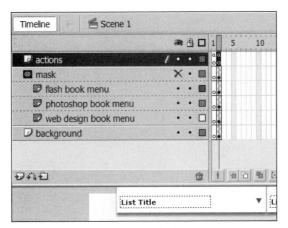

Figure 4-13. A view of the root timeline

Our bottom layer is simply the background layer, where we've placed a large, slightly grayed background. This is just here to make the stage area very distinguishable from the menus.

Above the background layer, you'll see a layer for each of our three menu frames. Each of these three layers holds one instance of MC ScrollingMenuFrame. As noted earlier, they are positioned so that just the bottom tab portion enters the viewable stage area. Going from left to right on the stage, the names given to these instances are flashBookMenu_mc, photoshopBookMenu_mc, and webdesignBookMenu_mc, respectively.

Above these three layers is the mask layer, which simply encompasses the entirety of the stage. This ensures that the menu clip is truly tucked away from view when it's in the hidden state. This is why we embedded the font outlines to the title_txt field, since masked dynamic text fields don't appear otherwise.

> *If you assign the mask dynamically with ActionScript, which we don't do here, you can mask aliased fonts. To do this, simply use the* setMask() *method.*

Finally, the actions layer resides at the top of the layer stack. Viewing the frame actions on frame 1, you see we have instantiated three data arrays, similar to what we did in Chapter 3 for our selection system. These arrays will define the data that goes into each menu item within our menu frames. As you can see, we've added a varying amount of menu items for each frame to demonstrate how the scrolling system handles menus of different quantities.

```
var flashBookData:Array = [{title:"Advanced Flash Interface Design"},
    {title:"Flash 3D Cheats Most Wanted"},
    {title:"Flash 8 Essentials"},
    {title:"Flash Cartoon Animation"},
    {title:"Flash Math Creativity"},
    {title:"Foundation ASP.NET 2 for Flash"},
    {title:"Foundation Flash MX"},
```

```
        {title:"Foundation Flash MX 2004"},
        {title:"Foundation Flash 8"},
        {title:"Foundation MX Express"},
        {title:"Foundation MX Studio"},
        {title:"Foundation MX Upgrade Essentials"},
        {title:"Foundation MX Video"},
        {title:"Foundation XML for Flash"},
        {title:"New Masters of Flash"},
        {title:"The Flash Usability Guide"}
    ];

    var photoshopBookData:Array = [{title:"40 Photoshop Power Effects"},
        {title:"Extreme Photoshop CS"},
        {title:"New Masters of Photoshop"},
        {title:"From Photoshop to Dreamweaver"},
        {title:"4x4 Beyond Photoshop"},
        {title:"4x4 Photoshop and 3D"},
        {title:"4x4 Photoshop and Flash"},
        {title:"4x4 Photoshop and Illustrator"},
        {title:"Photoshop Elements Express"},
        {title:"Photoshop Face to Face"}
    ];

    var webdesignBookData:Array = [{title:"Blog Design Solutions"},
        {title:"Constructing Usable Shopping Carts"},
        {title:"Foundation Dreamweaver MX"},
        {title:"Foundation Dreamweaver MX 2004"},
        {title:"Foundation Dreamweaver MX Ultra Dev"},
        {title:"Web Designer's Reference"},
        {title:"Web Standards Solutions"}
    ];
```

In frame 2, we simply call the doLoad() method on each of the three menus on the stage, passing in the data arrays created on frame 1 as well as the title we want to give each of the menus.

```
    /*
      Load the menu items into each menu
    */
    flashBookMenu_mc.doLoad(flashBookData, "Flash Books");
    photoshopBookMenu_mc.doLoad(photoshopBookData, "Photoshop Books");
    webdesignBookMenu_mc.doLoad(webdesignBookData, "Web Design Books");
    stop();
```

That's all there is to it. You've just finished building a usable navigation menu in Flash!

Summary

In this chapter, you've seen how to extend the selection system by applying it to the familiar website navigation menu. You should now have a good sense of how you can enhance some familiar concepts in HTML through Flash. Also, notice how easy it was to take the book selection system structure from the previous chapter and apply it to a new usability solution. Reuse of code will be a common theme in many of the chapters to follow.

Speaking of reuse, you may want to try a few things to tweak the behavior of the navigation menus we built in this chapter. Here are a couple examples:

- Modify the expand/collapse behavior of the menu frames. Although we've chosen to represent the expanding and collapsing of the menu through a few simple motion tweens, you might want to experiment with different visual representations instead. All you need to do is modify the enableMenu() and disableMenu() methods, compile, and test.

- Modify the scroll behavior. Try changing the equation to slow down or speed up the rate of acceleration of the mouse-position-based scroll.

Menus and selection systems are only a part of what makes up a functional web application. Once a user clicks an item, what happens next? In Chapter 5, we'll discuss another major component of usable web applications: how to load content in an informative way.

5 CONTENT LOADING

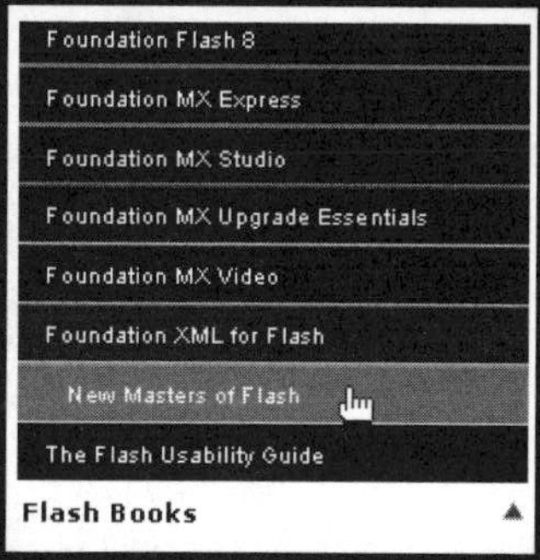

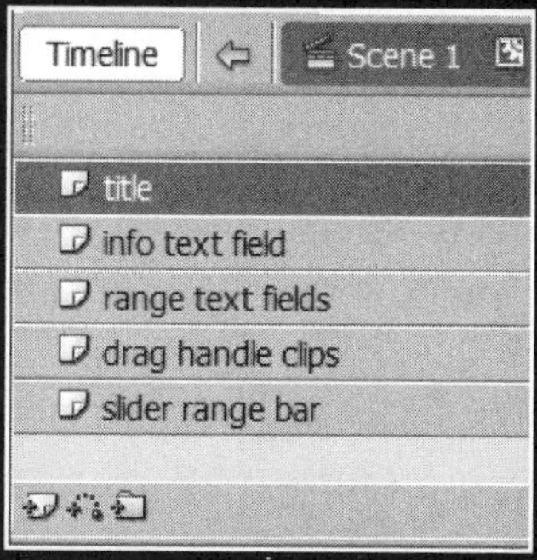

Foundation Flash 8
Foundation MX Express
Foundation MX Studio
Foundation MX Upgrade Essentials
Foundation MX Video
Foundation XML for Flash
New Masters of Flash
The Flash Usability Guide
Flash Books
Timeline
Scene 1
title
info text field
range text fields
drag handle clips
slider range bar
Address 1*
Address 2
City*
State
AL
Zip Code*
Work Phone*

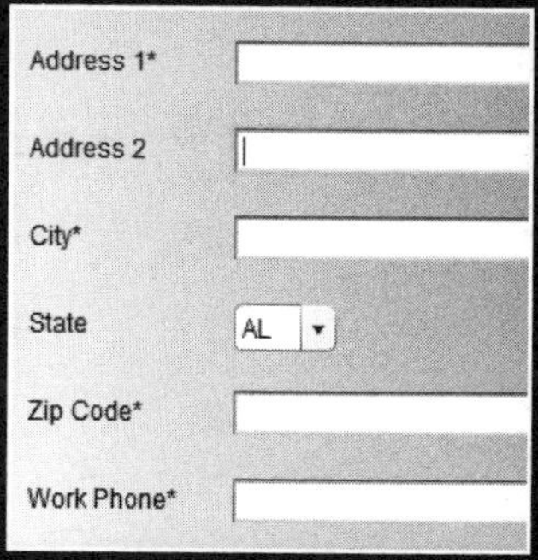

Whether searching for airline tickets or streaming a song to your machine, having to wait for your information to load has become one of the more fundamental annoyances on the Web. The constant battle between available bandwidth and file size remains as prevalent today as it was when we were first discovering the amazing possibilities of the Web years ago.

Certainly, things are getting better these days and will continue to get better as bandwidth limits rapidly expand. A 200KB HTML page would have been a pretty substantial download ten years ago (when the vast majority of home users dialed up with 28.8 Kbps modems), but would be considered relatively lightweight today, given the penetration of cable modems and dedicated LAN lines we see in homes and offices.

However, while the speed of file and data transfer is magnitudes above where it once was, we're also increasing our expectations about how much content can be delivered over a given time period. Downloading a high-quality MP3 may have taken more than an hour a decade ago. Now, if it takes more than a minute or two, most of us are ready to hit the Cancel button.

Undoubtedly, loading content will always be a usability issue, no matter how fast our connections are. That's because, while media producers are creating and distributing more load-intensive content to us, our expectation for downloads to be fast and painless will always remain.

As application developers, we have three main ways to assuage the problem:

- As much as possible, minimize the size of the files that will be downloaded.
- Keep the user entertained or informed while the content is being downloaded.
- Give users access to the portion of the content that is already downloaded, allowing them to use it more quickly, before the entire file reaches their machine. For example, this approach works well with streaming audio.

In this chapter, we'll show you how to harness the methods within certain loadable Flash objects to create informative loaders. In addition, we'll create an example of streaming content through a streaming audio player. Here's what we'll cover in this chapter:

- HTML's inherent loading problem
- Key characteristics behind designing usable loader interfaces
- The Sound, MovieClip, MovieClipLoader, XML, and LoadVars class methods and properties
- How to use the Model-View design pattern to build reusable loaders
- How to build a usable streaming audio player loader
- How to build a reusable movie clip loader for Flash Player 7 and later

Understanding HTML's inherent loading problem

In HTML, keeping a user informed of the load status of each page is not something developers typically consider. Instead, emphasis is placed on slimming down page file sizes by, say, reducing image quality or writing more efficient code. A user's general perception of a website is that every mouse click is *expensive*. Having to click three links to get to a point of interest on a site could mean three lengthy waits as each new page begins to load.

Because HTML doesn't give developers any kind of loading API, there's no feasible way to provide meaningful loading information to the user. Users are relegated to staring at a blank white screen or the load status bar in the corner of their browser, which is more often than not a poor resource for getting accurate loading information. This is HTML's *inherent loading problem*. It lacks an elegant way to inform a user of the load status of an HTML page.

More recently, with the increased use of Ajax-based applications, HTML developers have been able to circumvent the page-refresh issue by allowing users more capability to interact with a page, without requiring a complete redirect to a new page. But they still can't provide users with meaningful load-status information.

In Flash, a host of useful loading data is available for almost every loadable object. So, let's look at how you can harness Flash to build a loader solution that will give your users a better experience.

Developing a Flash loader solution

Because Flash *inherently* allows asynchronous actions to take place, and information about the load status of an object is easy to access, the Flash developer should consider what to display to users as they wait for new content.

One of the obvious things you can do is to load content even before a user requests it. In a Flash application that, say, contains five different interactive games, it would make sense for the application to begin loading each of the other four games while a user is currently in the midst of her selected game. When she has completed (or gotten bored with) her current game, she can move to another game that is ready to go, because the loading work was being done while she was busy with the first game.

However, you won't always get this lucky. It may not always be practical to load every possible object while a user is busy with other tasks. In these cases, the design of informative feedback while an object is loading will play a crucial role in the overall experience a user has with your application. In this chapter, we'll refer to this feedback object as simply a *loader*. Let's discuss what characteristics describe a successful loader.

The design of loaders

You can make many choices in building your loader. Here are the key questions to keep in mind:

- What sort of information should be displayed in a loader?
- What is the best way to visually represent this information?
- What can users do while the information they requested is loading?

Let's discuss some general issues related to designing effective loaders, from a usability standpoint.

Ensuring accuracy

A very basic, but sometimes overlooked, principle of designing loaders is accuracy. While it's certainly not optimal to show the user a blank white screen while content is loading, it's arguably worse to show users information that's inaccurate.

Many loaders aren't actually monitoring a download at all. Instead, they exist merely as a placeholder until the download of a file is completed. We're all familiar with the hourglass icon that appends itself to your mouse cursor when a load begins on your machine, as shown in Figure 5-1. The hourglass simply remains until the load is completed. At the very least, the hourglass lets us know that something is happening, in case we've forgotten that we requested a load-intensive process. However, it would be far more usable and effective if the pixels of sand actually correlated to the amount of the load process completed.

Figure 5-1.
The familiar hourglass icon indicating loading

You're probably also familiar with the web browser download dialog box, which displays an estimation of how much time remains for the download, as shown in Figure 5-2. Based on sporadic connection speeds from the client's machine and upstream bandwidth from the server's end, the estimation can sometimes be completely off or constantly readjusting. This is not good. A key point is that *it's better not to display something than to display something that is inaccurate.*

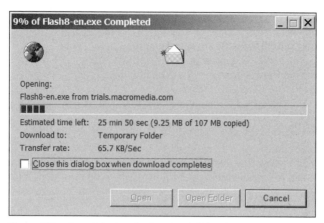

Figure 5-2. Internet Explorer's download dialog box

Adding visual appeal

As we've stated in previous chapters, one of the basic tenets of good usability design is that it provides a pleasurable experience. While waiting for a download can be tiresome, the least we can do as designers is to offer our users something aesthetically appealing to look at (although ideally, you should offer something of higher value to the user, as discussed in the next section).

You can find many examples of loaders that are actually interesting to look at, although much like Flash intros of yesteryear, staring at a pretty loader can get old very quickly. However, unlike Flash intros, loaders aren't just bells and whistles.

Allowing users to multitask

One of the major ways you can enhance the users' experience is to give them something else to do while they are waiting for the application to download. Flash can handle loading-related processes asynchronously with relative ease, which gives you the opportunity to provide users with mini-applications to use within the loader.

For example, a banking site might offer users a means of viewing the latest mortgage and account interest rates while waiting to check their account balances. Allowing users the option to begin completing other tasks as current ones are in mid-process is a great way to both increase their efficiency and divert their attention away from processes that are still completing.

General loader functionality

Regardless of how different loaders may appear, the functional code that sits behind them is, by and large, the same. The exciting part, from a development perspective, is that it's very easy to attach different interfaces to the same loader.

As a developer, you need only a few things to build your loader:

- You need to have some cue given to the loader to tell it that the file has begun loading.
- You need to know exactly how large the file is and how much of the file has been downloaded to the client in order to display loading information to the user.
- You need a cue that tells the loader the file has finished loading.

Fortunately for Flash developers, nearly every object that can be loaded into a Flash file has this exact information available from its API. These include the Sound, MovieClip, MovieClipLoader, XML, and LoadVars objects. This makes it very easy to get the exact data you need to create a loader. The difficult (and hopefully rewarding) part is in deciding how to visually represent the information you have in hand.

Commonly streamed objects

Many Flash objects that can be imported externally into a SWF provide methods for developers to use to monitor the download process. Let's take a brief look at some commonly streamed objects in Flash.

The Sound object

You can load MP3 files directly into Flash using the Sound object. It can be accomplished as simply as this:

```
var mySound:Sound = new Sound();
// Load an MP3 and stream it by setting the isStreaming value to true.
mySound.loadSound("mySong.mp3", true);
```

Let's look at some of the available properties and methods of the Sound class that will help you create your loader clips.

- Sound.loadSound(): The loadSound() method is used to initiate loading of a sound file. It accepts the URL of an MP3 sound and an optional second Boolean parameter to stream the sound. Once you've requested a sound to load, you can initiate a loader clip, and then use the properties and methods that follow to change the state of the loader.
- Sound.getBytesLoaded() and Sound.getBytesTotal(): The Sound object comes with getBytesTotal() and getBytesLoaded() methods that return integer values for the total size (in bytes) of the MP3 file being loaded and the amount of bytes that have already been loaded. By repeatedly requesting this information, you can make constant updates to your loader clip.

- Sound.onLoad(): The onLoad() event handler is invoked when a sound file completes loading. You can use this method to terminate your loader clip.

- Sound.duration: With the Sound object, you get the added benefit of knowing the length of time of the clip (or the portion that has been downloaded). The duration property returns the total length of a sound in milliseconds. This is just another display option you can use to give instant feedback for impatient users.

- Sound.position: Flash also gives developers access to the amount of time a sound clip has been playing, via the position property. When you play a streaming sound instead of waiting for the entire file to download, Flash will begin playing the clip when enough buffering has been given. You can use the position property to place, say, a marker on your preload display that represents the current time position of the streaming audio.

The MovieClip object

For most Flash projects, you'll probably be using loaders for movie clips. Separating a project into several smaller, component-style movie clips to prevent long download times is now commonplace in the development of large Flash applications. The following are the MovieClip object load properties and methods.

- MovieClip.loadMovie() and MovieClip.loadMovieNum(): The loadMovie() method is used to initiate a movie clip load into a parent movie clip. It accepts the URL of the SWF file (or, alternatively, a JPEG file) as well as an optional parameter to send and load variables. Once you've requested a movie clip to be loaded, you can initiate a loader clip and use the properties and methods that follow to change the state of the loader. The other option to loading SWF and JPEG files into the player is to use the loadMovieNum() method. This yields the same results as loadMovie(), but your target is actually a document level instead of a movie clip.

- MovieClip.getBytesLoaded() and MovieClip.getBytesTotal(): The getBytesTotal() and getBytesLoaded() methods return integer values for the total size (in bytes) of the movie clip being loaded and the amount of bytes that have already been loaded. You can take advantage of these values to determine what changes need to be made to your loader clip visuals.

- MovieClip._framesloaded and MovieClip._totalframes: The _framesloaded and _totalframes properties return integer values for the number of frames loaded and total frames in a movie clip. You can use either this pair of values or the previous pair and get the same total percentage of the clip being downloaded. These two properties come in handy when you would like to stream in a long timeline animation and begin playing it before it has downloaded entirely.

The MovieClipLoader class

The MovieClipLoader class was added to MX 2004 and is supported in Flash Player 7 and above. This class is specially tailored to loading *and* monitoring the load of SWF and JPEG files into the Flash Player, allowing you to create UI elements that can respond to its events and properties.

> *The advent of the* MovieClipLoader *object can be mainly credited to Flash guru Colin Moock, who petitioned for a better movie preloading API. The original petition for the* MovieClipLoader *object appears at* http://moock.org/blog/archives/000010.html. *This page provides an in-depth discussion of the faults and defects of loading files without this new class.*

The MovieClipLoader class provides a set of events and methods that allow you more accuracy and notification possibilities than movie clip properties alone. The following are the key methods of the MovieClipLoader class.

- MovieClipLoader.loadClip(): The object itself loads a SWF or a JPEG file using the loadClip() method. The loadClip() method accepts the path to the SWF or JPEG file being loaded, as well as the instance name of the clip in which to load the file.

- MovieClipLoader.addListener(): While a clip loads, the MovieClipLoader will inform any number of objects to the status of the load. The objects "listening" to these status updates can be added through the addListener() method by simply passing in the instance name of the listening object.

While it's all well and good that objects are listening to MovieClipLoader, it won't help you unless the objects know what they're listening for! That's why MovieClipLoader comes with a handful of event handlers—methods that you must define within each listening object, which are then called by MovieClipLoader. Table 5-1 shows a sampling of event handlers (the ones that we'll be using in our solution later in the chapter). More methods are available within the MovieClipLoader API. For the full list, refer to online resources or the *Macromedia Flash MX 2004 ActionScript 2.0 Dictionary* (Macromedia Press).

Table 5-1. Some MovieClipLoader event handler methods

Name	Description
onLoadStart()	Called when a load has begun
onLoadProgress()	Called during the load
onLoadInit()	Called when a load has completed
onLoadError()	Called if an error was encountered in attempting the load

With the MovieClipLoader class, you now have a built-in way to handle events such as 404 (File Not Found) errors and when a new movie clip's first frame has executed. Given this rather enlightened process for loading files into the Flash Player, we will show you an implementation of the MovieClipLoader class exclusively in the second solution described in this chapter.

The XML object

The XML object also contains an API for loading an XML file into Flash. More than likely, you'll be using this object when requesting data from a central database through XML for display in your Flash movie. Unless you're actually sending in huge amounts of data, however, loading an XML file will be a less-intensive process than loading an external sound or movie clip file, so displaying an informative loader might not be as essential. Here's a quick look at what the XML object has to offer.

- XML.load(): The load() method loads an XML file into Flash. It accepts the URL of the XML file that you wish to load. Once you've requested the XML file to load, you can initiate a loader clip and use the properties and methods that follow to change the state of the loader.

- XML.getBytesLoaded() and XML.getBytesTotal(): As you would expect, the getBytesTotal() and getBytesLoaded() methods return integer values for the total size (in bytes) of the XML file being loaded and the amount of bytes that have already been loaded. You can take advantage of these values to determine what changes need to be made to your loader clip visuals.

- XML.onLoad(): The onLoad() event handler is invoked when the XML file completes loading. You can use this method to terminate your loader clip.

The LoadVars object

The LoadVars object API works much like the XML object's API. LoadVars objects accept a text file that contains variable name/value pairs separated by the ampersand sign (as in *myVariable=myValue&myVariable2=myValue2*). As with the XML object, typically these text files will be much smaller than sound or movie clip files. Here's a quick look at what the LoadVars object has to offer.

- LoadVars.load(): The load() method loads a text file into Flash. It accepts the location of the text file that you wish to load. Once you've requested a text file to load, you can initiate a loader clip and use the properties and methods that follow to change the state of the loader.

- LoadVars.getBytesLoaded() and LoadVars.getBytesTotal(): The getBytesLoaded() and getBytesTotal() methods return integer values for the total size (in bytes) of the text file being loaded and the amount of bytes that have already been loaded. You can take advantage of these values to determine what changes need to be made to your loader clip visuals.

- LoadVars.onLoad(): The onLoad() event handler is invoked when the text file completes loading. You can use this method to terminate your loader clip.

Creating a usable audio clip loader

One of the most relevant places to consider building a loader clip is in a multimedia player. Audio and video files of any decent quality are still large enough to require a significant wait before they are completely downloaded to a user's machine, even these days. In this example, we're going to show you how to build a simple audio player loader with some distinctive usability features.

Our audio player will function in the same way as many standard players. It will have play, pause, and stop buttons, along with a volume controller. In this particular implementation, we won't talk much about the design or code behind these particular widgets, since they don't directly impact the loader portion, though they will be a part of our final solution for completeness.

Laying out the loader features

First, we need to consider what kinds of visual feedback will be most useful for the users during a download. For an XML file, you might want to display how many bytes of data have been downloaded. In an audio download, you could certainly do the same. However, letting a user know that two million bytes have been downloaded may not be as meaningful as relaying the fact that the first two minutes of a four-minute song have been streamed to the player. The latter is a far more informative and useful statement, because people are more accustomed to equating the size of a music file with its time length.

So, our first thought should be that all visual displays of loading information should relate in some way to the time length of the audio file being downloaded. Now, we should consider the specific pieces of data to display.

Our progress bar will serve a dual purpose. Not only will it show how much of the file has been streamed, but it also will be used as a timeline from which we can provide a seeker for users who wish to skip around the MP3 file. You're probably familiar with this feature if you've used any mainstream digital audio player.

When users drag the seeker to a different spot on the timeline, it would probably be helpful for them to see what the exact time position of that spot is before they decide to release the mouse button. Many audio players, such as Winamp and Windows Media Player, provide that information in the corner of the interface alongside the total time. For our player, we'll display a little flag that drags with the seeker and will display the new time position, as shown in Figure 5-3. This will keep a user's eyes and mouse arrow focused at the same spot, rather than making the user look at two different areas.

Figure 5-3. The display of an audio player with preloading information

Audio is one medium where you can give users content before the entire file has been downloaded. In Flash, it's incredibly easy to request an MP3 file be streamed rather than fully downloaded before playing. We'll take advantage of this in our audio player to minimize the wait for our users. They can begin listening and using our seeker even while the file is still downloading.

Finally, we'll provide a display for the current time position of the audio playback and the total duration of the audio file that has been downloaded.

So, in summary, here are the tasks we need to accomplish to complete our usable audio player loader:

- Create a horizontal progress bar that will fill as the MP3 file is streamed into the player. This progress bar will also act as a timeline for users who wish to jump around and listen to particular portions of an MP3 file.

- Build in a button that can be dragged along the timeline to jump around to different sections of the MP3 file. Next to the button, we'll indicate the exact time position that the MP3 will start playing if a user decides to release the button. This will allow users to more easily remember and reference specific portions of a song or audio clip, rather than just estimating its location along the timeline.

- Because the MP3 file will be streaming, we will show two time statuses: the time where the MP3 is currently playing and the total duration of the MP3 that has been downloaded.

Building the audio player

Now that we've laid out foundations for a usable loader, let's roll up our sleeves and start building! Of course, the fun of using (and building) an audio player isn't just in seeing it stream. We need plenty of other functionality, like pausing, stopping, rewinding, fast-forwarding, volume control . . . you get the idea. In this solution, we'll focus on how to build the audio loader, but we'll also discuss some of the other components that go into a basic audio player.

In our explanation of designing the audio player's visual assets, we'll reference the completed FLA file (Chapter5a_Final.fla). If you're building your own player from scratch, follow along with us and use Chapter5a_Final.fla as a handy reference. You can do this by downloading the Chapter5a_Final.zip file from the book's page on www.friendsofed.com, and then exporting the files within the ZIP file into a directory on your machine.

Open Chapter5a_Final.fla in the /source/fla/ folder. You should notice on the root timeline a layer called player, which contains a movie clip that houses our usable audio player. For reference, you can find the audio player in the movie clips folder within the library (Window ➤ Library). We've given it a name of MC AudioPlayer. Double-click the audio player so you can see all the pieces that are needed for it to function.

The bottom layer, labeled skin, houses the skin for this audio player. If you're building one from scratch, feel free to use our skin as a template. We've left it available within the /source/images/ directory of the code download for this chapter (named skin.jpg). The size of our skin is 352 width × 110 height; naturally, you should set the size of your stage to this. Import the skin into Flash (File ➤ Import ➤ Import to Stage) and set the position of the skin to the (0,0) on the stage.

5

Notice how our skin contains a display box at the top (which we'll use to house basic information for the streaming audio clip) as well as a timeline bar. We'll overlay the loader information on top of these areas. Note that we've built the skin in Adobe Photoshop to take advantage of its superior stylization capabilities. The beveled and inset look of the timeline bar, display box, audio control buttons, and volume control give it a very nice realistic look and feel. Remember that usability isn't just about functionality, but about aesthetics as well!

Next, let's move on to the assets we need for our loading bar. Above the skin layer, we'll add the following:

- The progress bar clip
- The seeker clip
- The information display text fields
- The volume dragger clip
- The audio player buttons
- The time position indicator clip

Let's look at how all of these are implemented now.

Adding the progress bar clip

Directly above the skin layer lie two layers: the progress bar layer and a mask layer, as shown in Figure 5-4. The progress bar layer contains a movie clip called MC ProgressBar. Double-click this clip to edit it.

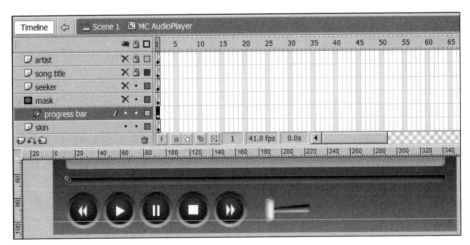

Figure 5-4. The progress bar clip

Here's how we've set up the progress bar and mask layers:

1. Create a solid black rectangle that is 330 pixels high by 6 pixels wide. The upper-left corner of the rectangle should sit at the (0,0) registration point for this clip. In code, we'll reset the clip's _xscale value appropriately to achieve the loading effect. You'll need to make sure your rectangle's left edge sits at the 0 x-position of the registration point, or else it won't scale properly during the load.

2. With the clip created, position it just over the timeline bar area of the skin. In our case, it is positioned at (12,63) on the stage. Also, we've given it an instance name of progressBar_mc, which, as always, can be done by filling in the instance name text field in the clip's Properties panel (select the clip and go to Window ➤ Properties).

3. Set the _alpha property of the clip in the Properties panel to 40% so that you still see the beveled quality of the timeline behind the progress bar as it grows. It will give the progress bar a much more natural look.

4. You can create a mask layer by adding a new layer on top of the progress bar layer, right-clicking over the layer name area, and then selecting mask. The layer underneath (the progress bar layer) should now become masked by whatever shape you have in the mask layer.

5. In the mask layer, create a rectangle that mimics the timeline's rounded edges (using the Set Corner Radius option, which will appear in the lower-left portion of your toolbox when creating a rectangle). This gives a cleaner finish on both the left and right edges of the progress bar clip as it appears to fill up the beveled timeline of the skin.

Because our mask layer covers just the area of the timeline and we aren't concerned with modifying the progress bar's y-value, the height of your progressBar_mc clip is not particularly important, as long as it covers the timeline.

Adding the seeker clip

Above the mask layer, we have the seeker layer, which will contain a movie clip (MC Seeker) that will appear to sit on top of the progress bar clip. We set up this layer as follows:

1. We imported a Photoshop-produced seeker that has rounded edges and is light in color to contrast nicely with the timeline. Any design will do, as long as it is large enough to be easily draggable and contrasts well with the timeline underneath it.

2. Position the seeker clip so that its left edge is at the exact same pixel position as the left edge of the loading bar.

3. In the Properties panel, give the seeker clip an instance name of seeker_mc.

Building the information display text fields

Now, we'll build the various text fields that will display information about the song or audio file, as well as the download progress to the user. Figure 5-5 shows roughly where we positioned each of these text fields.

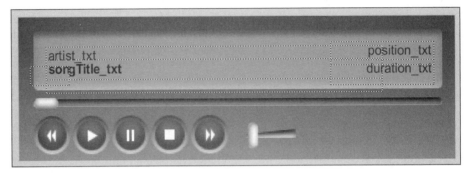

Figure 5-5. The information display text fields

Here are the steps for adding the text fields:

1. Above the seeker layer, create a layer called song title and make a dynamic text field with an instance name of songTitle_txt. Ours is set to Arial, 10-pt font, bold.

2. Above the song title layer, create a layer called artist and make a dynamic text field with an instance name of artist_txt. Ours is set to Arial, 10-pt font.

3. Above the artist layer, create a layer called duration and make a dynamic text field with an instance name of duration_txt. Ours is set to Arial, 10-pt font.

4. Finally, above the duration layer, create a layer called position and make a dynamic text field with an instance name of position_txt. Again, Arial, 10-pt font will do the trick!

For both the song title and artist, we'll grab this information from the Sound.ID3 object (ID3 is a tagging standard that contains basic identification information for an MP3). You'll see how this works in our discussion of the code.

The position_txt and duration_txt text fields will constantly update during the download process. The position_txt field will show the current time position of the audio clip once it begins playing, and the duration_txt field will display the total length of the downloaded portion of the clip.

Adding the volume button clip

Every good audio player should also have an adjustable volume control. Notice the triangular-shaped beveled volume region to the right of the audio buttons of our skin. As with most audio players, the thinner portion of the triangle denotes lower volume and the thicker portion indicates higher volume.

Above the duration layer resides the volume dragger layer, which will contain a movie clip (MC VolDragger) that will appear to sit on top of the progress bar clip. These are the steps for adding this layer:

1. In our example, we've imported a Photoshop-produced volume button similar to our seeker graphic. Again, the rounded edges and light color contrast nicely with the skin. In your implementation, make sure the button is large enough to make it easy for users to drag as well as being easily distinguishable from the skin.

2. Position the MC VolDragger clip so that its left edge is at the exact same pixel position as the left edge of the loading bar.

3. In the Properties panel, give the MC VolDragger clip an instance name of volumeDragger_mc.

Adding audio player buttons

Above the volume dragger layer, we've made a layer called audio player buttons. Because we already have the visual buttons embedded within the skin, all we need here are invisible hotspots on top of the movie clips above the skin, so that we can assign actions to them in code. These are the steps for the play button movie clip:

1. Directly over the play button, create a circular movie clip with an instance name of play_mc.

2. Set the _alpha to 0%, so that you can't see it but it will activate the playing of the currently loaded music file.

Similarly, we've created play previous (rew_mc), pause (pause_mc), stop (stop_mc), and play next (fwd_mc) movie clips, all with 0% _alpha transparencies in the audio player buttons layer.

Note that even though we refer to these as "buttons," we've made them Flash movie clips as opposed to buttons. Since movie clips have the same event handlers as buttons (onRollOver(), onPress(), onRelease(), and so on), it doesn't really make a difference in this case which type of object you choose.

> As a side note, we won't be implementing the previous and next buttons, as this audio player will play just one song. We'll leave it to you to add in this functionality at your leisure. Of course, an audio player that plays just one song isn't that usable, but our real goal here, as the chapter title suggests, is to demonstrate how to build an intuitive loader.

5

Creating the time position indicator clip

Last, but not least (perhaps *most* in fact!), sits the time position indicator layer above the audio player buttons layer. The time position indicator clip (named MC TimePositionIndicator in our library) on this layer will follow the seeker when a user drags the seeker to a new location. Double-click the time indicator clip, and you should see the timeline layout, similar to Figure 5-6.

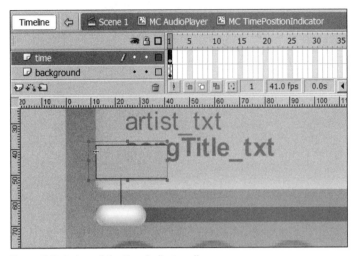

Figure 5-6. A view of the time indicator clip

Here are the steps to take if you're making this from scratch:

1. On the bottom layer of the time indicator clip, (labeled background in our solution), place a background graphic (we've chosen a yellow background to contrast against the rest of the skin) with a line pointing downward toward the seeker.

2. Above this layer, create a layer named time and make a dynamic text field that is positioned over the rectangle. We've again set ours to Arial, 10-pt font. Give this text field an instance name of time_txt.

3. Give the time position indicator clip an instance name of timeIndicator_mc within the parent player clip.

That's all there is to building the actual player! Yes, it definitely had a lot of different parts involved, but now we're ready to sit back and code in the functionality behind this player. We'll do that next, and then finish off the solution by discussing a few small details you need on the root timeline (including actually linking the audio player to a class file) to get the audio running.

Using the Model-View design pattern

Now that we have our audio player clip built, it's very tempting and easy to fall into the trap of rushing into code development to watch the loader in action. But we're going to be a bit smarter about that! As you know by now, this book is not just about designing applications for usability, but also about building code for reuse and maintainability. To that end, we'll now introduce a general design pattern for a reusable audio loader code base.

A design pattern is nothing more than a generic solution to solve a recurring situation in code development. The design pattern we discuss here would be equally applicable to building an XML loader, or as you'll see, building any application that could benefit from having different interfaces attached to the same bits of data.

As we mentioned earlier, grabbing the necessary bits of data to build an informative loader is not the hard part. Once you've loaded an MP3 file into the Sound object, all this information is instantly available to you from the Sound API. In fact, if you were to build a 100 different audio loader user interfaces, the load process and status updates for the load would stay *exactly* the same! It makes no sense to ever have to rewrite this code again, once you've written it the first time.

The interesting challenge lies in how you represent the data that's returned to you from the constant updates you'll want from the load process. Our theoretical 100 different interfaces could very well have 100 different interpretations of the load-status data. This is the part of the code that should change every time you want to try out different functional interfaces.

In this scenario, a common practice among advanced Flash developers is to separate the data construction (which we'll refer to as the *model*) from the interface (which we'll refer to as the *view*). In the *Model-View design pattern*, our model will be in charge of loading an MP3 and then tracking the progress of the load until its completion. It will then tell the view when a new update has been made to the loading data, at which point, the view will decide how to represent these changes to the interface. The view can also ask the model to change based on user inputs (for instance, dragging the seeker to another location on the timeline). Figure 5-7 shows the incredibly basic schematic diagram for a typical Model-View design pattern implementation.

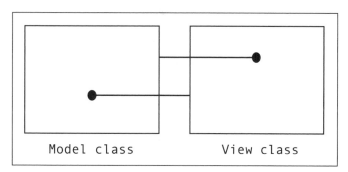

Model class   View class

Figure 5-7. In the Model-View pattern, the model loads and stores data calculations, passing it to the view class. Both classes contain a reference to each other, so they can easily communicate and give or receive requests as needed.

Once we build the model, it can easily partner with any new view we build in the future. Now that's good reuse!

> The Model-View pattern of development also has a slightly more complex relative called the Model-View-Controller (MVC) pattern. In the MVC design methodology, the controller is in charge of receiving user inputs from the view and modifying the model accordingly. In the Model-View pattern, the view just talks directly to the model.
>
> The MVC pattern is most useful for larger-scale development projects and/or projects involving a few more developers, where the separation of tasks becomes a higher priority. Plenty of wonderful tutorials of the MVC model are available, such as Colin Moock's analog/digital clock example in his book Essential ActionScript 2.0 (O'Reilly). For more information about variations of implementing the MVC design pattern on the Web, visit http://c2.com/cgi/wiki?ModelViewController.

What about maintainability? Well, the other main benefit of separating the model from the view is that it becomes much easier to debug the loader. If we had combined these two classes into one larger class, it would be harder to assess whether a particular bug stemmed from the actual data being loaded or from the interface's interpretation of the data. By separating the classes, we can more easily see where the bugs lie.

In our case, we'll embed all the data behind the Sound object's loading process (including the Sound object itself) in a model class, along with some fundamental audio status properties and methods. Let's go ahead and build this class first.

Building the loader model

Open the `AudioFileLoader.as` file within the /source/classes/ folder of the chapter download. This class represents the model for our audio player in the Model-View pattern. Let's go through each portion of this file and see how we've built it. As always, feel free to rewrite the class file yourself.

We'll start by creating instances of a Sound object as well as a reference back to the view class we'll build in just a moment. We haven't built the view yet, but we're going to name this class AudioPlayer. Here are the first few lines of code:

```
class AudioFileLoader {

    private var mySound:Sound;
    private var view:AudioPlayer;
```

Additionally, we'll want to keep track of what percentage of the audio has been loaded and played back. We'll also have a variable that will store the amount of seconds the audio has been playing. We'll make this its own attribute, so that if a user wants to skip to a different portion of the audio track, all the view has to do is pass in the amount of seconds from the beginning to skip to, and the model will reset itself accordingly. So, these variables follow:

```
private var percentLoaded:Number;
private var percentPlayed:Number;
private var secondsOffSet:Number;
```

We'll need a few more variables. The isBuffered, isPlaying, and isStopped variables act as status Booleans, letting us know whether the audio has buffered enough to begin playing, whether it is playing at the current moment, and whether the user has actually clicked the stop button, respectively. You'll see shortly why these are necessary bits of information. In addition, because the model is going to constantly update the view on status changes to the load, we'll use the setInterval() method to continually recalculate our load data. We'll use the loadIvl variable to store the generated ID from setInterval() so we can clear it from memory after the load is finished. Add these variables next:

```
private var isBuffered:Boolean;
private var isPlaying:Boolean;
private var isStopped:Boolean;
private var loadIvl:Number;
```

After the properties, we include a bunch of get/set methods, which are publicly accessible methods for grabbing the values of private variables. We need these so that the view class (coming up next) can access the private properties we just set. Add these methods next:

```
public function get getSecondsOffSet():Number
{
  return secondsOffSet;
}

public function set setSecondsOffSet(_sec:Number):Void
{
  secondsOffSet = _sec;
}

public function set setView(_view:AudioPlayer):Void
{
  view = _view;
}

public function get getPercentLoaded():Number
{
  return percentLoaded;
}
```

```
public function get getPercentPlayed():Number
{
  return percentPlayed;
}

public function get getDuration():Number
{
  return mySound.duration;
}

public function get getPosition():Number
{
  return mySound.position;
}

public function get getAlbum():String
{
  return mySound.id3.album;
}

public function get getArtist():String
{
  return mySound.id3.artist;
}

public function get getVolume():Number
{
  return mySound.getVolume();
}
```

After this, we add in the constructor method for this class, along with an init() method that will set the initial values for the properties above. Note that we set the mySound property's volume to 50 (on a scale to 100) using a setVolume() method that comes later in the code.

```
function AudioFileLoader()
{
  init();
}

private function init():Void
{
  mySound = new Sound();
  mySound.setVolume(50);
  isPlaying = false;
  isBuffered = false;
  isStopped = false;
  secondsOffSet = new Number();
}
```

Our checkLoadStatus() method will recalculate the percentage loaded, percentage played, and seconds the audio has been playing each time we enter it. Notice that if the audio has been stopped by the view (in other words, the user has clicked the stop button), it resets the percentPlayed and secondsOffSet values to 0, because the Sound.position attribute will actually give us the position of the stream the sound last played, which is not what we want here. Our load-status checker will also set the isBuffered and isPlaying to true when the file first begins streaming. Finally, we'll make a call to the view to update the interface based on the new data (this method will be called in updateAssets(), and will be created in the view's class file later on). Here's the checkLoadStatus() method that follows:

```
private function checkLoadStatus():Void
{
  percentLoaded = mySound.getBytesLoaded()/mySound.getBytesTotal();

  if (isStopped)
  {
    percentPlayed = 0;
    secondsOffSet = 0;
  }
  else
  {
    percentPlayed = mySound.position / mySound.duration;
    secondsOffSet = mySound.position / 1000;
  }

  if (!isBuffered && mySound.position != 0 && mySound.duration!=0)
  {
    isBuffered = true;
    isPlaying = true;
  }

  view.updateAssets();
}
```

After this method, we'll add the critical load() function. This method will simply take in an MP3 file path and pass it to our Sound object to begin streaming. We'll then make repeated calls to the checkLoadStatus() method through our loading interval that will be in charge of updating the loading information and telling the view to update itself. Here, we've set the interval to 100 milliseconds per status check, which is certainly fast enough to make the updates appear continuous.

```
public function load(_mp3File:String):Void
{
  mySound.loadSound(_mp3File, true);
  if(!loadIvl)
  {
    loadIvl = setInterval(this, "checkLoadStatus", 100);
  }
}
```

Our next set of methods is pretty self-explanatory. The start() method will accept a secondsOffSet parameter and will play the sound at that position. We can use this in our view later on to reset the play position when a user moves the seeker to a different location in the timeline. The play(), pause(), stop(), and setVolume() methods are also shown here, and they do exactly what their respective function names suggest. Add these methods to round out our class:

```
public function start(_secondsOffSet:Number):Void
{
  secondsOffSet = _secondsOffSet;
  mySound.start(secondsOffSet);
}

public function play():Void
{
  isStopped = false;

  if (!isPlaying)
  {
    isPlaying = true;
    mySound.start(secondsOffSet);

    if(!loadIvl)
    {
      loadIvl = setInterval(this, "checkLoadStatus", 100);
    }
  }
}

public function pause():Void
{
  isStopped = false;

  if (isPlaying)
  {
    isPlaying = false;
    mySound.stop();
  }
}

public function stop():Void
{
  mySound.stop();
  isStopped = true;
  isPlaying = false;
  percentPlayed = 0;
  secondsOffSet = 0;
```

```
        checkLoadStatus();
        clearInterval(loadIvl);
        loadIvl = undefined;
    }

    public function setVolume(_vol:Number):Void
    {
        mySound.setVolume(_vol);
    }
}
```

That completes the `AudioFileLoader.as` class. Once again, notice that all the preceding code describes the status of the MP3 file and nothing about how this is represented on the interface. Now, let's get to the class that will take this information and expose it in a meaningful way to users.

Building the loader view

Open the `AudioPlayer.as` file within the /source/classes/ folder of the chapter download. This class represents the view for our audio player in the Model-View pattern. Again, feel free to start this file from scratch as you follow along.

Because this class controls the elements of our audio player interface, we'll have it extend the `MovieClip` class. At the top, we import a few classes that will help us do some tweens on the elements of this player. More on this in a bit. For now, add this to your class:

```
import mx.transitions.easing.*;
import mx.transitions.Tween;

class AudioPlayer extends MovieClip {
```

Next, we'll lay out all the movie clips and text fields we created for the audio player clip. Remember all of these elements reference the objects that we built within the MC AudioPlayer movie clip.

```
        private var play_mc:MovieClip;
        private var pause_mc:MovieClip;
        private var stop_mc:MovieClip;
        private var timeIndicator_mc:MovieClip;
        private var volumeDragger_mc:MovieClip;
        private var progressBar_mc:MovieClip;
        private var seeker_mc:MovieClip;

        private var artist_txt:TextField;
        private var songTitle_txt:TextField;
        private var duration_txt:TextField;
        private var position_txt:TextField;
```

Next, add the following variables to the class. The isSeeking variable will be set to true when a user is dragging the seeker. You'll see why we need this later. The initSeekerX and initVolDraggerX store the initial x-position of the seeker and volume dragger clips. The seekerIvl and volIvl variables will store the setInterval() values for intervals that will be initiated when a user drags the seeker and volume buttons, respectively. Finally, we include a reference back to the model, AudioFileLoader.

```
private var isSeeking:Boolean;
private var initSeekerX:Number;
private var initVolDraggerX:Number;
private var seekerIvl:Number;
private var volIvl:Number;

private var audioFileLoader:AudioFileLoader;
```

Next, we will add the class constructor. The constructor for our audio player will set the initial seeker and volume dragger x-positions before calling an init() method. The init() method will attach this view to the model, make our time indicator clip invisible to start, set our seeking Boolean to false, and call two new methods—setStates() and setVolumeDragger()—that will set the interactive properties for the loading.

```
function AudioPlayer()
{
  initSeekerX = seeker_mc._x;
  initVolDraggerX = volumeDragger_mc._x;
  init();
}

private function init():Void
{
  timeIndicator_mc._alpha = 0;
  audioFileLoader = new AudioFileLoader();
  audioFileLoader.setView = this;
  isSeeking = false;
  setStates();
  setVolumeDragger();
}
```

Next, we will write the setStates() method, which will house all the interactive functionality behind the audio player. The play, pause, and stop buttons simply call the play(), pause(), and stop() methods we built in the model class. They don't have to do anything more than that. You may think, for example, that the pause button should also tell the seeker to stop moving down the timeline. But remember that all the updates to the view will occur in the updateAssets() method! Begin with these lines:

```
private function setStates():Void
{
  play_mc.onPress = function() {
    _parent.audioFileLoader.play();
  }
  pause_mc.onPress = function() {
    _parent.audioFileLoader.pause();
  }
  stop_mc.onPress = function() {
    _parent.audioFileLoader.stop();
  }
```

Let's now consider what should happen when we move the seeker bar. First, our time indicator clip should appear. In the seeker_mc clip's onPress event, we'll tween in the timeIndicator_mc clip, setting its _alpha property to 100 over the duration of half a second.

Then we'll use the startDrag() method to allow users to drag the seeker only across the timeline. To do this, we set the upper and lower boundary points of the drag to the exact _y position the seeker is currently on (so it cannot move up or down). The leftmost position a user can drag the seeker is the initial seeker position (this is why we needed to store the initSeekerX variable in the beginning). The rightmost position of the seeker will be the total width of the load status clip's progressBar_mc (remember that we positioned the progressBar_mc movie clip on the exact same pixel as the seeker) added to the initial x-position of the seeker. However, we also need to subtract the width of the seeker itself from the width of the progressBar_mc clip so that the seeker's right edge doesn't extend past the end of the progress bar.

We'll also need to set up an interval to recheck the time position of the seeker, so that we can fill in the time position within the timeIndicator_mc clip. In the setInterval() method within the code that follows, we'll call a new method, doSeekerCheck(), to handle this work. Finally, we'll set this class's isSeeking Boolean to true. You'll want to add this code next, in the setStates() method.

```
    seeker_mc.onPress = function() {

        var myTween = new Tween(_parent.timeIndicator_mc, "_alpha",
➥   Regular.easeOut, _parent.timeIndicator_mc._alpha, 100, .5, true);

        this.startDrag(false,_parent.initSeekerX,_y,_parent.initSeekerX
+ _parent.progressBar_mc._width - _parent.seeker_mc._width, _y);

        if (!_parent.seekerIvl)
        {
          _parent.seekerIvl = setInterval(_parent, "doSeekerCheck", 41);
        }

        _parent.isSeeking = true;
    }
```

When a user releases the mouse button after dragging the seeker, we need to do three things:

- First, we need to rehide the time indicator clip by tweening its _alpha property back to zero.
- Second, we will call stopDrag() on the seeker clip, so that it no longer is attached to the user's mouse movements, and set the isSeeking property to false.
- Finally, we'll call a custom method called doStreamChange() (yet to be built) to actually change the play position of the audio file.

Add this code next inside the setStates() method:

```
seeker_mc.onReleaseOutside = seeker_mc.onRelease = function() {

    var myTween = new Tween(_parent.timeIndicator_mc, "_alpha",
➥ Regular.easeOut, _parent.timeIndicator_mc._alpha, 0, .5, true);

    clearInterval(_parent.seekerIvl);
    _parent.seekerIvl = undefined;
    _parent.isSeeking = false;
    _parent.doStreamChange();
    this.stopDrag();
}
```

Finally, we'll add in similar methods to the volume dragger clip:

```
volumeDragger_mc.onPress = function() {

    if (!_parent.volIvl)
    {
      _parent.volIvl = setInterval(_parent, "doVolumeChange", 41);
    }

    this.startDrag(false, _parent.initVolDraggerX, _y,
➥ _parent.initVolDraggerX + 30, _y);
    }

    volumeDragger_mc.onRelease = function() {

    clearInterval(_parent.volIvl);
    _parent.volIvl = undefined;
    this.stopDrag();
    }
}
```

Next, we'll code in the doSeekerCheck() method that we call using setInterval() when the seeker is pressed. It will fill in the time position of the seeker when a user drags it and also keep the time indicator clip hovering over the seeker clip. To get the correct time position, we simply need to know how far down the progress bar the seeker position is and multiply that percentage by the total duration of the sound file. Note that because the duration is returned in milliseconds, it would be pretty impractical to just return this value as is. Telling a user that the seeker is positioned at 15,000 milliseconds into an audio file is far less informative than if we spent a little time and created a method to convert 15,000 milliseconds into 2:30. So, we'll wrap that value into a method called getTimeFromMSecs(), which will simply accept a number of milliseconds and return a much nicer, readable display. Add this code next:

```
private function doSeekerCheck():Void
{
  timeIndicator_mc._x = seeker_mc._x;
  timeIndicator_mc.time_txt.text = getTimeFromMsecs(((seeker_mc._x
➥ - initSeekerX) / (progressBar_mc._width - seeker_mc._width)) *
➥ (audioFileLoader.getDuration));
}
```

Now, let's add in the doStreamChange() method, which is called when a user releases his mouse button after dragging the seeker. Recall the start() method from the model class. It accepted a number of seconds from the beginning of the streamed audio to begin playback. Wherever the seeker happens to be released, we can recalculate the number of seconds that its position corresponds to and pass it to the model's start() method.

Notice that the math here is virtually the same as the math to create the time indicator clip's text display. The only difference is that instead of converting milliseconds into a usable time display, we divide by 1,000 to get the number of seconds offset that playback should begin.

```
private function doStreamChange():Void
{
  var secondsOffSet:Number = ((seeker_mc._x - initSeekerX) /
➥ (progressBar_mc._width - seeker_mc._width)) *
➥ (audioFileLoader.getDuration / 1000);
    audioFileLoader.start(secondsOffSet);
}
```

The getTimeFromMsecs() method that doSeekerCheck() calls is added next:

```
private function getTimeFromMsecs(_msec:Number):String
{
  var numSeconds:Number = _msec / 1000;
  var numMinutes:Number = Math.floor(numSeconds / 60);

  numSeconds = Math.floor(numSeconds - (numMinutes * 60));

  if (numSeconds < 10)
    return numMinutes + ":0" + numSeconds;
  else
    return numMinutes + ":" + numSeconds;
}
```

Next, add these methods. The first method was called in the init() method and initializes the volume dragger's x-position. The latter is called via setInterval() when the volume dragger is pressed.

```
private function setVolumeDragger():Void
{
  volumeDragger_mc._x = initVolDraggerX + (30 *
➥ (audioFileLoader.getVolume / 100));
}

private function doVolumeChange():Void
{
  audioFileLoader.setVolume(((volumeDragger_mc._x -
➥ initVolDraggerX) / 30) * 100);
}
```

So, what have we done so far? We've set the interactive functionality of our play, pause, and stop buttons; defined how the seeker clip functions and changes the playback of the audio; and defined how the volume dragger clip functions and modifies the volume. But we haven't finished AudioPlayer.as yet. We still need to construct two more major methods.

First, the class needs a public method that we can use to load the MP3 file. Of course, we already built such a function in our model class called load(), right? However, back on the Flash stage, our audio player clip links to the view, not the model. So, in order to pass a file to the model, we'll just write a method that simply passes a given MP3 file to the model.

```
public function load(_mp3File:String):Void
{
  audioFileLoader.load(_mp3File);
}
```

Second, we need to create the updateAssets() method that redefines all of our visual loader assets. Recall that the model calls this method after completing its update on the loader data. The updateAssets() method will do the following manipulations to the loader interface:

- Set the artist and song title text fields if they have not been set yet.

- Change the width of the loader clip to correspond to the percentage of the download completed.

- Change the position of the seeker clip to the percentage of the downloaded portion played only if the user is not currently dragging the seeker. (Now you see why we need the isSeeking Boolean!)

- Modify the position and duration time text fields.

The following code accomplishes these four tasks. To find the new width of the loader clip, we just request the model's percentLoaded property and multiply this value by 100. This resulting value is the _xscale for the recalculated progress bar. We'll again rely on the trusty Tween class to apply a smooth transition as the progress bar fills the timeline.

Similarly, we can ascertain the x-position of the seeker clip by requesting the model's percentPlayed property and multiplying this value by the total width of the progress bar minus the width of the seeker clip itself. Again, notice we set the seeker clip's x-position only when a user is not currently dragging the clip (when the isSeeking Boolean is set to false).

Getting the position and duration time text displays is simply a matter of grabbing the model's getPosition and getDuration properties. We'll once again use the getTimeFromMSecs() method to output more readable time displays.

```
public function updateAssets():Void
{
    artist_txt.text = audioFileLoader.getArtist;
    songTitle_txt.text = audioFileLoader.getAlbum;

    var myTween = new Tween(progressBar_mc, "_xscale",
➥ Regular.easeOut, progressBar_mc._xscale,
➥ audioFileLoader.getPercentLoaded * 100,1, true);

    if (!isSeeking)
    {
        var myTween2 = new Tween(seeker_mc, "_x", Regular.easeOut,
➥ seeker_mc._x, initSeekerX + audioFileLoader.getPercentPlayed *
➥ (progressBar_mc._width - seeker_mc._width), .1, true);

        duration_txt.text=getTimeFromMsecs(audioFileLoader.getDuration);
        position_txt.text=getTimeFromMsecs(audioFileLoader.getPosition);
    }
}
}
```

With that, the loading portion of our view is complete.

> We haven't presented the code that affects the volume change for the audio loader, because we've focused on the loader portion. However, the full code for both the model and view is available from this chapter's ZIP file.

5

Putting it all together

Now, all we need to do is link the audio player clip we built to the model-view code that we've written. The audio player is tied to the view class, and the view and model class work together to drive the functionality behind the clip. So, in the Flash library, right-click the audio player clip and select Linkage. . .. From here, export the clip to ActionScript and fill in AudioPlayer as the AS 2.0 class to which to link.

Now, with our audioPlayer_mc clip already on stage, we can write one simple line of code to set the player in action. Create a new layer called actions and, on the first frame, add the following:

```
audioPlayer_mc.load("http://www.friendsofed.com/books/1590595947/
➥ sample.mp3");
```

Obviously, you can substitute any MP3 file you prefer. But, there you have it: a usable loader tied to a Flash-based audio player!

A note on the Model-View design implementation

Now that we've finished the build of our basic audio player, we do want to mention one thing regarding how we implemented the Model-View design pattern. In our code, we had to include a variable for the view within the model class and a variable for the model within the view class. This may not be the best way to implement a Model-View pattern, because it forces a dependency on each of the two classes having knowledge of the other.

More advanced Flash readers may be familiar with using events to communicate from one object to another without each object even knowing about how the other object was implemented. In the Model-View scenario, you could get rid of the dependencies each class has on the other. Instead, any changes to the view, such as a button click or seeker drag, would dispatch an event. The model would listen for events and act accordingly.

We'll show you an implementation of event broadcasting in the next loading solution, and you'll find a more in-depth discussion of the EventDispatcher class in Chapter 7, so stay tuned! For now, though, let's move on to one more example of loading content using the MovieClipLoader object.

Building a reusable movie clip loader

As we explained earlier in this chapter, the latest Flash Players (from version 7 on up) now support the use of the MovieClipLoader object, which ships with current versions of the Flash software. MovieClipLoader gives you a more tailored and accurate API to work with than the traditional load properties and methods of the MovieClip class.

Since loading SWF and JPEG files into either a movie clip or document level is arguably the most common loading procedure in Flash, we'll now show you how to devise a reusable loader object that will take advantage of MovieClipLoader.

In this example of a reusable loader, we'll describe how to build a custom loader movie clip and a linked class that uses the `MovieClipLoader` object to both perform the load and inform the custom class of what's going on during the loading process. This clip will have two means of informing the user how much of the file has actually loaded: a progress bar and percentage loaded information text. Our goal here is to write a fairly simple class and build an intelligent interface that you'll be able to use over and over again, and tweak to your heart's creative content. Figure 5-8 shows what our end product will look like.

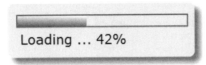

Figure 5-8. Movie clip preloader clip showing a progress bar and percentage loaded text field

Download this section's source code, `Chapter5b_Final.zip`, from the book's page on www.friendsofed.com, and export the files within the ZIP file into a directory on your machine.

Open `Chapter5b_loader_Final.swf` from the /source/swf/ directory, and you'll see that we're loading a simple JPEG file into the Flash Player and showing the load status with our loader. Obviously, this is a very simple application, but it is intended to be reused in more complex applications without needing to spend much time implementing it.

First, let's first consider what we need for this loader:

- As was the case for the audio loader, we'll need a progress bar to reflect visually how much of the JPEG file has been loaded.

- When the load has completed, we'll need to remove the preloader and notify any clips that are waiting that the loaded file is completely loaded and ready to be shown and/or accessed.

- For our second notification to the user, the text "Loading . . . *x*%" will reflect the same information as just noted, only in text format.

- In case the requested file is not found, we'll alert the user by showing some "file not found" text. Of course, you should always debug your project to make sure that all files requested actually exist on the server, but sometimes a name mismatch occurs or a file is missing. This will alert users to click ahead and not make them wait any longer than necessary.

The code portion of our example will extend the `MovieClip` class and contain a `MovieClipLoader` object, which handles the internals of the loading procedure and provides us with easy access to the methods and properties we'll need to accomplish the loader's tasks. Let's get started and see how we can use `MovieClipLoader` to help us create this usable loader!

Setting up the loader graphics

Open Chapter5b_Loader_Final.fla from the /source/fla/ directory of the chapter's source and open the library (Window ➤ Library). Double-click the MC MovieClipLoaderUI symbol to take a look at its internals, as shown in Figure 5-9.

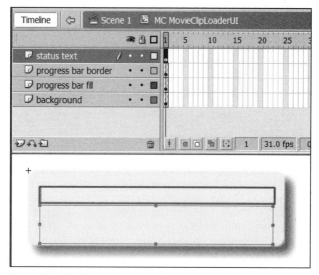

Figure 5-9. The timeline layers of the movie clip loader UI clip

Following are the steps we've taken to create the graphics.

1. On the first layer, named background, we've made a rounded-rectangle graphic using the Set Corner Radius option with the drop shadow filter (see Chapter 4 for details on Flash 8 filters) applied to make it stand out from the rest of the application. This graphic is converted to a movie clip named graph_bg, and the existing instance on the stage has been named bg_mc in the Properties panel. Next, the instance is aligned to the lower-left corner of the stage orientation crosshairs at (0,0). This will make it simpler to place accurately on the stage at runtime.

2. We then create two new layers above the background layer named progress bar fill and progress bar border. With the rectangle tool selected and the Object Drawing option toggled to off, we've created a long and skinny rectangle with a border and fill, which can be separated. The border and fill are both converted into separate movie clips named graph_border and graph_fill respectively. The graph_border instance is then placed on the progress bar border layer, and the graph_fill is given an instance name of progressBar_mc. Lastly, we set the _width value of progressBar_mc to 1, so that it's invisible at runtime.

3. Having built the background, shadow, progress bar, and its border, all that's left to create is a dynamic text field for our loading text display. The very top layer of this movie clip is named status text and contains a dynamic text field with an instance name of progress_txt.

That should do it for the actual graphics. Now, let's move to the code and see how we can use MovieClipLoader to drive the functionality of this loader clip.

Coding the reusable loader clip

First, we need to link the loader clip to its associated AS2 class file. In the Flash library, right-click MC MovieClipLoaderUI and select Linkage. From here, click Export for ActionScript and type MovieClipLoaderUI in the AS 2.0 class input field. MovieClipLoaderUI will be the class that includes all of the necessary functionality for the loader clip to work. Let's build that now!

Building the MovieClipLoaderUI class

The MovieClipLoader object will be responsible for the load and gives our UI class information about the load status. The UI class that we're going to build, MovieClipLoaderUI, extends the MovieClip class and uses the loading and status events of MovieClipLoader to update progressBar_mc and progress_txt within our freshly built MC MovieClipLoaderUI clip. Open MovieClipLoaderUI.as from this chapter's source code directory (under /source/classes/).

Let's start our discussion by detailing the properties of this class:

- mLoader is an instance of the MovieClipLoader class.
- owner is the object that will actually use this loader to load in a new file.
- callBack is the function defined by owner that will be called by the loader when it has completely loaded the file.
- targetClip is the movie clip into which we'll load our file.
- loadUrl is the path to the file that we wish to load.
- progressBar_mc and progress_txt are references to the interface elements that we discussed in the previous section, and these will display the status of our load.

Here's how the class begins:

```
class MovieClipLoaderUI extends MovieClip
{
  private var mLoader:MovieClipLoader;

  private var owner:Object;
  private var callBack:Function;

  private var targetClip:MovieClip;
  private var loadUrl:String;

  private var progressBar_mc:MovieClip;
  private var progress_txt:TextField;
```

Now let's add the first method of this class, init(). This will eventually be called by the object using the loader (owner), and it passes in the integral parameters that the loader needs to do its job.

```
public function init(_loadUrl:String, _targetClip:MovieClip,
➥ _owner:Object, _callBack:Function):Void
{
  loadUrl = _loadUrl;
  targetClip = _targetClip;
  owner = _owner;
  callBack = _callBack;
  initLoad();
}
```

The initLoad() method, called in the preceding init() method and added next, initiates the load (as you might suspect!). This method first assigns a new MovieClipLoader to mLoader, then adds this clip to mLoader's list of listening objects using addListener(). This will tell mLoader to inform the clip of all of its status updates, as you'll see soon. Finally, we tell mLoader to load loadUrl into targetClip.

```
private function initLoad():Void
{
  mLoader = new MovieClipLoader();
  mLoader.addListener(this);
  mLoader.loadClip(loadUrl, targetClip);
}
```

Defining MovieClipLoader's event handlers

Next, we're going to define all those event handler methods (see Table 5-1 for a refresher) in our MovieClipLoaderUI class that are called by mLoader.

First, let's implement the onLoadStart() method. In response to the start of the load, we assign an onEnterFrame script to progressBar_mc. We give progressBar_mc a variable, dest, which will be a number with a value between 0 and 100 corresponding to the percent of the file loaded. The script inside the onEnterFrame function is just a nice easing equation, which will make progressBar_mc adjust its new _xscale value with a pleasing and smooth motion. Think of this approach as a quick alternative to using the Tween class from our audio loader example.

```
public function onLoadStart(_targetClip:MovieClip):Void
{
  progressBar_mc.dest = 0;
  progressBar_mc.onEnterFrame = function()
  {
    _xscale += (this.dest - this._xscale) * .5;
  }
}
```

Following this, we'll write the onLoadProgress() method. It accepts three values as parameters. The first, _targetClip, is a reference to the movie clip or document level into which we're loading our file. The _loadedBytes and _totalBytes parameters correspond to the amount of bytes already loaded and the total size of the file being loaded (also in bytes).

In the body of the method, the first thing we do is divide loadedBytes by totalBytes to get a number between 0 and 1, corresponding to the amount that has loaded. We then multiply this number by 100 and round it up, to get an actual percentage of the load somewhere between 0 and 100. Next, we update the variable dest on progressBar_mc, which will ease its _xscale to that value. Finally, we concatenate the percentage value with "Loading . . ." and "%" and assign it to progress_txt text value.

```
public function onLoadProgress(_targetClip:MovieClip, _loadedBytes:
➡ Number, _totalBytes:Number) :Void
{
  var percent:Number = Math.ceil((_loadedBytes/_totalBytes) * 100)
  progressBar_mc.dest = percent;
  progress_txt.text = "Loading ... " + percent + "%";
}
```

After this, we define the onLoadInit() method. In response to this event, our loader clip's job is finished, and we will call our next method, removePreloader().

```
public function onLoadInit(_targetClip:MovieClip):Void
{
  callBack.apply(owner);
  removePreloader();
}
public function removePreloader():Void
{
  progressBar_mc.onEnterFrame = undefined;
  mLoader.removeListener(this);
  _visible = false;
  delete mLoader;
  this.removeMovieClip();
}
```

The removePreloader() method does the cleanup and removal of the loader clip. First, we remove the onEnterFrame function on progressBar_mc, and then we remove the listener from mLoader. This is important when we use the MovieClipLoader class more than once in the same project. If we did not do this, the listener would still react to the subscribed events, *even if they weren't interested in anything else being loaded!*

Next, we delete the mLoader completely and set _visible to false on the loader clip before calling removeMovieClip(), in case it was dynamically attached. We perform both of these operations because in some instances, you won't attach the loader clip dynamically, but you'll still want it to disappear from the view.

Finally, we define the onLoadError() method. In the case that the file we're trying to load isn't found, we should tell the user about our mistake by setting the progress_txt text property to "file not found". This is a very clean and easy way to handle the veritable 404 error in Flash.

```
public function onLoadError(_targetClip:MovieClip, _errorCode:String)
{
  progress_txt.text = "file not found";
}
}
```

Putting the loader clip to work

So now that we've built the loader from the bottom up and taken a look at the code that drives the whole thing, let's actually see how it gets implemented, shall we? Go back to the first frame of Chapter5b_Loader_Final.fla and open the ActionScript editor.

```
import mx.transitions.easing.*;
import mx.transitions.Tween;

this.createEmptyMovieClip("picHolder_mc", 1)
picHolder_mc._alpha = 0;

this.loadFinished = function()
{
  var fadeTween = new Tween(picHolder_mc, "_alpha",
➥ Regular.easeOut,  picHolder_mc._alpha, 100, .5, true);
}

this.attachMovie("MC MovieClipLoaderUI", "preload_mc", 2,
➥ {_x:122, _y:218});
preload_mc.init("../images/pic_1_full.jpg", picHolder_mc, this,
➥ loadFinished);

stop();
```

In this example, we've imported the mx.transitions classes to help tween the _alpha property of the image we're loading. We then create an empty movie clip on the _root timeline, naming it picHolder_mc, and set its _alpha property to 0.

The custom function loadFinished(), invoked by the MovieClipLoader object when the loader clip has completely loaded its file, creates a new tween, which blends the _alpha property of our picHolder_mc using a nice smooth transition.

The next step is to actually attach a loader clip to the stage. We call it preload_mc and pass its _x and _y values in at instantiation, which is a quick way to position it on stage. The final step here is to tell the loader clip to get busy. The init() method of the loader clip we've built, you'll recall, takes four parameters: a URL to the file we want to load, a target where it should be loaded, a reference to the timeline that should react when it's completely loaded, and the function on that timeline that should be invoked. In our chapter's example, we're loading an image from the Internet, so that we can see the loader clip in action.

> *Unfortunately, the* `MovieClipLoader` *class does not work with the* Simulate Download *option (*View ➤ Simulate Download*) when you test the movie (*Control ➤ Test Movie*) in Flash MX 2004. For this reason, in order to actually see the download progress in action, you'll need to view the example from a web server. This quirky bug is fixed in Flash 8.*

Now, test your movie, and you should see your loader clip in action!

A case study: A basic image gallery

5

So now that we've built a very basic loader and seen it work, let's take a look at how to integrate and use it in an application with a little more meat.

For this case study, we've created a fairly simple image gallery, which is based on the selection application we built in Chapter 3 and the loader movie clip we built in the previous section of this chapter. Go to this book's page on the friends of ED website (www.friendsofed.com) to see our gallery. You should see something similar to Figure 5-10.

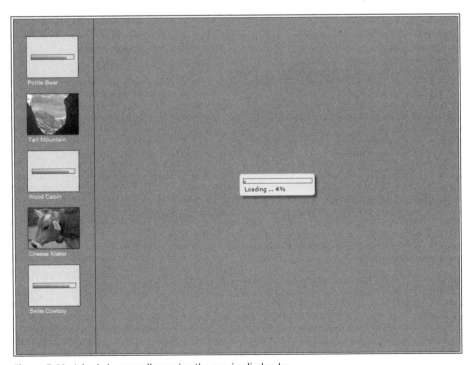

Figure 5-10. A basic image gallery using the movie clip loader

As you can see from the example, the application first loads five thumbnail images on the left side of the screen simultaneously. When you click one of the thumbnails, a full-size image is loaded on the right side. You'll notice two uses of the loader clip in this example. The first loads in the images in our thumbnail items, and the second loads the full-size image. Neither of these two uses requires any additional coding or extending of the MovieClipLoaderUI class. Notice that each of the thumbnails loads individually at its own respective rate (depending on the size of the thumbnail), so users don't need to wait for the entire page to load to see the images.

Now, open this example's source FLA, Chapter5b_Gallery_Final.fla, in the /source/fla/ folder from the code download files. We won't go as in depth with the construction of the essential clips as we've done in other solutions. You have the source files at your disposal!

This application consists of three main components: a selection system that we've customized to load images into its button Items, a full-size image viewer movie clip, and loaders implemented for both. Let's first look at the thumbnail items and how they go about loading their image.

> In a nutshell, to construct the selection system for the image gallery, we extended our UIButton class and our SelectionSystem from Chapter 3. The resulting subclasses, ThumbItemButton and SimpleImageGallery, take care of the user interactions by handling mouse events, showing selections, and telling the FullsizeViewer_mc movie clip to load a particular image. For more details about the selection system, refer to Chapter 3.

Loading the thumbnails

In Chapter5b_Gallery_Final.fla, open the main library and double-click MC ThumbItemButton to view the internals of the thumb item movie clip. The third layer from the bottom, labeled preloader, has a slimmed-down version of last section's loader clip.

We've essentially duplicated the original loader clip (which we still use in MC FullSizeViewer) and removed the background graphic and the load-status text fields, so that only the progress bar remains. We've also resized the border and fill graphics (border_mc and progressBar_mc) to fit the dimensions of the thumbnails. You should also see a layer titled thumbHolder. This is a blank movie clip, which we designate as the target of our loader.

Now, under the chapter's /source/classes/ directory, open ThumbItemButton.as. If you've read Chapter 3 in this book, this should look very familiar to you. However, we've added two main methods in this subclass to handle the loading of the thumbnail image. Let's take a look at these new methods.

The first, loadThumb(), simply tells our loader clip to load the image specified in the thumb item's itemData object (passed in via init() method) into thumbHolder_mc, and that this thumb item is the owner of the loader clip.

```
private function loadThumb():Void
{
  thumbHolder_mc._alpha = 0;
  preloader_mc.init(itemData.thumb, thumbHolder_mc, this,
➥ thumbImageLoaded);
}
```

Keep in mind that as the owner of the loader clip, it will now be notified when the load has completed successfully, so that it can proceed with any updates to the clip being loaded.

Next, we define the thumbImageLoaded() event handler method. This method responds to the event called when the image has finished loading by fading thumbHolder_mc in with a nice, smooth transition.

```
public function thumbImageLoaded():Void
{
  fadeTween = new Tween(thumbHolder_mc, "_alpha", Regular.easeOut,
➥ thumbHolder_mc._alpha, 100, .5,true);
}
```

That's it! Pretty simple, eh? It is worth noting that when the loader clip has finished its job and performs its cleanup method, removePreloader(), the loader clip is not removed from the stage, as it was not dynamically attached. If you refer back to the MovieClipLoaderUI class, you'll see that its visibility is set to false, which accomplishes the task at hand.

Loading the full-size image

The next place we use our new loader clip is in the movie clip MC FullSizeViewer. The instance of this clip lives on the root timeline and is named fullSizeViewer_mc. This clip has a corresponding class, FullSizeViewer, which extends the MovieClip class and defines a public method, loadImage(), which the SimpleImageGallery class calls to load a new image. Go ahead and open the FullSizeViewer.as file under the /source/classes/ directory of this chapter's source. We start the code with our usual importation of transition classes and instantiation of properties:

```
import mx.transitions.easing.*;
import mx.transitions.Tween;

class FullSizeViewer extends MovieClip
{
  private var border_mc:MovieClip;
  private var preloader_mc:MovieClip;
  private var picHolder_mc:MovieClip;
  private var bg_mc:MovieClip;
  private var fadeTween:Tween;
```

```
public function FullSizeViewer()
{
  border_mc._visible = false;
}
```

Then we add the loadImage() method. This method's body should look very familiar to you by now. It creates an empty movie clip in which to load an image, and then attaches a loader clip to handle the load sequence. We no longer need to pay attention to how the loader clip works—just attach it to the stage and let it do its thing!

```
public function loadImage(_image:String):Void
{
  border_mc._visible = false;

  this.createEmptyMovieClip("picHolder_mc", 1);
  picHolder_mc._alpha = 0;

  this.attachMovie("MC MovieClipLoader", "preloader_mc", 2);
  centerClip(preloader_mc);
  preloader_mc.init(_image, picHolder_mc, this, imageLoaded);
}
```

Our imageLoaded() definition (highlighted in the preceding code and defined next) is called when loading of the full-size image is completed. As you can see from the browser example, each image has a border wrapped around it. This is just a single graphic in Flash that first swaps depths with the image clip, and then is dynamically sized based on the width and height of the image we've just loaded.

```
public function imageLoaded():Void
{
  border_mc._visible = true;
  border_mc.swapDepths(101);
  border_mc._width = picHolder_mc._width;
  border_mc._height = picHolder_mc._height;
  centerClip(border_mc);
  centerClip(picHolder_mc);
}
```

Next is the centerClip() method, which centers elements within the loader clip based on its width and height compared to the width and height of bg_mc. Let's take a look at how the centerClip() performs its simple magic.

```
private function centerClip(_clip:MovieClip):Void
{
  _clip._x = (bg_mc._width - _clip._width) * .5;
  _clip._y = (bg_mc._height - _clip._height)* .5;
}
}
```

One of the clips that we have in the MC FullSizeViewer clip is a simple rectangle clip that spans the entire area that we've designated as our stage for showing the full-size images. So, based on the width and height of that graphic (which never changes) and the dimensions of the clip we would like to center (passed in as a parameter), we can deduce where the clip needs to be to appear centered on the stage. To accomplish this, we subtract our positioned clip's _height or _width property from the _height or _width property of the clip to which we would like to center (bg_mc), and then split that value in half. This is a convenient little piece of code that you may want to pull out from this class and keep for reuse in your other projects!

With that, the gallery sample is finished. So, as you can see from the ease and convenience of the loader clip we've created, it's a simple task to add it into your projects to create some aesthetically pleasing and usable loaders.

Summary

5

Loading content is an integral and sometimes frustrating part of the Web experience. In Flash, you have the unique ability to create informative loaders, display content before it has completely loaded, and also let users accomplish other tasks while content is loading.

While a lot of coding was involved in this chapter's examples, you've also seen that you can structure your code so that building future loaders is incredibly easy because your code is reusable. Fashioning new interfaces without having to rewrite the data portion of the load lets you focus the development process on the user interface rather than on the code. It's our job as Flash developers to use these tools and techniques to make the inevitable download waits as bearable as possible!

Loading content intelligently is, of course, only the beginning of your users' interaction with your applications. In the next few chapters, we'll examine what happens after the load. Coming up next in Chapter 6, we'll explore how users can view and more efficiently interact with the data presented to them.

In the previous chapter, you saw how to design and construct informative loaders to bridge the gap in time between a user's requests and the machine's downloading of information. Of course, once that information has loaded, the loader clips have faded away, and the dust has settled, then the application truly begins. So, what techniques can we use now to allow users to best view and interact with this newly downloaded data?

We could spend thousands of pages trying to discuss every possible kind of tool involving data displays you could feasibly build in Flash. With each one, we could have a slightly different answer to our posed question. So, instead of trying to cover a lot of different applications too abstractly, we've decided to focus on data display and interaction using one fairly common web application as an example: *the online store*. We'll do this by examining how the classic "inventory and shopping cart" scenario is implemented via HTML and find ways of improving this metaphor using Flash.

In this and the next chapter, we're going to replace the old-fashioned methods of how users interact with store inventories in HTML by employing some usability techniques that can be uniquely achieved in the Flash environment. In this chapter, we'll cover how to set up an inventory display grid for a set of store items (using the shopping cart metaphor as an example), as well as using drag-and-drop functionality to achieve multiple tasks with our items. In Chapter 7, we will expand on the inventory display grid from this chapter by covering innovative and far more seamless ways to allow users to filter and refine their choices before adding items to their cart.

As you read through these discussions, keep in mind that a vast number of different Flash applications could profit from employing inventory display and selection techniques. Although we are discussing an implementation of an online store, consider how these techniques (and even more generally, the thought process behind these techniques) may apply to your own Flash applications. Usability is as much art as it is science. Our intention is to let the discussion and examples here spark ideas for your own Flash-enhanced projects.

Let's roll up our sleeves and start thinking about usable inventory view and selection devices. Here's what we'll cover in this chapter:

- Metaphor-based design and the shopping cart metaphor
- Limitations of HTML-based inventory display and selection devices
- How to design drag-and-drop functionality in Flash to improve on the shopping cart metaphor
- How to build a reusable, elegant inventory display grid in Flash
- The architecture of drag-and-drop functionality using class interfaces

A brief interlude into metaphor-based design

Before we get into the guts of a usable store inventory and selection implementation, we would like to take a brief interlude and talk about *metaphor-based design*. This is one of the more notable concepts in usability engineering, and since there's some good overlap between this concept and our chapter example, we think it's appropriate to give it some airtime.

We'll define metaphor-based design as nothing more than *creating an interface that mimics a physical-world mechanism*. The inventory view and shopping cart scenario is one of many real-world metaphors that engineers have assimilated to the Web. By looking at the usability benefits (and consequences) of metaphor-based design, we can better draw conclusions as to how to best implement the online store inventory view and selection process we'll tackle in the rest of this chapter.

Technology is laden with interactive metaphors adopted from the physical world. From the concept of desktops and files to e-mail, metaphors help us more easily learn how to interact with sometimes initially unintuitive concepts on the Web. They help us adapt to new environments by representing them in a more familiar physical form. The essence of a really good metaphor implementation is one that does the following:

- Helps users quickly grasp how to accomplish a task
- Hides the underlying functional implementations from the user
- Doesn't get too grounded in the physical-world example as to hinder the advantages inherent to the Web

It's easy to see why a metaphor can help users grasp new concepts on the Web faster. By and large, nearly every online store during the dot-com era incorporated the concept of a shopping cart because it immediately made sense to most people. They were comforted by understanding how to shop and knowing that they could click a link to add an item to a cart without having to purchase that item immediately.

This comfort blends into the second real benefit of metaphor-based design. The shopping cart scenario also means that potential customers don't have to concern themselves with how the actual functionality behind the interface works. A "shopping cart" is nothing more than a list of selected quantities of items that are stored either in a client-side cache or in some intermediary state on the server (that is, the use of application session variables or database tables). How this data is actually stored is both unhelpful and unnecessary information to be giving the user. By masking functional implementations through metaphorical interfaces, we keep an application's complexity away from the user, and instead, make it intuitive (one of our basic tenets of usability!).

However, it's also very easy to stick to a metaphor too closely. A clear example of this is brought up in *About Face 2.0: The Essentials of Interaction Design* by Alan Cooper and Robert Reimann (Wiley). We'll do our best to paraphrase their example here.

We're all familiar with the metaphorical "paper-based" calendar accessible from most operating system desk trays. Paper-based calendars are organized in pages by month. In the physical world, breaking down the calendar pages into months makes sense, as it makes pages a reasonable size and the calendar, as a whole, relatively portable to carry around in briefcases, pockets, and so on. Most computer-based calendars act the very same way. The benefit is that users instantly understand how to read and interact with such an implementation. However, the traditional month-segmented calendar limits us from seamlessly tying a week together that is separated by two months; for example, using the calendar shown in Figure 6-1 to schedule something from August 28 to September 4. A better, more usable desktop calendar could simply implement a continuous scrollbar instead of adhering to the real-world concept of monthly pages.

Date
October
2005
S M T W T F S
1
2 3 4 5 6 7 8
9 10 11 12 13 14 15
16 17 18 19 20 21 22
23 24 25 26 27 28 29
30 31

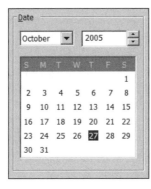

Figure 6-1.
A desk tray calendar that follows the physical-world paper calendar too closely. You're still forced to change the settings to an entirely new month to see September 1, rather than being able to continuously scroll through each week.

In summary, a successful metaphor-based design helps the user more easily intuit an interface without hindering the ways in which technology can improve its physical-world counterpart. With these parameters in mind, let's now move to the meat of our chapter discussion and see how HTML-based shopping carts fare as a metaphor.

Understanding the HTML shopping cart metaphor

In the real world, items in a shopping cart can be checked out at the cashier or put back on the shelves. Similarly, items in an online shopping cart can be purchased or removed. Figure 6-2 shows a typical online shopping cart implementation.

A9.com users save 1.57% on Amazon. Learn how.
Added to your Shopping Cart:
Foundation XML for Flash (Foundation)- Sas Jacobs
Paperback
$26.39
- Quantity: 1
Other items in your Shopping Cart:
Podcast Solutions: The Complete Guide to Podcasting (Solutions)- Michael Geoghegan
Paperback
$16.49
- Quantity: 1
Subtotal: $42.88
Edit shopping cart

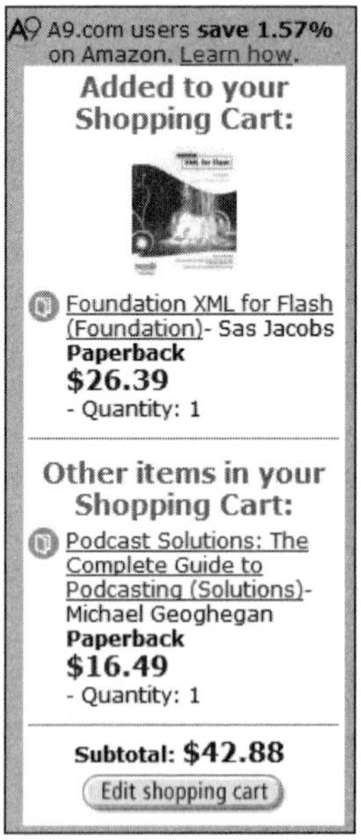

Figure 6-2.
Amazon.com's right-margin shopping cart view gives you a quick look at their cart without having to go to a separate page, but you still need to click through to another page for detail views or to remove an item.

However, one of the major disadvantages to the HTML shopping cart scenario is the stop-and-go nature of browsing through inventory items and adding them to a cart. Here is a typical workflow when adding an item to a cart:

1. Browse through a grid of items on a web page, as shown in Figure 6-3.

Figure 6-3. Red Envelope employs the classic inventory grid layout. You must click the link underneath each image to go to a detail view and to add the item to a shopping cart.

2. Select a particular item to view.

3. Be redirected to some item detail page.

4. To add an item to the cart, click another button, as shown in Figure 6-4, and wait for the server to process the transaction.

Figure 6-4. Most online stores require you to click a button to add an item to a shopping cart. This also requires a round-trip from the client to the server and a browser refresh.

5. Be redirected to a page displaying a full list of items that are in the metaphorical shopping cart.

6. Be presented with further options to search for more items, and if you're lucky, a link to redirect you to the original list of items you were browsing through.

The stop-and-go feel of adding items to a cart in HTML can be frustrating and incredibly inefficient. Shoppers are constantly bombarded by page redirects and server refreshes at every corner. The workflow and constant round-tripping from client to server makes the metaphor of placing and removing items from a shopping cart a weak one at best. It doesn't have the fluid feel of a real shopping scenario.

What you've just seen is how many metaphors tend to degrade on the Web. We get some hints of the metaphor, but only to the extent that they remain feasible to implement. One of the sore spots of HTML design is that it tends to be too rigid a model to really take advantage of all the positive characteristics of the physical-world metaphor. We rely on the user to conform to the inflexibility of HTML architecture, rather than find ways to better implement the metaphor.

> Exacerbating the problem with the HTML shopping cart workflow is the fact that this constant round-tripping usually has little "bang for the buck." For instance, when a user adds an item to a shopping cart, we typically store the ID of the item along with the ID of the user in some database table. This involves a call to another page, a database connection, a database submission, and a re-rendering of the entire HTML page to display the update. Yet, all that has been passed down to the server is a few bytes' worth of data (the item ID and perhaps some other small bits of information, depending on the particular application structure).
>
> A better-performing solution would be to store these cart items on the client's machine until users are ready to purchase their items. While you could store data on the client side using cookies in HTML, you don't always see this done because cookies are browser-dependent and could potentially be rejected. As HTML developers, we're more willing to risk tarnishing the user experience in exchange for the assuredness of storing cart items securely on the server side.
>
> In Flash, we could easily store this light piece of data on the client side as an ActionScript array (or for the more ambitious, in some hand-built object), and not need to worry about browser dependencies of the client-side cookie. Only when the user is ready to purchase an item do we submit everything to the server, in one bulk load.
>
> Note that we've omitted the actual storing and submission of items in the shopping cart from this chapter's solution to focus on the other aspects of usability in this chapter.

In Flash, we don't need to conform (at least not nearly as much) to a few development options. It allows us, instead, to flex our creative muscles and implement innovative interactions that better fit a real-world metaphor. The great thing about Flash is that we can better mold a real-world concept into the online world. We don't need to mask metaphors behind rigid HTML components and settle for just giving metaphorical terms to otherwise old-hat HTML design.

Now, let's try to improve the real-world shopping scenario in Flash and see how we can provide a much better-fitting design.

Devising a better shopping cart solution in Flash

To circumvent the problem points with the HTML design, our general usability goal should be to make the entire interface more seamless, like a real shopping experience would be. Instead of the stop-and-start nature caused by constant server round-trips we're accustomed to in HTML, let's find a way to build on the interactive metaphor of putting items into a cart that is fluid and continuous.

One easy way to achieve this goal is to implement *drag-and-drop functionality* with the inventory items. Going back to Figure 6-3, suppose that when a customer drags her mouse off an item, she were able to then "carry" the item around to different areas of the application interface. If she then dropped the item over some shopping cart panel, it would immediately be added to her cart. Drag-and-drop plays off the metaphor of picking up an item and placing it into a real shopping cart.

Remember that one key to good metaphor-based implementations is to not constrain yourself to the metaphor too closely if it means limiting the ease of use of your application. So, one way we could extend the metaphor is to allow the customer to, say, drag a copy of the item over a detail panel. When a customer releases the item, specific product information could be displayed. Although there isn't a strong parallel physical-world concept of placing an item over some apparatus that will then display detailed product information about the item (you might consider those price-checking bar code scanners as a rudimentary form of this), it is something we can implement in the online world to add to the usability of our application.

To be smart, however, we shouldn't just limit user interactions to solely drag-and-drop actions. For instance, what would happen if you just clicked an item instead? Traditional HTML web applications would probably send you to a new page showing a detailed description and perhaps an enlarged photo of the item. In a usability-enhanced Flash application, we can just as easily make the clicking of an item invoke the same response as dragging the item over the detail panel.

Let's take these general ideas and see how they could work in a real application. To demonstrate, we've built a book store inventory catalog with items that can be seamlessly dragged into a different portion of the application, depending on what the user wants to do.

Download the `Chapter6_Final.zip` file from this book's download page at www. friendsofed.com and export the files within the ZIP file into a directory on your machine. Then open the `Chapter6_Final.swf` file in the `/source/swf/` folder.

6

You should see the shopping catalog application, as shown in Figure 6-5. Because the concept of drag-and-drop in a web application may not be obvious to new users, we've included a set of simple instructions at the top of the page to get users started on the right path.

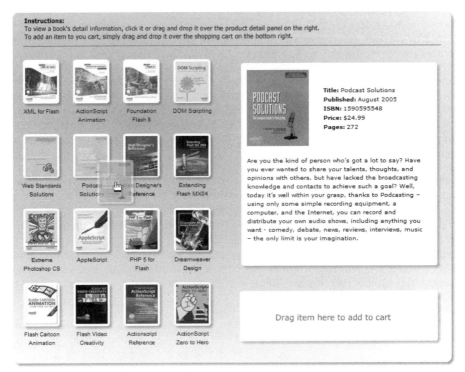

Figure 6-5. A usability-enhanced shopping catalog with draggable inventory items, including a detail panel and shopping cart

Use your mouse cursor to drag over a book thumbnail item to other parts of the application. Notice that when you drag the mouse off the item, a semitransparent copy of the item attaches to your mouse arrow. Now, by dragging it over the detail panel, you should see the panel highlight itself. This makes it clear that you can drop the item copy here to get more information. The same concept applies to the shopping cart clip in the lower right. Drag-and-drop a book thumbnail over the cart, and you should see the cart accept the item.

Also, try releasing your book thumbnail while it's not over either the detail or cart panel. You'll see that the item snaps back to its original position and fades out of view. This makes it clear to the user that no changes have taken place. You'll find that such attention to *little details* can make a *huge usability difference*!

You might be wondering whether or not drag-and-drop is actually a usability enhancement for viewing and selecting items in an inventory. After all, drag-and-drop interactions, while a staple on desktops (such as moving files from one folder to another), are not common on the Web. Some may argue that introducing this new kind of metaphor will confuse, and possibly deter, customers from using such an application.

While that's certainly a possibility, remember that our definition of usability also involves an ingredient of innovation. As long as the benefits of innovative design outweigh the drawbacks of ramping up a user's understanding of the application, we feel it is well worth it. Stepping outside the traditional bounds of web design is critical to enhancing usability.

Of course, another critical key is your user base. More advanced Web users will probably welcome and benefit from the change more readily than users who are comfortable with old staples. You may want to have a group of people representative of the kinds of users who would interact with the real application test a demo to determine whether it's truly the right design decision.

Notice the improvement on the usual HTML solution. The multistep, one-way process of clicking an item to view its detail, and then clicking a button to add it to a cart, and then finding your way back to the inventory view is replaced by a user-controlled workflow. If you want to learn more about an item, you just click it or drag it over the detail panel. If you know what you want, you can just drop it over the shopping cart icon. The user now has more leverage in deciding how to interact with the store inventory, leaving behind the rigid workflow we see in HTML-based inventory selections.

Now that you've seen the final solution, it's time to turn our attention to how to build it. As you probably have noticed in this solution, we haven't fully developed the shopping cart. Our intention in this chapter is to keep the focus on how to build drag-and-drop functionality so that any object within your application can respond to something being dropped over it. For now, the shopping cart responds with a simple "Item added to cart!" message. In a public-ready solution, you would obviously want to display the cart items in an elegant way.

In Part 3, we'll show you a fully functioning online book store solution that uses the same metaphor in this chapter, but with a fully developed shopping cart. It will also allow a user to add multiple copies of a book to the cart (or any other customization for that matter). So, if you wanted to purchase three *ActionScript: Zero to Hero* books, you could drag three copies into the cart, or you could drag a book item into the detail panel, and then key in a *3* in a Quantities field before clicking an Add to cart button.

Building the Flash solution

If you carefully examine the kinds of interactivity going on in the solution, you should notice a lot of subtle interactions occurring. Building the application involves the following:

- Extending the selection system classes we discussed in Chapter 3 to create an inventory grid (similar to Figure 6-3)
- Adding the drag-and-drop functionality with the book thumbnails
- Creating a methodical way to add in new "droppable" areas (such as the detail panel and shopping cart)

We'll employ an object-oriented methodology by using a construct called an interface to build the droppable areas. But, before we get to the code, let's examine the various Flash assets we'll need to get this application off the ground.

Creating the Flash UI assets

Open Chapter6_Final.fla from the /source/fla/ folder extracted from the ZIP file for this chapter's example. You'll notice that our root timeline is fairly simple. We have a background layer, which is a subtle gray-to-white gradient fill, intended to give the entire application a nice textured feel. In the layer above this, labeled instructions, we provide a quick set of instructions regarding the drag-and-drop functionality. On the top layer, we include an instance of a movie clip whose symbol name is MC Interface. This houses pretty much all of the components of this application. Open this clip so you can see how the interface is composed.

Let's see what elements reside in each layer of our store catalog application interface.

The cart layer

On the bottom layer, labeled cart, resides our shopping cart movie clip. This clip will have a symbol name of MC Cart and an instance name of cart_mc. It's also linked to the AS2 class file Cart.as, which we'll discuss later. If you double-click into this clip, you will notice three layers, as shown in Figure 6-6.

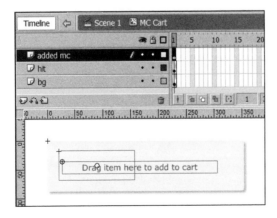

Figure 6-6.
The timeline for the basic cart movie clip

The bottom layer, bg, holds a background image for the cart with a white background to contrast with the darker main background image. We employ a drop shadow filter here (Chapter 4 discusses using filters in Flash 8) to make it stand out from the main background even more.

The next layer, hit, contains a rectangular movie clip with an instance name of hit_mc. The clip is centered on top of the background and is about 80% of the background's area. This clip will serve as the active hit area for the cart. In other words, only when an item has made contact with any portion of hit_mc will the cart "accept" the item if dropped. The _alpha property of the clip has been set to 0 to make it invisible to the user.

You might be wondering why we've decided to make this hit area somewhat smaller than the actual size of the background of the cart. Quite simply, a customer who really wants to add an item to his cart will undoubtedly drag the item toward the central portion of the cart. In order to have the action of adding an item actually activate, a significant portion of the item must be over the icon. This prevents accidental additions to the cart when, say, a user has decided to not select an item but doesn't realize that a corner of that item has hit the cart area. This forgiving nature is a standard quality of good usable interaction design.

Finally, on the top layer, we add an MC Added Item clip (instance name of added_mc) that, for the purposes of this solution, will display a status message to the user. When an item has been added to the cart, the "Item added to cart" message will display. Otherwise, "Drag item here to add to cart" will display. Again, while we haven't implemented it here, in our fully functioning book store application in Part 3, we'll make the cart actually store the item.

The product detail layer

Let's now move back to the MC Interface timeline. Above the shopping cart layer, we have the product detail layer. This layer holds an instance of the MC ProductDetail clip called productDetail_mc. MC ProductDetail provides the placeholders for the product information data we'll pass to it when an item is dropped over its surface. Its associated AS2 class, ProductDetail.as, defines the code that presents the selected book's information. Double-click the MC Product Detail clip to see what's inside, as shown in Figure 6-7.

First, you'll notice the bottom layer of our product detail clip, named bg, contains a background image that is light gray with a drop shadow filter underneath it. This helps to better distinguish the panel from the background of the application, even when no product information is being displayed.

On the layer above this is the hit layer, for our defined hit area. This is the actual area that will trigger the drag-and-drop sequence. As we did for the cart, the hit_mc movie clip is centered on top of the background and is slightly smaller than the background area. And, just as in the cart layer, we've set this clip to 0% _alpha so that it's invisible to the user.

Above this is a layer called image, which holds an empty movie clip called imageHolder_mc. This clip will hold the larger-sized image that corresponds to the selected thumbnail item. We've placed it toward the upper-left area of our product detail panel.

6

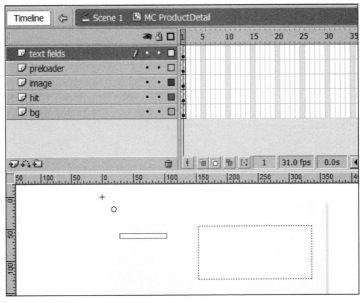

Figure 6-7. The timeline for the product detail clip

In the preloader layer above the image layer, we have an instance of a MC MovieClipLoaderUI clip called preLoader_mc. This loader will be in charge of displaying load-status information as the image of the product is loading. MC MovieClipLoaderUI is, in fact, the very same loader clip we built in Chapter 5!

Above the preloader layer, we have a text fields layer that holds text fields for the various pieces of textual information associated with each book. In this case, we'll leave it fairly simple. The description_txt field will post a brief paragraph about the book selected, and the info_txt field will display the title, number of pages, ISBN number, and price for each book.

The product grid layer

Back on the MC Interface timeline, in the product grid layer, is an empty movie clip called MC ProductGrid. This empty clip will be a container for all of the book item thumbnails. We've labeled the instance of this clip grid_mc in the Properties panel. Also, we've linked this movie clip to an AS2 class we'll construct called ProductGrid. ProductGrid.as will be in charge of structuring the book thumbnail items into the classic inventory grid layout.

> *Where else have you seen an empty movie clip used to hold a collection of items? That's right. Once again, we will be taking advantage of the work we did in Chapter 3, extending the SelectionSystem class to create ProductGrid!*

You'll notice a script layer on top of the main MC Interface layer set. This layer contains a bit of ActionScript code that will initialize the product grid and the resulting drag-and-drop functionality. We'll get to this at the very end of our solution discussion after you've seen how to code these clips' underlying functionality.

The thumbnail item clip

Of course, without having an actual clip that represents an inventory item, this chapter wouldn't go very far! So, the last piece of the puzzle, as far as our UI goes, is to create a thumbnail item clip along with a clip that will appear as a copy when a user drags the item to another location. We've separated these two into different clips, rather than just reusing the same one for the copy because some elements of the base thumbnail aren't really needed. From a usability point of view, we should show just enough information about the original inventory item so users see what they are dragging. Let's explain.

As shown in Figure 6-8, the draggable item doesn't retain the title display below it. By *not* including the title underneath the draggable item, the bounding area (the area that must pass over the cart's hit_mc clip to activate it) is simply a clearly defined rectangle. Had we included the title, the invisible rectangular area surrounding the title text field would also become part of the bounding area, making it a bit more confusing for a user to handle.

Figure 6-8.
When dragging a book item to another destination, we include only the image of the book itself rather than the text. Including the text is just unnecessary overhead from a visual standpoint. Additionally, the draggable item has an intuitive rectangular bounding area for our hit tests when we drag over the shopping cart or product detail panel.

Double-click MC ThumbItemButton from the Library panel to see its composition. Starting at the very bottom layer, bg, we have a background graphic that has rounded corners and a drop shadow filter to give it a nice, raised effect when we place it against the background of MC Interface. Above this layer is the thumbholder layer, which contains an empty movie clip into which our book thumbnail image will load. We've given this an instance name of thumbHolder_mc.

Above the thumbholder layer, you'll see yet another instance of MC MovieClipLoaderUI called preloader_mc, which will be in charge of monitoring the loading of the book thumbnail image to this clip. While our book thumbnails will be quite small in size, don't forget that many items will be loading asynchronously. Even if it's just a split second, it's comforting to see a loader bar appear instead of just a blank item; it lets users know that the application is working.

Finally, the title layer contains an instance of the MC Title clip, labeled as title_mc. This clip simply contains a dynamic text field called title_txt.

Notice that we have linked this clip to a class named ThumbItemButton. In conjunction with the ProductGrid, it will form a selection system with the added drag-enabling functionality we'll work on in the code base for this chapter.

The draggable thumbnail item clip

Now, take a look at MC ThumbDragItem by double-clicking it from the Library panel. The guts of this clip are very similar to what you saw for the MC ThumbItemButton. The only visual difference here is that we've removed the title text layer, as we noted earlier. Also, note that this clip is linked to a class named ThumbDragItem.

Coding the solution

Now that we have taken a thorough look at our various assets, let's get started with the code development. We'll forewarn you that this is one of the more complex programmatic solutions you'll see in this book! It involves a bunch of separate pieces that work together to create the final solution. Rather than going through every line of code from every class we create (as we do for some of our simpler implementations), we'll elaborate on only the more integral pieces of code that drive this application.

We will go back and forth between classes a few times so you get a better understanding of where and how these classes integrate with one another. Of course, you have the complete source code available from the ZIP file for this chapter, so if you're one of those types that learns better through brute-force code surveying, feel free to simply scan through our solution and use our discussion here as an aid. To keep you steered on the right path in our code discussion, here's a road map of our basic approach:

- We'll set up the ProductGrid class (based on the SelectionSystem base class from Chapter 3) and show you how to implement a well-structured grid layout for our various book item thumbnails.

- We'll outline the ThumbItemButton class (based on the UIButton base class from Chapter 3) and explain how it defines where to position each instance of MC ThumbItemButton. You'll see how this class works with the ProductGrid class to create the book thumbnail dragging effect.

- We'll set up a DragDropManager class, whose job will be to monitor when a user drags or drops a book thumbnail item over an area of the interface. We'll also discuss the ThumbDragItem class, which works in tandem with DragDropManager to sense when the dragged item lands over another part of the application. DragDropManager will then be responsible for telling the product detail panel and the cart that a user has dragged or dropped something over their surface, so that they know to react in their own predefined manner.

- We'll create the classes for the product detail panel and shopping cart objects. For simplicity's sake, we'll refer to these objects as *droppable UI objects* in our code discussion. We'll show you how to use an object-oriented concept called *interfaces* to better structure your code for these classes.

- We'll put it all together by creating an instance of DragDropManager, registering our droppable UI objects with it, and then passing a book data array to the ProductGrid class to create the inventory view.

Creating the grid layout structure

If you recall from Chapter 3, we built two extendable classes (SelectionSystem and UIButton) that form a basic, reusable selection system. Whether it's a set of navigation links or a set of store catalog items, as in this case, we can use our selection system base classes to handle the initial load, attachment, and positioning of items into a container clip.

We will override two key methods here in the extension of these two classes. Recall that the attachButtonItems() method within the SelectionSystem is in charge of actually attaching the UIButton elements to a container clip and then passing whatever information the UIButton needs to function. We will modify this method to pass it an additional set of information that it needs to position itself in the grid layout. Secondly, we'll overwrite the setPosition() method within the UIButton class to take this new information and convert it to the exact (x,y) pixel location of where it should position itself on stage. After doing these two modifications, we'll have the code ready to structure our items in the inventory grid layout you see in Figure 6-5. So let's get started!

MC ProductGrid is the clip that acts as a container for all of our book thumbnail items. Since we've already built the methods to handle the load of individual items within the SelectionSystem class, we'll need to extend this class through MC ProductGrid's linked class ProductGrid. Our focus in this discussion will be on how to extend and customize this base class to set up our product grid layout.

What's unique about the MC ProductGrid clip (compared to other ways we've extended SelectionSystem) is the way the items within the clip will be positioned. Because it will be a grid layout, rather than a straight left-to-right or top-to-bottom layout, we'll need to do a little more work to determine how the book thumbnail items will position themselves. In ProductGrid.as, inside the /source/classes/ folder of the chapter download, we add a few private variables.

```
private var itemsPerRow:Number = 4;

private var currentRow:Number = 0;
private var currentColumn:Number = 0;

//space between rows and columns
private var horizSpace:Number = 16;
private var vertSpace:Number = 6;
```

We have an itemsPerRow variable to determine the number of rows in our book grid layout. As you can see in Figure 6-5, our grid is 4 × 4. So, we'll set this value to 4. Because the SelectionSystem class will load our book thumbnail items one at a time, we'll also need to keep track of the current row and column assigned to each book thumbnail item, namely currentRow and currentColumn. Think of these values together as the table cell within the 4 × 4 grid. Finally, we'll want to adjust how much horizontal and vertical space should fit between each column and row. The horizSpace and vertSpace variables will store this data. In this case, we'll set the horizontal padding between items to 16 pixels and the vertical padding to 6 pixels.

Now, recall from Chapter 3 that the SelectionSystem class uses an attachButtonItems() method (called through its doInit() method) to loop through a passed-in array of data to

FLASH APPLICATION DESIGN SOLUTIONS: THE FLASH USABILITY HANDBOOK

populate its associated parent movie clip with items. The attachButtonItems() method not only attached each new item clip to the stage, but also called an init() method defined within the UIButton class, which provided a generic object with all the essentials it needed to function. In our specific case, we'll need to pass into this init() method some *additional* way of letting the eventual ThumbItemButton class know where to place itself within this MC ProductGrid container clip. To accomplish this, we'll modify the init() method in the ThumbItemButton class to include a fourth parameter. We'll override the attachButtonItems() method as follows:

```
public function attachButtonItems():Void
{
  for(var i:Number = 0; i < systemData.length; i++)
  {
    //get placement object according to counts
    updateGrid(i);

    //attach a clip
    var item:MovieClip = attachMovie("MC ThumbItem", "Item_" + i, i,
    {id:i});
    item.init(this, i, systemData[i], getItemPositionObj());
    listItems.push(item);
  }

  //by default, select the first UIButton item and display its detail
  //in the product detail panel using initDetail()
  setSelection(0);
  initDetail();
}
```

Notice a couple methods called in this class (emphasized in the preceding code) that we haven't yet defined. First, the updateGrid() method will be in charge of updating the currentRow and currentColumn variables as each new book thumbnail is attached to the grid. Notice that when we pass in the current index of the item to this method, it will use the mod function (%) to figure out if the currently loaded item needs to move to a new row. If index % itemsPerRow evaluates to 0 (that is, the index divides into the number of rows evenly), we know that the placement of that particular item must be in a new row. Here is the updateGrid() method:

```
private function updateGrid(_index:Number):Void
{
  if(!(_index % itemsPerRow))
  {
    currentColumn = 0;
    currentRow++;
  }
  else
  {
    currentColumn++;
  }
}
```

The other new method is getItemPositionObj(). This method returns the essential positioning information for each of the thumbnail items, which is assigned to the new fourth parameter of ThumbItemButton's init() method. This information will come in the form of a generic Object instance populated with grid position information. Here is the getItemPositionObj() method:

```
private function getItemPositionObj():Object
{
  var obj:Object = new Object();

  obj.horizSpace = horizSpace;
  obj.vertSpace = vertSpace;

  obj.grid_x = currentColumn;
  obj.grid_y = currentRow;

  return obj;
}
```

Notice that the returned object in this method contains the horizontal and vertical padding between each item in our grid, along with the row and column number for the clip. This is enough information to calculate the exact _x and _y positions for the book thumbnail item. In our discussion of the ThumbItemButton class, we'll show you how a thumbnail item will use this information to position itself accordingly on stage.

These methods complete the ProductGrid class to create the easily recognizable grid interface for our book item inventory. We'll dig back into this class later on when we delve into our dragging functionality discussion, so you may want to leave this file open if you're following along using the chapter solution.

But, before we get to dragging, let's round out our implementation of the grid layout by implementing the necessary functionality in our ThumbItemButton class.

Setting the position of the thumbnails

Just as we've extended the selection system class to take advantage of its loading methods for ProductGrid, we'll also create the class linked to our MC ThumbItemButton clip to extend UIButton (our generic button item class from Chapter 3). Open ThumbItemButton.as inside the /source/classes/ folder of the chapter download and let's go through the particular way we extend this class to fully implement our grid layout.

Remember that our ProductGrid class will call this class's init() method. Here, you see the inclusion of the fourth parameter _gridObj, our generic object passed from ProductGrid's getItemPositionObj() method:

```
public function init(_selectionSystem:SelectionSystem, _id:Number,
  ➥ _itemData:Object, _gridObj:Object):Void
{
  gridObj = _gridObj;
  super.init(_selectionSystem, _id, _itemData);
  loadThumb();
}
```

We won't do the positioning work just yet. Instead, we'll simply set the passed-in _gridObj to a private property gridObj (while not shown, in our class code, we added gridObj as a private property we define in the class).

Recall from Chapter 3 that our clip's stage position is set by invoking the setPosition() method within the parent UIButton class. Once again, we'll override the method in the ThumbItemButton class to implement the positioning specific to this particular solution. Here's how we've coded the setPosition() method:

```
private function setPosition():Void
{
  _x = Math.round((gridObj.grid_x * _width) +
➥ (gridObj.horizSpace * gridObj.grid_x));
  _y = Math.round(((gridObj.grid_y-1) * _height) +
➥ (gridObj.vertSpace * (gridObj.grid_y-1)));
}
```

Notice that the setPosition() method takes the grid_x and grid_y values from gridObj and calculates the true _x and _y position for the book thumbnail. To calculate the appropriate _x position, we need to take the total width of one book thumbnail item (its _width + gridObj.horizSpace buffer width) and multiply it by its column position within the grid (grid_x). We can calculate the appropriate _y position in a similar fashion.

In a nutshell, that's the essential code needed within our grid and book thumbnail item clip classes to generate our simple but well-designed grid layout. This demonstrates where *reusability* of code helps us out. We've extended both the SelectionSystem and UIButton classes from Chapter 3 to handle the loading and selection states of our store catalog collection, and we just needed to override the SelectionSystem.attachButtonItems(), UIButton.init(), and UIButton.setPosition() methods to create this new grid layout format.

Now, let's move on to perhaps the more visually interesting portion of the code: our usable drag-and-drop functionality.

Creating the drag-and-drop functionality

You learned from our usability discussion that what's a little different about our drag-and-drop functionality is that you don't simply drag-and-drop a book thumbnail item; rather, you drag a *copy* of the item (the ThumbDragItem clip). What this implies is that we can't simply use the built-in startDrag() and stopDrag() functions on each book thumbnail to accomplish the task, because they apply to dragging the original item.

Take a look at ThumbItemButton.as once again. We've overwritten the handlePress() and handleRelease() methods from the extended base UIButton class. Recall that these methods are invoked when a user presses the item and releases the item, respectively. The handlePress() method will call a new method in our button class, startDragTest(). The handleRelease() method will call a new method called stopDragTest(). Let's take a look at these two new methods now.

```
private function startDragTest():Void
{
  this.onMouseMove = function()
  {
    if(!this.bg_mc.hitTest(_root._xmouse, _root._ymouse, false))
    {
      stopDragTest();
      SelectionSystem.cueDragDropManager(id);
    }
  }
}

private function stopDragTest():Void
{
  this.onMouseMove = undefined;
}
```

It may seem a bit confusing what we're doing here, but it's actually quite simple. When a user has pressed the mouse button on a particular book item, we set up an onMouseMove() event handler that waits to see if the mouse cursor rolls *off* the book thumbnail item. From a usability perspective, whenever this happens, it's a sure sign that the user wants to drag the item to some other destination. If so, we kill the event handler through the stopDragTest() method and tell the ProductGrid class to help create the dragging effect through a method called cueDragDropManager().

Let's move back to ProductGrid.as and take a look at our rather thin cueDragDropManager() method:

```
public function cueDragDropManager(_id:Number):Void
{
  _parent.dragDropManager.attachDragItem(systemData[_id]);
}
```

Now, if you aren't confused, you should be! One thing we haven't discussed yet is how we set up not only the dragging effect, but how other objects in our application interact with an item that is dragged or dropped over their respective surfaces. In essence, we need some sort of class that observes the entire application, knowing when to start a drag of a thumbnail item and signaling to other objects in the application when a user drags or drops the item over their surfaces. In this solution, we've built a class called DragDropManager to do this work. The _parent.dragDropManager is a reference to an instance of this class that will be created on the timeline of the MC Interface clip (our master clip for the whole inventory application).

> We use _parent here because we know beforehand that we're going to create this DragDropManager class instance on the same parent timeline as the ProductGrid instance. This isn't the best way to make our code reusable, as it now places a dependency on where we put the DragDropManager instance if we want to reuse this code. But we do this here to simplify the code for this solution.

So, now we know that when a user drags off a particular book item, we invoke some method called attachDragItem() from the instance of DragDropManager, passing with it the book thumbnail's item data (systemData[id]). This class's attachDragItem() method then creates that thumbnail item copy you saw in Figure 6-8.

To examine the DragDropManager class, open the DragDropManager.as file inside the /source/classes/ folder of the chapter download. First, let's quickly go through a few properties this class will need in particular for the attachDragItem() method to work:

```
private var targetClip:MovieClip;
private var linkage:String;
private var dragEnabled:Boolean;
private var dropEnabled:Boolean;
private var dropAreas:Array;
private var hitClip:DropArea;
```

We'll need a target movie clip, targetClip, that tells us to which movie clip's timeline the draggable book item thumbnail will be attached. In this case, it will be the MC Interface clip instance itself. Also, we'll need the linkage name, linkage, of the movie clip we want to use as the draggable item. In this case, it will be the MC ThumbDragItem movie clip. Of course, we could easily just hard-code these names within the DragDropManager class but, always with an eye toward reuse, we'll abstract these as variables. The other variables will be discussed a little later in this section.

Later on, when we write the initialization code within the timeline of MC Interface, we'll pass this data into the DragDropManager's constructor, which is shown here:

```
public function DragDropManager(_targetClip:MovieClip, _linkage:String)
{
  targetClip = _targetClip;
  linkage = _linkage;
  dropAreas = new Array();
}
```

Now, let's take a look at DragDropManager's attachDragItem() method.

```
public function attachDragItem(_itemData:Object):Void
{
  targetClip.attachMovie(linkage, "dragItem_mc", 1000);
  targetClip.dragItem_mc.doInit(_itemData);

  Mouse.addListener(this);
  dragEnabled = true;
}
```

Here, we attach an instance of the linkage movie (in this case it will be the MC ThumbDragItem clip) onto the master interface clip for this application. Also, we call a doInit() function that's defined in ThumbDragItem.as, passing along the original book thumbnail item's data object which then loads the copy of the book thumbnail image to this MC ThumbDragItem instance.

The DragDropManager class also has the responsibility of telling our droppable UI clips (the product detail panel and cart panel) what to do when a user drags this newly attached draggable item. Going back to our set of private properties for this class, we have an array called dropAreas, which will store a list of these droppable UI clip paths.

Now, notice that in the attachDragItem() method, this class also registers itself as an event listener of the Mouse object. What this means is that any event handler actions that can be invoked through the Mouse object, such as onMouseMove() and onMouseUp(), will also call the methods of the same name in our DragDropManager class. In our code, the onMouseMove() method will invoke testForHit(), a method that cycles through each of the droppable UI clips within our dropAreas array and sees whether our book thumbnail item has made contact with any of them. Here's the implementation of the onMouseMove() and testForHit() methods:

```
public function onMouseMove():Void
{
  testForHit();
}

private function testForHit():Void
{
  for(var i=0; i<=dropAreas.length-1; i++)
  {
    var testClip:DropArea = dropAreas[i];

    if(testClip.getHitArea().hitTest(targetClip.dragItem_mc))
    {
      testClip.setEngageDrop(true);
      hitClip = testClip;
      dropEnabled = true;
      disableOtherDropAreas();
      break;
    }
    else
    {
      disableAllDropAreas();
    }
  }
}
```

The essential calls are highlighted in the preceding listing. While the mouse is dragging the MC ThumbDragItem clip around the application, this code will cycle through each object in the dropAreas array to see whether the dragged item has made content with a droppable area (if(testClip.getHitArea().hitTest(targetClip.dragItem_mc) { }). We'll explain the getHitArea() method a bit later. For now, you should just know that it simply returns a movie clip that represents the active hit area for the droppable UI clip.

If the dragged item has made contact with a droppable area, with the call to testClip.setEngageDrop(true), the droppable UI movie clip can display an effect to show the user that the thumb item can be dropped over its surface. In this application, the product detail panel slightly fades. We'll explain the setEngageDrop() method in more detail in our discussion of droppable UI areas in the next section. Also, we store the reference to the droppable UI movie clip in another private property called hitClip, so that when a user decides to drop the clip, our DragDropManager class will remember which clip should respond to the drop. The class's dropEnabled Boolean is set to true, indicating that the thumb item is ready to drop over one of the droppable UI areas. You'll see how we use this Boolean in just a moment.

Did you also notice that we've set the variable testClip to a DropArea type (not a MovieClip type as you might expect)? DropArea is an *interface* we'll implement next. If you're not yet familiar with interfaces, we'll explain them in detail in just a bit. For now, all you need to know is that setEngageDrop() (along with getHitArea()) will be defined in every movie clip within the dropAreas array, by virtue of the fact that it is a type of DropArea.

It's worth mentioning how DropArea objects are added to the dropAreas array. This is done with a simple public method within DragDropManager called addDropArea(), shown here. We'll add these drop areas to the array after creating an instance of DragDropManager on the MC Interface clip's root timeline, in the "Putting it all together" section later in this chapter.

```
public function addDropArea(_dropArea:DropArea):Void
{
  dropAreas.push(_dropArea);
}
```

Of course, now that we have a method that will sense when a user has *dragged* an item over a droppable UI area, we also will need one that will sense when a user has *dropped* an item over a droppable UI area. This is where testForDrop() comes in. Here's the testForDrop() method within the DragDropManager class:

```
private function testForDrop():Void
{
  if(dropEnabled)
  {
    hitClip.doDrop(this);
    targetClip.dragItem_mc.remove();
    dropEnabled = false;
    Mouse.removeListener(this);
  }
  else
  {
    removeDragItem();
  }
}
```

Again, the essential calls are highlighted in the preceded listing. First, with `hitClip.doDrop(this)`, the droppable UI movie clip can display an effect to show the user that the thumb item has been dropped over its surface (we'll discuss the `doDrop()` method later in the upcoming section about the droppable UI areas). Notice that this line is invoked only if `dropEnabled` is set to true. This was set in the `testForHit()` method. The `if/else` statement is necessary because if `dropEnabled` is not true (meaning that the current item being dragged is not actually over any droppable UI clip), we call the `removeDragItem()` method, which will then create the "snapback" effect of the draggable book item we discussed earlier in the chapter.

Although we won't go into detail about the implementation of the snapback effect, for posterity, here is the method that does the trick within the `ThumbDragItem` class. We first set the original x- and y-positions of the draggable book thumbnail item in the `doInit()` method that is loaded from when we attached the clip in the `DragDropManager` class. Here, we snap the clip back to this position using a few tween calls:

```
public function returnToOrigin():Void
{
  xTween = new Tween(this, "_x", Regular.easeOut, _x, origX,.2, true);
  yTween = new Tween(this, "_y", Regular.easeOut, _y, origY,.2, true);
  fadeTween = new Tween(this, "_alpha", Regular.easeOut, _alpha, 0, .3,
➥ true);
  fadeTween.addListener("onMotionFinished", this);
}
```

So, in a nutshell, we've now created the structure for how items are dragged and dropped. If you recall, we've saved two methods that are owned by our droppable UI clips for later: `setEngageDrop()` and `doDrop()`.

Building the droppable UI areas

Our next step in the process is to build the classes that are linked to our *droppable UI clips* (the clips that a book thumbnail item can drop into): the product detail and the cart. We've combined the discussions of these two classes together because, if you think about it, both need to define the same actions:

- They need to change their physical states when a draggable book item touches their respective hit areas, so the user knows that by releasing an item, it will interact with the respective object.

- They need to define what actually happens when a draggable book item is dropped over their hit area. For instance, the product detail clip would then display information pertaining to the item, whereas the cart would add the item to the user's checkout list.

- And finally, they actually need to define what part of the UI should be considered the active hit area. Recall from how we created the cart and product detail panels in the Flash environment that we added invisible hit_mc clips to define the active hit areas.

6

For the OOP whizzes out there, you might be thinking about defining an *interface* that contains these three methods, and then having the product detail and cart classes implement them. Well, that's what we're about to do!

Be careful not to confuse the term *interface* here with the design of graphical interfaces. An interface, in OOP terms, is a construct that can be implemented by a class that creates the shell of methods that are both required and further defined by the classes that implement it. Essentially, an interface is a contract that the implementing class agrees to conform to which aids in cross-class communication. If you're still a little confused, it will make a whole lot more sense if we actually look at our interface code.

Open the `DropArea.as` interface. You can see it's rather skinny, defining only three methods.

```
interface DropArea
{
  public function setEngageDrop(_engage:Boolean):Void;
  public function doDrop():Void;
  public function getHitArea():MovieClip;
}
```

The first method, setEngageDrop(), will define what happens to the clips when an item has been dragged over a droppable UI clip's hit area. It expects a Boolean value that tells the object whether the thumbnail item has come in contact with the object. The second method, doDrop(), will define what happens when an item is dropped over a droppable clip's hit area. The final method, getHitArea(), simply returns a reference to the movie clip within the droppable UI clip that represents its active hit area.

> *You can see why this construct is called an interface. When a class implements an interface, it defines the methods that are created from the interface. The interface itself has no knowledge of what the method definitions look like. It only knows that the methods are defined within each respective class. In essence, it is an "interface" to all the classes that implement it. We can safely assume any class that implements* DropArea *will have the* setEngageDrop(), doDrop(), *and* getHitArea() *methods ready to go!*
>
> *The other great benefit is that we can now type an object as a* DropArea *object, as we did in the* DragDropManager *class. When doing so, we can reference the* setEngageDrop(), doDrop(), *and* getHitArea() *methods with the knowledge that they are implemented for any kind of* DropArea.

In our specific case, we use an interface as a class contract. If we wanted to add more droppable UI clips in the future, they must define these three methods in their own class definitions. If they don't adhere to the contract, when we go to compile our Flash movie, we'll get compilation errors. Quite simply, it helps us ensure that each droppable UI clip will define its hit area as well as what happens when an item is dragged or dropped over one of its hit areas.

> *Note that in this particular chapter example, things would work perfectly fine if we didn't have a* DropArea *interface but just ensured that the* setEngageDrop(), doDrop(), *and* getHitArea() *methods existed in each of our droppable UI clips. However, adding in the interface helps us remember what methods we need to define. If we didn't have the* DropArea *interface, we would not get compilation errors if we had forgotten to define these methods in a droppable UI clip, which makes debugging the code a lot more difficult.*

Now that we have the DropArea interface handy, let's see how easy it is to implement it for each of our three droppable UI clips.

The most basic implementation of either of the droppable UI clips is with the MC Cart clip. Open Cart.as in the /source/classes/ folder, the class linked to the MC Cart clip. Notice that it not only extends the MovieClip object, but it also implements the DropArea interface. Here is the implementation of the three interface methods:

```
public function setEngageDrop(_engage:Boolean):Void
{
if(_engage)
{
  _alpha = 60;
}
else
{
  _alpha = 100;
}
}

public function doDrop():Void
{
  setEngageDrop(false);
  added_mc.play();
}

public function getHitArea():MovieClip
{
  return hit_mc;
}
```

Notice that when the user drags a clip over the cart, setEngageDrop() simply readjusts its _alpha channel to 60% transparency. Otherwise, it will be set to the normal 100% transparency. When a user drops a clip into the cart, we play the added_mc clip, the simple text-based clip that just displays the message that the item was added to the user's cart.

6

Next, let's look at our implementation of the interface for the MC ProductDetail clip. Open ProductDetail.as in the /source/classes/ folder. Some of the properties shown here make sense only in the context of the entire class file.

```
public function setEngageDrop(_engage:Boolean):Void
{
  if(_engage)
  {
    _alpha = 60;
  }
  else
  {
    _alpha = 100;
  }
}

public function doDrop():Void
{
  setDetail(_parent.grid_mc.getSelectedData());
  setEngageDrop(false);
}

public function setDetail(_detailObj:Object):Void
{
  detailObj = _detailObj;

  info_txt.htmlText = "<b>Title: </b>" + detailObj.title + "<br>" +
➡ "<b>Published: </b>" + detailObj.published + "<br>" +
➡ "<b>ISBN: </b>" + detailObj.isbn + "<br>" +
➡ "<b>Price: </b>$" + detailObj.price + "<br>" +
➡ "<b>Pages: </b>" + detailObj.pages + "<br>";

  description_txt.htmlText = detailObj.description;

  imageHolder_mc._alpha = 0;
  preloader_mc._visible = true;
  preloader_mc.init(detailObj.fullsize, imageHolder_mc, this,
➡ imageLoaded);
}

public function getHitArea():MovieClip
{
  return hit_mc;
}
```

The setEngageDrop() method is exactly the same as it was in the Cart.as file. However, the doDrop() method will call a setDetail() method, which will then populate the info_txt and description_txt fields. Both are shown in the preceding code.

So, with that, we've shown you with fairly broad strokes how to implement the code behind our droppable UI clips, You should see that by using an interface, we ensure that the three critical methods—setEngageDrop(), doDrop(), and getHitArea()—are implemented properly.

As we mentioned at the onset, we've taken you through only the critical methods that drive the drag-and-drop interface. Other methods and properties sprinkled throughout the code files do bits of work that haven't been discussed in this chapter. We encourage you to comb through all of our source files to see how everything works!

Putting it all together

If you're still with us now, you deserve a pat on the back, or perhaps a hug. There's no doubt that this was one of the more intense discussions of code, but sometimes good usability requires some fairly intricate code development!

Now that we have defined all the critical parts that will implement our grid layout and drag-and-drop functionality, we need to add just a bit of initialization code to our FLA file to get the ball rolling.

If you head back up to the script layer of our MC Interface clip within Chapter6_Final.fla and view our frame actions, you'll see that this is where we create a new instance of the DragDropManager. We use the addDropArea() method to add in our droppable UI clips. When added, they are immediately included in the dropAreas array (discussed earlier) using the addDropArea() method.

```
var dragDropManager = new DragDropManager(this, "MC ThumbDragItem");
dragDropManager.addDropArea(productDetail_mc);
dragDropManager.addDropArea(cart_mc);
```

We then create an array of data for our book inventory items, called productData. This looks very similar to the selectionData array from Chapter 3, only here we've included the title, ISBN, publication date, description, and book thumbnail image path into each element of the array. The array is rather lengthy, so we've omitted it from this chapter, but it's available in the source code. Note that in a more robust implementation, you might consider an external XML file to pass in the data from a store database.

Finally, we write this one short, but powerful, line of code to begin the attachment of book inventory items to our MC ProductGrid instance:

```
grid_mc.doInit(productData);
```

Just like that, we've set the wheels in motion!

6

Summary

In this chapter, we've demonstrated a Flash solution for data display and interaction using the example of an online store. As always, we suggest that you think about new ways to extend the functionality we've shown you in this chapter. For instance, consider the following:

- Use sound to indicate successful thumbnail drops. While sounds can be annoying if they're too obnoxious, subtle ones can make it more obvious when a user successfully adds an item to a cart for instance.

- Make other objects draggable. Think about other ways you might use the drag-and-drop paradigm to enhance the user experience. How about if you could drag the product detail panel into the cart and have it create the same functionality as when you drag the corresponding book thumbnail item into the cart?

- Modify the grid layout structure. Our current grid layout allows for only 16 thumbnail items at a time. What methods could be employed to allow for more items? Perhaps you could use a mouse-position-based scroll, as we did for our menus in Chapter 4. Or, perhaps you could implement a numbered paging system that could load other pages asynchronously, and switch grid views through numbered page links.

Now that we've completed our look at setting up an inventory view and selection device, let's expand the store concept a bit further and talk about effective ways of filtering content for users. That's coming up in Chapter 7!

7 DATA FILTERING

In Chapter 6, we looked at an innovative solution for displaying and working with an inventory of data. You saw how, in HTML, the inventory view and selection is a multistep process involving several waiting periods and page refreshes. We demonstrated how to implement drag-and-drop functionality for inventory items in Flash to improve user efficiency and give the application a much more seamless and responsive feel. In this chapter, we're going to examine another essential aspect of most web applications: searching and filtering data. (In this chapter, we'll use the terms *searching* and *filtering* almost interchangeably. We'll tend toward *searching* when we're simply talking about the act of finding the item or items and use *filtering* when we're referring to the mechanism that a user employs to search data.)

The ability of an application to filter data is one way to make it "smart." It gives users the power to manage the kinds of data they want to see. Without any way to filter the items in, say, a catalog of books, users are left with the burden of wading through a number of items before deciding what to purchase.

However, bear in mind that just because an application provides users a way to filter data based on a specific set of criteria, it doesn't necessarily mean that the application is any easier or more pleasurable to use. Often, the tools we're given to filter data don't coincide with the ways we actually think about filtering data. That's what we'll address in this chapter. How can we make an application smart as well as being pleasurable to use?

Here's what we'll cover in this chapter:

- How users want to search vs. how they have to search
- Opportunities for improving HTML search applications
- How to design a seamless, responsive filtering application in Flash
- How to use the EventDispatcher object to apply responsive filtering

Examining the limitations of standard searches

Let's take a moment to think about how we, as consumers, usually go about searching for things. If you were to go to your local bookstore, you might have an idea of the type of book you wish to purchase. You may have a few specific criteria, but not necessarily an exact idea of what you want to buy. On top of that, other external factors could affect your decisions while you're shopping. For instance, a sale on all hardcover books might sway you toward a particular novel you weren't thinking of purchasing. As consumers, we browse, we examine, and we weigh many factors before coming to the decision of what item or items ultimately end up in our possession.

Let's see how this common search behavior works on the Web. Take, for example, a basic HTML search form that might be used on an online real estate site, as shown in Figure 7-1. It includes parameters such as a minimum purchase price, maximum purchase price, number of bedrooms, location, and type of housing. Near these form elements is a submission button that redirects you to a page with item views that matched the criteria you've chosen.

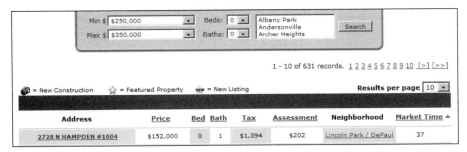

Figure 7-1. A common search form and results page from a real estate site

Considering that the purchase of a home is probably one of the most significant financial decisions people make in their lifetimes, it's pretty unreasonable to expect that home buyers have a solid, unbending set of criteria for their dream home. For instance, they may consider purchasing a home for a premium value if it's located in a more prime section of town, or they might expect more bedrooms in a less ideal area for the same price.

In considering all these factors, home buyers have two choices when it comes to using the HTML search form in an effective way:

- Search each specific scenario one at a time.
- Perform much broader, less-filtered searches.

So, a home buyer might simply perform a search for each set of criteria, one step at a time, as illustrated in Figure 7-2. She might first keep the location, bedrooms, and type of housing constant, and increase her price range. After viewing all the matched options, she returns to the search page, inputs everything, but this time varies the price range even further. After enough iterations of this process, she might tackle changing a second para-meter. Instead of varying the price range, she varies the number of bedrooms based on location. For each less ideal location, she wants an extra bedroom or two included in the search criteria.

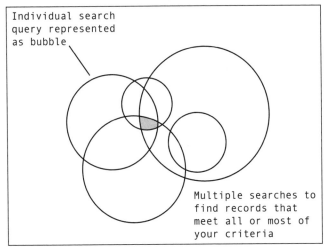

Figure 7-2. Workflow for searching via multiple queries

As you can see, this method requires a good bit of searching and researching. As you know by now, each submission and refresh is costly to the user. In addition, having to consider all the variable parameters for each variation is rather difficult. In the end, our home buyer might decide to do one of two things: pare down her own criteria for her dream house to simplify the search process or try another method.

The second choice our prospective home buyer has is to broaden her search criteria. Instead of varying parameters and searching multiple times, she selects the maximum range possible for all criteria. Of course, this means that she will get back a much larger result set than desired. Most of the homes returned from the filtering process probably won't match her initial criteria in every way. It then becomes a matter of refiltering the returned data manually. She'll most likely go through each of the many homes that meet any of her criteria and throw away the ones that don't match all (or enough) of her criteria. Figure 7-3 illustrates this search method.

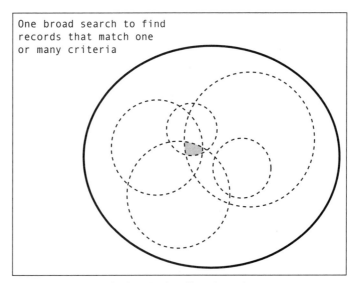

Figure 7-3. Workflow for broader, less-filtered searches

Home buying isn't the only case where you might expect users to have variant criteria based on a multiple set of factors. Take, for instance, the process of booking a flight online. An airline passenger might be flexible in booking a flight for the night before or leaving a day later, depending on the cost of the flight and the number of layovers.

As you can see, the way we search doesn't always parallel the interfaces we're given to search. We are forced to bend our own rules to work with the web application. Not only does this render the application less usable, but it also may prevent us from finding that dream home or that perfect airline ticket purchase.

Improving filtering with Flash

Using Flash, we can improve the less-than-ideal HTML filtering tools in several ways. First, we can improve the performance and feedback of filtering by storing data on the client. Additionally, we can design an enhanced filtering interface to make it easier for users to specify their criteria and see not just the matches, but the near matches as well.

Storing data on the client

One of the problems with HTML searching is that every time we perform a search, the application makes a trip to the server to return the results that match our criteria. Every round-trip to the server requires a page redirect, a new database connection, the return of data back to the server, and the rendering of an entire HTML page. This is an expensive hit for the usability of our application. Considering that a user might want to change only some of the criteria on future searches (for instance, lowering just the maximum price range in a real estate application), having to requery criteria that hasn't changed is unnecessary and inefficient.

Our Flash approach will take advantage of the fact that we can easily store all the values of a particular item that are "filterable" on the client side. In the real estate example, it would be very easy to do one initial query that returned all the available properties within a database and store the price, location, bedroom count, and housing type within an array or a custom-built Flash object. Subsequent filterings on these homes wouldn't require a server trip. Instead, we can write a bit of code to loop through each home and remove those that don't match all of our criteria. By filtering on the client side, the home buyer gets near instantaneous feedback on how changing one parameter affects the matching results.

Of course, in a true real estate application, the database might contain hundreds, if not thousands of properties. Returning all of these records to the Flash application at once could result in a lengthy wait for the user. Moreover, displaying a thousand properties on a page would be hard to do in a readable way. In this case, we have a couple of suggestions.

First, you should design your application so that your initial base of search results is as manageable as possible. For instance, you could create a set of navigation items that sort the results accordingly. Clicking each of these items would return a smaller subset of initial inventory a user can filter. In this case, navigation just becomes an initial way to filter down your master set of data. You'll want to choose your navigation system carefully, though. Pick a navigation theme that most users have a strong bias toward, to prevent them from constantly having to drill back up the search chain. For instance, you could create a set of navigation items that categorized properties by neighborhoods, since location is something most home buyers have a strong opinion about.

7

Another solution is pagination. This just means that you break up the results into chunks and show a certain number of records at a time, along with a paging mechanism to view the next or previous page of results, as shown in Figure 7-4. This is a near universal piece of functionality that you'll see on popular sites, such as Amazon.com and Google. But, if you're results list spans dozens and dozens of pages, users aren't going to be inclined to sift through all of them. If you're working with a data set even near the scope of an Amazon.com or Google search, this may just be inevitable and acceptable, since users know that they are searching an incredibly vast database. However, we recommend that, at all costs, you avoid pagination when you can, and instead work toward reducing the number of search elements on a page by providing more search options or search options with greater specificity.

Figure 7-4. An example of pagination

In our chapter solution, we'll assume that we have a manageable set of data to start. In a real-world application, you'll want to retrieve your data through connecting to a database via XML or integrating your application on top of a PHP or .NET application.

Using sliders to filter search criteria

Improving filtering performance and feedback is crucial, but that's not the only way we can enhance the usability of a searching function.

In the usual, hard-and-fast rules of HTML, select boxes and radio buttons typically paint the search landscape. In Figure 7-1, the drop-down select boxes for the minimum and maximum price ranges for real estate go by increments of $50,000. The designers for this search form obviously found the $50,000 increment to be a happy medium between giving the user the option to search within a specific price range and managing the overall length of the drop-down box. Searching in $100,000 increments may be too wide a range to be of great use, while searching in $1,000 increments would create a rather lengthy, difficult-to-use search drop-down component.

Once again, HTML design pigeonholes a particular interactive function into an HTML construct that only partially fits the users' needs. It's certainly conceivable that home buyers might have a price range narrower than $50,000. But, in order to make an HTML select box usable, developers must compromise the search criteria.

As we mentioned in Chapter 6, one of the basic advantages to Flash is that we don't need to force a functional concept into one of only a few rigid components. We can better parallel how a user thinks about searching and filtering data with how a user *actually does* filter data.

So, let's define a mechanism that takes advantage of client data storage and Flash's seamless response capabilities. In our enhancement, we'll reintroduce the book store catalog system we began building in Chapter 6.

Our approach will be to employ movable sliders to filter data. Users can change their search criteria by dragging the slider handles within each filtering component to an appropriate range of values that best suits their needs.

To see how the sliders work in the basic book-searching function, download the `Chapter7_Final.zip` file from this book's download page at the friends of ED website (www.friendsofed.com) and export the files within the ZIP file into a directory on your machine. Open the `Chapter7_Final.swf` file within the /source/swf/ subdirectory. You'll see a pair of sliders corresponding to different search parameters for the online book catalog we built in Chapter 6, as shown in Figure 7-5.

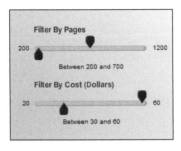

Figure 7-5.
A slider component allows seamless filtering of, in this case, a catalog of books.

Each slider contains two drag handles, which can move along the slider to specify the range of values for a particular search criterion. The drag handles have a large base with a pointed edge, so that users can both see precisely where the handle position is set and also have an easy time rolling the mouse over the surface area of the handle before they drag it.

In the Filter By Pages and Filter By Cost sliders in Figure 7-5, users can choose a value anywhere in between these boundary cases by dragging the sliders to their ideal range of values. Directly underneath the sliders lies a textual description of the filter. To the right and left of the sliders are the minimum and maximum values for the page count and price ranges.

Notice, too, that when you move the left slider to the right, thereby increasing the minimum number of pages, it will go only as far as the location of the right slider. The same is true when you try to drag the right slider to the left: it will go only as far left as the location of the left slider. This ensures that the range of values has a true minimum that is smaller than (or equal to) the maximum value.

The most apparent interaction improvement with a slider is the seamless feel it provides the filtering application. If the HTML real estate example we presented earlier in this chapter had employed a Flash interface using sliders, consider how much easier it would be for home buyers to find the homes that best matched their criteria. Instead of forcing home buyers to search in $50,000 increments, they could simply use the slider to pinpoint a much more specific (or broader) target price range. You can immediately see how much easier and useful this is than clicking a drop-down box and selecting from a specific range of price values.

7

Now, imagine having all of the search criteria implemented with sliders. A home buyer could set all of the criteria to her most ideal settings (the perfect price, location, number of bedrooms). If she finds that none or too few of her criteria meet her needs, she could then decide to be more lenient on price. Instead of having to go back to a search page and reinput and resubmit all of her search parameters, she only needs to grab the price range slider and change it appropriately.

> *Sliders aren't optimal for all kinds of criteria. A slider probably won't work best for a set of discrete location options, and they certainly won't work for keyword searches. Sliders will work best for criteria that have a "lowest" to "highest" concept. A range of price values and the number of bedrooms are both perfect candidates for sliders. For other criteria, consider implementing different selection devices, such as a scrolling list (see Chapter 4) or a search box.*

Fading in and out inventory results

As you manipulate the sliders to change your search criteria, notice that items that no longer fit your set of criteria fade out, but they are not totally invisible. This gives you a better sense of not just which items match all of your criteria, but also which items *have just missed your criteria*. You can quickly readjust your sliders to see which items didn't meet which requirements. Figure 7-6 shows how the filtering devices and inventory responses look.

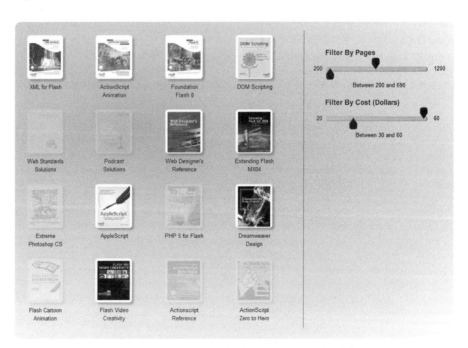

Figure 7-6. The book item inventory, with searchable parameters on the right

This fade effect is a further luxury we can provide with seamless filtering. In many traditional HTML applications, searches are entirely hit-or-miss. An item must match all of your criteria in order for it to display in your results. Those that match most of your criteria are given the same treatment as those that match none of your criteria: they aren't displayed at all. Some searches will do partial matching and relevance ranking, but these searches still don't allow you to quickly change parameters from the results list.

Being able to see items that match almost all of your criteria is certainly a valuable tool. For example, a home buyer who has decreased the maximum price of her dream home might see that the one property she likes best now fails to match all of her criteria. After reconsidering, she might end up deciding to put in an offer for that house, despite the fact that it does not meet every one of her criteria. In the HTML version, she may not have realized or considered the home because of its all-or-nothing filtering behavior.

Reviewing the filtering enhancements

In summary, our Flash solution will improve filtering as follows:

- Filter data on the client side, rather than round-tripping to the server each time users change their criteria.
- Use sliders for criteria to give filtering a more seamless and responsive feel.
- Fade out (but not remove) items that no longer match a given set of criteria. Users will be able to see which items match, as well as which items almost match by seeing items fade and come into view as they modify the criteria.

All these enhancements will make it easier for a user to quickly filter search parameters without the limitations we've become accustomed to in HTML! Let's get started, shall we?

Building the Flash solution

Once again, if you haven't done so yet, download the `Chapter7_Final.zip` file (from `www.friendsofed.com`) and export the files within the ZIP file into a directory on your machine. We'll start by going over the interface objects we need to construct before showing you how to approach the code development.

Creating the Flash UI assets

Open `Chapter7_Final.fla` in the /source/fla/ folder. A significant portion of the clips contained within our Flash library should be quite familiar to you. In particular, we've reused the MC ProductGrid and MC ThumbItemButton clips from Chapter 6. If you're taking the approach of skipping to various chapters and haven't read Chapter 6 yet, it might be a good idea to read through that chapter if you're interested in the particular way we've implemented the book catalog system.

7

From a UI perspective, only one major piece of the puzzle here is truly new: our slider movie clip for filtering data. Let's take a few moments to see how we've built the different parts of this fairly simple but incredibly powerful clip.

The filtering slider

The parts of the slider are actually incredibly simple. They bear some resemblance to the progress bar and seeker clips we built in our audio player sample from Chapter 5, although since no loading concept is involved, the filtering slider is even less complicated! Figure 7-7 shows the timeline layers of the data filter slider clip.

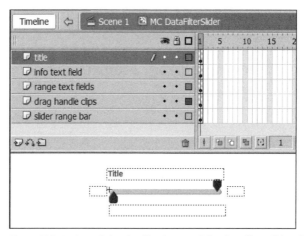

Figure 7-7. A view of the timeline layers of the data filter slider clip

Within the Flash library (Window ➤ Library), open the MC DataFilterSlider clip.

The bottom layer, labeled slider range bar, contains a rectangular clip with an instance name of sliderBar_mc positioned at (0,0). This slider bar clip (180 width × 8 height) is nothing more than a background graphic that our draggable clip will appear to slide along to change the value of a specific property. We've given our bar slightly rounded edges using the Set Corner Radius tool in the toolbox, and we've also added a drop shadow filter (see Chapter 4 for details on Flash 8 filters) to make it easily visible from the background of the main application. Click the movie clip and go to the Filters panel (Window ➤ Properties ➤ Filters) to see the settings for the drop shadow.

The second layer, drag handle clips, contains two instances of the graph_dragHandle movie clip, named dragHandleLeft_mc and dragHandleRight_mc. The dragHandleLeft_mc instance is positioned at (0,2), so that its left edge lies flush with the left edge of the slider bar. It has also been flipped vertically so that its pointer points up toward the slider bar. The dragHandleRight_mc instance is positioned at (166, −16), so that its right edge lies flush with the right edge of the slider bar and points toward the bar. Both drag handle clips have a bevel filter added to them to make them stand out from the background and appear to be raised from the slider bar. Go to the Filters panel to see the settings for the bevel filter.

Above the drag handle clips layer, in the range text fields layer, we've added the text fields that will display the range for the slider's values on the left and right sides of the clip. The instance names are min_txt and max_txt. As is customary in most of the applications in this book, we've set these to Arial 10-pt font, using the anti-alias for animation font rendering to give the values a very crisp and smooth look and feel.

Above this layer, in the info text field layer, we've added a text field named filterVal_txt, which will display the current range of the particular search criterion. We've positioned it directly beneath the slider bar, where it will be easy to view, regardless of the position of the drag bar clip.

Finally, in the title layer, we add in a title_txt text field to the top layer to give us a place to describe the kind of data the slider will filter.

When you view the linkage properties for this clip (right-click the clip in the library and select Linkage), you'll see we've linked MC DataFilterSlider to an AS2 class named `DataFilterSlider.as`. We'll dig into the code for this shortly.

Back on our root timeline, notice that we've included two instances of the MC DataFilterSlider clip on stage. We've positioned the filtering devices in the upper-right corner of our application, as shown earlier in Figure 7-6. On the pages datafilter layer, we've given the MC DataFilterSlider clip an instance name of pageFilter_mc. On the price datafilter layer, we've given another instance the name priceFilter_mc.

The product grid

The other key movie clip in the mix is the actual book catalog. In the layer labeled product grid, we've included an instance of MC ProductGrid (discussed in detail in Chapter 6) named grid_mc. Just as in the example in Chapter 6, we'll simply pass it an array of data that contains the information it needs to display a full-fledged book inventory view.

Now, let's move on to our code implementation to see how to put the filtering devices in action.

Building the filtering slider code

Functionally speaking, all of the book items in the catalog need to react to changes made to the filtering devices, and you should keep that in mind as you read about their code implementations. Here is the basic course we'll take to design the code that will drive this solution:

- We'll begin by building a DataFilterManager class that will act as a central managing class for each of our distinct filtering devices (in this case, the page and price filters).

- We'll create a DataFilterSlider class that will link to our MC DataFilterSlider clip. This class will notify the DataFilterManager class when a change to its parameter has been made, so that the manager can then notify the book item thumbnails to update their physical appearance (either faded or unfaded) based on the changed criterion.

- We'll discuss the EventDispatcher component that comes with Flash. The DataFilterManager class will use the power of the EventDispatcher component to transmit changes in the filtering sliders to the book items.

- Finally, we'll complete the solution by actually showing how DataFilterManager employs the EventDispatcher object to make the solution work.

Building the DataFilterManager class

Our first job will be to build a central managing class that will monitor all of the various filtering sliders in our application. Remember that the DragDropManager class in Chapter 6 kept track of all the UI components that a book item could be "dropped" over and managed the interactions that occurred with the drag-and-drop functionality. In a similar fashion, we'll use the DataFilterManager class to keep track of the various book item filtering properties in our application and *manage* what happens when the filter sliders are used. It will need to notify the book grid when a user changes a particular filter so that the grid can update itself, fading out all the items that don't match the given set of criteria.

Open the DataFilterManager.as class located in the /source/classes/ directory of our solution example. Here are some of the specific tasks this class will need to perform:

- Allow a way to "register" our different filtering properties to this central manager.

- Provide a method for a filter device to report back to this central manager when a user has made an update, passing along the new value of the filterable property.

- Send the newly updated property value to the book items to have them change accordingly.

Our DataFilterManager, like the DragDropManager class from the previous chapter, will be a stand-alone class that will be instantiated at runtime within the main timeline of the application. We'll add this bit of instantiation code when we put the solution together at the end of this chapter.

DataFilterManager will include one private property, a generic object called filterCriteria that will store each type of filter (a page filter and a price filter) for reference. When we say "storing a type of filter," we don't mean the instance name of the filter slider clips, but an object that represents the filtered data itself. The object in this solution will be called FilterType. The filterCriteria object will store multiple instances of this FilterType object.

FilterType is a very skinny class that just defines all the pertinent properties that the manager class needs to know about regarding each filter. You can look at FilterType.as in the /source/classes/ folder, but it just holds variables for the minimum and maximum values of each filter, as shown here:

```
class FilterType
{
  public var minVal:Number;
  public var maxVal:Number;
}
```

The DataFilterManager will also need the help of another custom class, EventBroadcaster, to report changes in the filtering sliders to the book items. We'll discuss this class thoroughly later in the chapter, in the "Using the EventDispatcher object" section. So, we'll import two external classes into this one. This is how we begin the DataFilterManager class:

```
import EventBroadcaster;
import FilterType;

class DataFilterManager
{
  private var filterCriteria:Object;

  public function DataFilterManager()
  {
    filterCriteria = new Object();
  }
```

The first public method we'll add to the class is our filter registration method. Any number of filtering devices can be added to the DataFilterManager instance by registering their filter type via registerFilterType() and passing in a string that will represent the type of filter being registered.

```
public function registerFilterType(_type:String):Void
{
  initializeCriteria(_type);
}
```

This method takes a string as a parameter, which is a custom-defined name of the type of filter that will be updated by the filtering clips. It then calls the initializeCriteria() method, which will create a new FilterType attribute of filterCriteria, using the type string as the attribute identifier, and set the initial minimum and maximum values to 0 for now. Here's the initializeCriteria() method, which we add next:

```
private function initializeCriteria(_type:String):Void
{
  filterCriteria[_type] = new FilterType();
  filterCriteria[_type].minVal = 0;
  filterCriteria[_type].maxVal = 0;
}
```

Next, we add the update method, updateFilterCriteria(). The update method's job will be to accept a filter type and a new minimum and maximum value for the filter. It will then update the filterCriteria object with the new values and send the newly updated values to the book items to have them change accordingly. The way we send this information to our book items is highlighted in the following code. We'll use the mx.events.EventDispatcher component, part of the Flash MX component framework, to do the bulk of the work for us. Those of you unfamiliar with EventDispatcher might be a bit confused about what's going on here. But, let's hold off on this line of code for now, as we'll return to it in "Using the EventDispatcher object" a bit later. For now, it's enough to know that this line will initiate the book items to change their appearance based on a property change.

```
public function updateFilterCriteria(_type:String, _minVal:Number,
➡ _maxVal:Number):Void
{
  filterCriteria[_type].minVal = _minVal;
  filterCriteria[_type].maxVal = _maxVal;

  EventBroadcaster.getInstance().broadcastEvent("doFilter",
➡ filterCriteria);
  }
}
```

Now with the DataFilterManager class completed, let's move on to the class that directly controls how each filtering device will work: the DataFilterSlider class.

Creating the DataFilterSlider class

The DataFilterSlider class implements the functionality behind our sliders. Open the DataFilterSlider.as class within the /source/classes/ folder. Naturally, we build this class as an extension off the MovieClip object, since it links to the MC DataFilterSlider movie clip on stage.

```
class DataFilterSlider extends MovieClip
{
```

This class contains numerous private variables. First, we create the instances of all the assets within the MC DataFilterSlider clip we constructed earlier:

```
private var dragHandleLeft_mc:MovieClip;
private var dragHandleRight_mc:MovieClip;
private var sliderBar_mc:MovieClip;
private var filterVal_txt:TextField;
private var min_txt:TextField;
private var max_txt:TextField;
private var title_txt:TextField;
```

Next, we'll create variables that will help define and display the range of values possible for a particular book item filtering criterion. The minVal and maxVal variables will store the *absolute* minimum and maximum range values possible for the particular filter criteria.

```
private var minVal:Number = 0;
private var maxVal:Number;
```

Recall that each instance of the MC DataFilterSlider slider object will actually be initialized with its data through the DataFilterManager class. Here, we'll include a filterID string that will be passed to DataFilterManager to register its filter to a new instance of FilterType. Also, we keep a reference of the DataFilterManager object as a property of the DataFilterSlider object so that we can easily pass new updates to the values of the filter back to the manager. This bit of code goes next:

```
private var filterID:String;
private var dataFilterManager:DataFilterManager;
```

Then we add in the constructor and an onLoad() method that will initialize the mouse events of the drag handles, calling an initDragHandles() method defined later in code.

```
public function DataFilterSlider()
{
}

public function onLoad():Void
{
    initDragHandles();
}
```

Following this, we'll define the initialization method for this class. The doInit() method initializes the values and properties of the slider filter. Here is the definition of doInit():

```
public function doInit(_filterID:String, _filterTitle:String,
➡ _minVal:Number, _maxVal:Number,
_dataFilterManager:DataFilterManager):Void
  {
    minVal = _minVal;
    maxVal = _maxVal;

    min_txt.text = minVal.toString();
    max_txt.text = maxVal.toString();
    title_txt.text = _filterTitle;

    filterID = _ filterID;

    dataFilterManager = _dataFilterManager;
    dataFilterManager.registerFilterType(_filterID);

    updateFilterValues();
  }
```

The important points here are that we provide doInit() with the custom name of the type of filter this slider will control, the title of the filter shown to the user, the minimum and maximum value ranges possible for the filter, and a reference to the instance of the DataFilterManager class that will be managing all the filters for us. Notice that we call registerFilterType() from the instance of the DataFilterManager class to register this filter.

Next, we call a method named updateFilterValues(). This function calculates the new range of values for the filter criterion by figuring out how far to the left, as a percentage, each drag handle is located down sliderBar_mc, and then multiplying this decimal by the range between the minimum and maximum values. Then we add on the minimum value (since that value may not always be zero) to come up with the final value for the criterion in question.

We also populate the filterVal_txt text field with a readable phrase describing the new value. To cap it off, the method will call updateFilterCriteria() from our DataFilterManager class, passing in the newly calculated range values for the filter. Remember that this method updates the value of the criteria, and then informs our book items to update their appearances based on the new property change.

```
private function updateFilterValues():Void
{
  var valueDif:Number = maxVal - minVal;

  // left side
  var uiLeftPercent:Number = dragHandleLeft_mc._x
➡ /(sliderBar_mc._width - dragHandleLeft_mc._width);
  var filterLeftVal:Number = (valueDif * uiLeftPercent);
  var leftVal:Number = Math.round(minVal + filterLeftVal);

  // right side
  var uiRightPercent:Number = dragHandleRight_mc._x
➡ /(sliderBar_mc._width - dragHandleRight_mc._width);
  var filterRightVal:Number = (valueDif * uiRightPercent);
  var rightVal:Number = Math.round(minVal + filterRightVal);

  // update text
  filterVal_txt.text = "Between " + leftVal.toString() + " and " +
➡ rightVal.toString();

  dataFilterManager.updateFilterCriteria(filterID, leftVal,
➡ rightVal);
}
```

Next, we define the initDragHandles() method called in the onLoad() method from earlier in this code discussion. This method defines the onPress() and onRelease() event handler methods for both drag handle clips.

```
private function initDragHandles():Void
{
  var ref:MovieClip = this;

  dragHandleLeft_mc.onPress = function()
  {
    ref.dragHandleLeft();
  }
```

```
    dragHandleRight_mc.onPress = function()
    {
      ref.dragHandleRight();
    }

    dragHandleLeft_mc.onRelease =
    dragHandleRight_mc.onRelease =
    onMouseUp = function()
    {
      ref.killDrag();
    }
  }
```

The new methods defined here—dragHandleLeft(), dragHandleRight(), and killDrag()—are written next and complete the code for this class. In a nutshell, dragHandleLeft() and dragHandleRight() define the physical area where a user can move the drag handles and also assign the onMouseMove() event handler to the updateFilterValues() method. Here we've assigned the left drag handle's drag area so that it cannot go any more to the right than the x-position of the right drag handle. Similarly, the right drag handle cannot be dragged any more to the left than the x-position of the left drag handle. When users move the mouse during a drag, repeated calls are made back to updateFilterValues() so that they immediately see the new values for the criteria that they are updating. The killDrag() method removes the drag functionality.

```
    public function dragHandleLeft():Void
    {
      dragHandleLeft_mc.startDrag(false, 0, dragHandleLeft_mc._y,
➥ dragHandleRight_mc._x, dragHandleLeft_mc._y);
      onMouseMove = updateFilterValues;
    }

    public function dragHandleRight():Void
    {
      dragHandleRight_mc.startDrag(false, dragHandleLeft_mc._x,
➥ dragHandleRight_mc._y,
➥ sliderBar_mc._width - dragHandleRight_mc._width,
➥ dragHandleRight_mc._y);
      onMouseMove = updateFilterValues;
    }

    public function killDrag():Void
    {
      stopDrag();
      onMouseMove = undefined;
    }
  }
```

With that, we've covered all the integral properties and methods for our DataFilterSlider object! We're almost on our way to completing this filtering application. But there's still the little matter of our book items. They'll need to fade in and out according to each newly updated set of criteria provided by the DataFilterManager class. Let's see how the EventDispatcher object can help the book items listen for changes that the DataFilterManager object receives from the filters.

Using the EventDispatcher object

The EventDispatcher object, found within the mx.events package, gives developers an easy way to dispatch events from one object (a dispatcher) to any number of other objects (listeners). You can set up an object to be a dispatcher by initializing it from the EventDispatcher object, using the static initialize() method.

```
EventDispatcher.initialize(objDispatcher);
```

You can then add to or remove listeners from the dispatching object. In the following code, the just-initialized event dispatcher object named objDispatcher adds aListeningObject to listen to the event named eventName. In the next line, we remove aListeningObject as an event listener.

```
objDispatcher.addEventListener(eventName, aListeningObject);
objDispatcher.removeEventListener(aListeningObject);
```

Finally, you can dispatch an event to all of its listening objects as follows:

```
objDispatcher.dispatchEvent(anEvent);
```

The anEvent parameter is a generic object instance that stores the name of the event being dispatched (in a string property called type). Since it is really just a generic object, you can also pass along any other bits of information a listening object would need to know about the event by adding that data to the anEvent object. When dispatchEvent() is called, each listening object will invoke its own defined method with the same name as the dispatched event, and will automatically have the event object available by defining it as a parameter to the method.

```
aListeningObject.anEventName(_anEvent:Object) { // Insert code };
```

In our solution, we've created a generic Event class (Event.as in /source/classes/) to support the event dispatcher model. It includes the mandatory type string that stores the name of the event to be dispatched, along with a params object that will store any additional parameters a particular event should include.

```
class Event
{
  public function Event() {}

  public var type:String;
  public var params:Object;
}
```

While the EventDispatcher object has its merits, it doesn't give us quite the amount of flexibility we're seeking. Any object that wants to add itself as a listener to a dispatched event from another object needs to know where that other object exists, so that it can assign itself as an event listener. Remember that, in our case, we want each book thumbnail item to listen to a DataFilterManager object for changes to the filtering criteria. We could initialize DataFilterManager as an event dispatcher, but then the book items would have to know where the DataFilterManager object exists to listen for its changes.

Wouldn't it be nice if there were a way that objects could freely dispatch events, and listeners could listen for events without needing to know where they're coming from? Well, there is a way, which we'll show you right now.

We'll enable this functionality by creating a generic EventBroadcaster class (EventBroadcaster.as in /source/classes/) that implements both the Event and EventDispatcher objects. This class is simply a type of EventDispatcher that can be accessed in the *same way* from anywhere in code. Its only job will be to manage the dispatching of events and the objects who listen to those events. We make it globally accessible by creating a getInstance() static method that ensures that only one EventBroadcaster instance is ever created during a user's session. The getInstance() method either creates an instance of EventBroadcaster (if it's the first time it has ever been called) or returns the created instance of EventBroadcaster. Those of you familiar with object-oriented design patterns should recognize this as the *Singleton design pattern*.

> *The Singleton design pattern is useful to use in a class that will require only one instance. Because the* EventBroadcaster*'s sole purpose is to provide a global way of managing the dispatching of events from an object to other listening objects, it becomes the perfect candidate for a singleton.*

The main benefit to this class is that it no longer obligates the objects that dispatch events to know which object is listening to them, and vice versa. It will help make our code more flexible and scalable.

Within the class, the broadcastEvent() method allows us to actually dispatch an event. It takes the name of a method to call, along with an associated data object. It then inserts these values into an instance of Event (the name of the method in the Event.type variable and the data object in the Event.params variable) before broadcasting the event to its listeners using the EventDispatcher.dispatchEvent() method. Essentially, it lets us now dispatch events without having to first bind the name and data associated to the event into an object. Instead, it does that work for us!

The entire class is shown here.

```
import Event;
import mx.events.EventDispatcher;

class EventBroadcaster
{
    private var dispatchEvent:Function;
    public var addEventListener:Function;
    public var removeEventListener:Function;
```

```
        private static var eventBroadcaster;

        public static function getInstance():EventBroadcaster
        {
          if ( eventBroadcaster == undefined )
          eventBroadcaster = new EventBroadcaster();

          return eventBroadcaster;
        }

        private function EventBroadcaster()
        {
          EventDispatcher.initialize( this );
        }

        public function broadcastEvent(_eventName:String, _params:Object)
        {
          var event:Event = new Event();
          event.type = _eventName;
          event.params = _params;

          dispatchEvent( event );
        }
    }
```

The real advantage here is how easy it is to now have our DataFilterManager interact with each book item thumbnail when a user changes the criteria settings with the slider components. We'll harness the EventBroadcaster class above to broadcast an event from DataFilterManager that will be listened to by all of the book thumbnail items. Let's see how we go about doing this.

Implementing the EventBroadcaster class

Here is the updateFilterCriteria() method from the DataFilterManager class once again. Remember that this method is called upon initializing each new MC DataFilterSlider clip and is repeatedly called when a user drags any one of the sliders.

```
        public function updateFilterCriteria(_type:String, _minVal:Number,
    ➡ _maxVal:Number):Void
        {
          filterCriteria[_type].minVal = _minVal;
          filterCriteria[_type].maxVal = _maxVal;

          EventBroadcaster.getInstance().broadcastEvent("doFilter",
    ➡ filterCriteria);
        }
```

In the bold line of code, we call the static getInstance() method to access the lone instance of EventBroadcaster. We then broadcast an event named doFilter, passing along with it our filterCriteria object, which holds the names and value ranges of each criterion (page count and price) for this application. Now, any object registered to listen to the doFilter event with EventBroadcaster will initiate its own doFilter() method every time this line of code is called.

So, our next step is to define a doFilter() method in the book thumbnail items' supporting class. This method will ensure that when the DataFilterManager instance broadcasts the event through EventBroadcaster, each book thumbnail item will check to see if the data range within the filterCriteria object meets the value of each book thumbnail item.

Modifying the ThumbItemButton class

Open the ThumbItemButton.as file within the /source/classes/ folder for this chapter's solution. Notice that this is the very same class file we used to create our book thumbnail items that made up the book catalog in Chapter 6. It's also the same class that sits behind the book thumbnail items in this solution. However, in the init() method, we add this line of code to register a book item instance as a listener to the doFilter() message broadcasted:

```
EventBroadcaster.getInstance().addEventListener("doFilter", this);
```

Now, we simply need to create the doFilter() method, which will receive our generic Event object from the broadcastEvent() method of the EventBroadcaster class. The doFilter() method checks the range values of both the page counts and price values of the newly updated criteria set, and compares them to the page count and price value of the book item itself. If either the page count or price is out of the range of values set for the current criteria, we simply set its _alpha property to 20, creating the fading effect to show that the item no longer matches the given user-filtered criteria. Notice that by giving the doFilter() method the _event parameter, we now have access to the filterCriteria object passed by the DataFilterManager because it was assigned to the params property when it was dispatched through the EventBroadcaster instance.

```
public function doFilter(_event:Event):Void
{
  if (pages <= _event.params.pages.minVal || pages >=
➥ _event.params.pages.maxVal)
  {
    _alpha = 20;
    var filtered:Boolean = true;
  }
  else if (price <= _event.params.price.minVal || price >=
➥ _event.params.price.maxVal)
  {
    _alpha = 20;
    var filtered:Boolean = true;
  }

  if(!filtered)
  {
    _alpha = 100;
  }
}
```

7

Putting the pieces together

Now that we have all of our classes built, we'll need to write a few quick bits of code on our root timeline to set our filtering application in action. Follow along by opening Chapter7_final.fla once again and viewing the frame actions placed on the second frame of the top layer in the root timeline.

First, we need to create a new instance of DataFilterManager, and then initialize both of our search filter movie clips with their doInit() methods, passing along the title of the filters and their respective minimum and maximum range values.

```
// instantiate a new DataFilterManager
var datafilterManager:DataFilterManager = new DataFilterManager();

// instantiate the data filter sliders, passing in a reference
// to the data filter manager
pageFilter_mc.doInit("pages", "Filter By Pages", 200, 1200,
➡ datafilterManager);
priceFilter_mc.doInit("price", "Filter By Cost (Dollars)", 20, 60,
➡ datafilterManager);
```

What follows is a near repeat of what we've done in Chapter 6. We'll create an array of data (named bookData) that represents all the books in our inventory along with the essential values that are needed in this application (namely, a thumbnail image, the price, and page count of each book). We won't show you the entire array here, but one object of the array will look something like this:

```
{title:"Book",price:29.99,pages:490,thumb:"../images/bookimage.jpg"}
```

Finally, we load all this data into the grid_mc instance by calling the following line of code:

```
grid_mc.doInit(bookData);
```

That's it! You can test this movie and see the benefits of all of our hard work.

Summary

Although we've accomplished a great deal in this chapter, in reality, we've only touched the surface of the ways in which Flash can improve how users can search and filter data in a web application. We've provided a more usable experience by managing the data filtering on the client side and making the adjusting of criteria a seamless process for the user.

In your own applications, you might consider adjusting the fading of data objects based on how closely they match your criteria. We've empowered users by showing them not just book items that match their criteria, but also leaving the ones that don't. It might even be a greater benefit to users to see ones that match most of the criteria they pick. Consider varying the _alpha property of these book items based on how many criteria match. You could easily modify the doFilter() method within ThumbItemButton to keep a count of the number of criteria that match, and then set the _alpha property as a percentage of matched to total criteria parameters, for example. This gives users a much better idea of what items will most appeal to them. The more filtering devices there are, the better this method will work.

You might also devise filtering devices to accommodate other kinds of searching. For filters that might not best work with a slider, consider other ways to enhance their usability. For instance, a keyword search might entail providing a text box area that calls the updateFilterCriteria() method each time a letter is pressed, rather than requiring a user to click a submit button. A user typing in "Flash usability" will first be able to see all books related to Flash before seeing which of those are specifically related to usability as well. Also, because you're using the EventBroadcaster object, adding new kinds of filtering devices won't require complex coding surgery. You simply need to modify the doFilter() method of the ThumbItemButton class to accommodate for new kinds of filters, and then implement classes and clips for those new filters.

These are just a couple of the many possible modifications and extensions possible with our base application. In the end, our ultimate goal as usability designers is to avoid the often latent, all-or-nothing style of searching that we're accustomed to seeing in many search applications.

The terms *seamless* and *smart* define a lot about what we did in this chapter. In Chapter 8, those terms will again play an integral role as we examine ways of improving the usability of forms.

7

8 FORMS

| Foundation Flash 8 |
| Foundation MX Express |
| Foundation MX Studio |
| Foundation MX Upgrade Essentials |
| Foundation MX Video |
| Foundation XML for Flash |
| New Masters of Flash |
| The Flash Usability Guide |
| **Flash Books** ▲ |

| Timeline ⇦ 🎬 Scene 1 🖻 |
| 📄 title |
| 📄 info text field |
| 📄 range text fields |
| 📄 drag handle clips |
| 📄 slider range bar |

Address 1*	
Address 2		
City*	
State	AL ▼
Zip Code*	
Work Phone*	

The mention of the term *web form* may give some of you that sinking feeling in your stomach. Let's face it, nobody really enjoys filling out web forms, or paper forms for that matter. Yet, whether you're purchasing airline tickets to Hawaii, finding your perfect dating match, or most important, buying that new friends of ED Flash usability book (we suggest a bare minimum of two copies), forms are the most prominent way we interact with web applications today. Still, it's amazing how little the usability of forms has improved over the past decade.

In our experience with many web development firms, whenever a project calls for a form, developers often rehash the same code from older projects, without thinking twice about improving the usability of the form. Project to project, the same usability issues carry over and resurface. From poor validation techniques to bad tabbing structure, many forms are inefficient and a sheer pain to use.

In this chapter, we'll take a look at core ways you can improve the form experience. At the end, we hope you'll have gained a new perspective on how to create Flash-based forms that are much more enjoyable to use.

Here's what we'll cover in this chapter:

- The humanization of forms
- Common deficiencies in form validation
- Common deficiencies in form workflow
- Flash's UI components
- How to build a smooth and forgiving form in Flash
- How to use the Strategy design pattern to implement form validation

Humanizing forms

Perhaps part of the reason forms have improved little in recent years is because of the way designers and developers approach form development. How do you really make text fields, drop-down boxes, radio buttons, check boxes, and text areas any friendlier to the user? The first step is to change the way we think about forms.

Consider the relationship between a form and the user. In reality, the interactions you provide with a form are not all that different from those you might have with a ticket broker on the phone or a cashier at the grocery store. In these human-to-human interactions, as a customer or user, your main objective is to complete a task quickly and efficiently—whether it's purchasing that pair of Chicago Cubs World Series tickets or just buying your week's groceries at the supermarket. More than likely, your second objective is to have a pleasant and smooth experience. Long waits in the grocery store line or short-tempered ticket agents are experiences we would rather avoid and might even provoke us to seek products or services elsewhere.

When you interact with a form, you provide information to the application so you can obtain a product or service, your same goal as with the human interactions we just described. And, while your first objective is that your information is submitted accurately, your next objective is probably to have a tolerable time supplying that information.

As web professionals, we should consider the *behavior* of a form in much the same way as we would consider how a customer service agent, ticket broker, or cashier should act in front of a customer. By humanizing forms, it's much easier to see where they can be more polite, forgiving, and helpful to the user. Let's take a look at a few aspects of web forms, keeping in mind this concept of humanization, and see how we might improve them.

Improving form validation

Almost all forms offer some sort of validation response to ensure that the information input by a user is actually valid. Not including validation can lead to unusable data, errors in processing, and unhappy customers. It's perhaps the most obvious area of form development we can improve on to be more considerate of the user. Forms validate to check that required fields are filled out and user responses are legitimate (for example, a valid e-mail address or phone number). Offering validation responses does not, however, guarantee a usable web experience. Let's take a look at three key ways we can improve validation.

On-the-fly validation

In most HTML and Flash applications, the validation of a form control happens after a user has submitted the form. It's very likely that just a few errors will be returned in a long form, requiring the user to scroll back through to pluck out which items need to be fixed. We've become so accustomed to this kind of bulk validation that it doesn't seem strange to us at all. But imagine if a ticket agent requested all of your personal and credit card information over the phone. Just before processing your ticket purchase, he yells at you for not telling him your first name in the beginning, and you need to acknowledge your error before correcting it. Kind of odd, eh? Well, that's just about how most forms behave!

A form could easily behave in a more polite and considerate manner. Instead of waiting to tell you what you did wrong at the very end, it could offer a validation response after each form element is filled out. That way, when users get to the checkout line (or the submit button), they will have the comfort of knowing that there won't be any surprises when they are ready to submit the form.

Unobtrusive error handling

Some usability experts may argue this kind of on-the-fly validation may be a bit obtrusive. Users may not want to fill the form out in order, and instead decide to skip around to different sections on the page. What might happen here is that error messages will pop up each time the user leaves a form element that he plans to come back to later.

This brings up a second way to improve validation error handling. When you do show an error message to the user, make sure that it doesn't impede the user's progress. Many HTML forms use a JavaScript alert message to display form error messages. These alert boxes pop up on top of the form page and require users to click OK before fixing their errors. It's as if the form were reprimanding you for an innocent mistake, and forcing you to acknowledge it was your fault, rather than being polite about it!

Instead of requiring users to do anything to acknowledge they've made an error, make the error messages visible but not in a way that impedes the user from filling out the rest of the form. In this way, you can still validate on-the-fly without it becoming a hindrance to the user.

Smarter validation

While on-the-fly validation helps prevent users from having to retrace their footsteps at the end of a form, the true best-case scenario is to avoid validation responses altogether. Sometimes it's obvious what a user means by a provided input, even if it doesn't match the exact specifications that the form dictates.

For example, consider the infamous phone input field. In the U.S., phone numbers are given by a three-digit area code, followed by a seven-digit subscriber number. Figures 8-1 and 8-2 show the two most common implementations of the phone text input field. In Figure 8-1, the phone input field is split into three fields to make the format of the phone number obvious. In Figure 8-2, a single box is provided with a help note on the side, describing the way a user should key in the phone number.

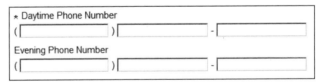

Figure 8-1. Multiple text fields for phone input

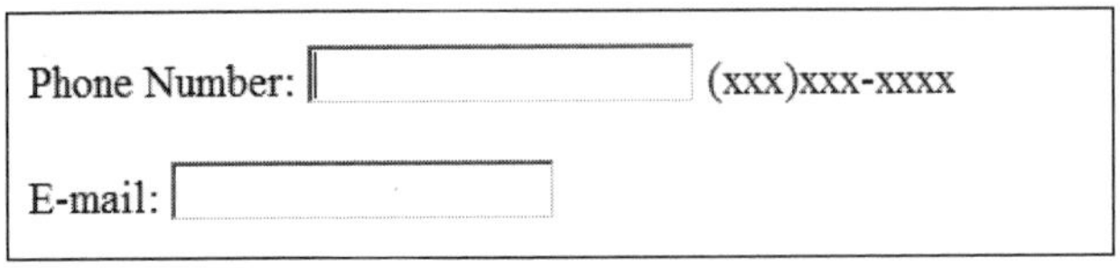

Figure 8-2. A single text field for phone input, with a format requirement

The multiple phone number input fields in Figure 8-1 give better context to the phone number. However, this setup forces you to tab from one input field to the next (although more sophisticated implementations automatically tab you into the next field).

The single text field in Figure 8-2 makes it easier for the user to type in a phone number, but the problem is that it accepts the phone number in only one format. While the accepted format for a phone number is in the form *(555) 555-5555*, there's no reason that it shouldn't also accept entries like *555-555-5555, 555.555.5555*, or even *5555555555*. Yet, as developers, we rarely build for this kind of flexibility into our applications.

Usually, a phone number that is not in the expected format is returned to the user as an error. While there may be good reason to request uniformity in user inputs to ensure the integrity of the data, in obvious cases where a user's intentions are clear, we can build validation controls with a judicious amount of flexibility.

Building for this kind of leniency is fairly simple. It wouldn't be too hard to post-parse a phone number that may not be in the correct format, even though the user's intentions were obvious. You could then pass back to the database (or whatever storage mechanism you're inclined to use) a cleaned version of the phone number, reparsed into the standard format, as illustrated in Figure 8-3. The great benefit here is that you've managed to keep the data in the format you want, while not annoying the users by making them do this trivial bit of reformatting work for you.

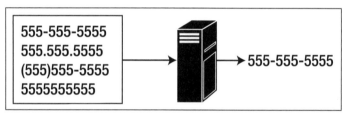

Figure 8-3. Post-parsing data after a text input is submitted prevents users from having to do the work.

Not to sound like we're eating our own words here, but in some cases, you do want to be careful about allowing a degree of flexibility in the validation of your data. Take, for instance, an open-ended birth date text field, where inputs like June 29, 1979, 6/29/79, and 6-29-1979 are all read as acceptable entries. However, what about 4/6/79? While in the U.S., this would be the sixth day of April in 1979, in Europe, this would be the fourth day of June in 1979. In this case, you want to let the user clearly know what date format you're expecting. A label such as MM/DD/YYYY next to the text field should convey this information.

Improving form workflow

Forms are not just about input fields and validation. Another major factor in form usability is how the form flows. Forms should flow in a natural way, providing users with an easy method of navigating from one element to the next. Just as a customer service representative might guide you through an ordering process by asking you questions at a consistent, steady pace, a form should do all the little things it can to make your experience smooth and easy.

Tabbing

Tabbing order is a key issue with forms. Any Internet user who has filled out enough forms in her lifetime knows that by hitting the *TAB* key, you can advance to the next form element, and by hitting *SHIFT+TAB*, you can go back to the previous element. Tabbing provides a very fluid way of keying in form elements. It prevents the constant shifting between mouse and keyboard that severely reduces user efficiency. Most HTML forms have a default tabbing order (given by the order of the form elements within the HTML source code), but it may not always be the best order for your purposes.

In Flash-based forms, tabbing doesn't come by default. You'll need to implicitly create the order of the tabbing. We'll show you one way to do that in this chapter's example.

Positioning

While tabbing helps create a more lucid keyboarding experience, an obnoxiously long form still requires you to adjust your vision down the screen. By the time you reach the bottom of the screen, each subsequent *TAB* press moves only to the next element above the screen division. The luxury you previously had of seeing what was coming next on the form list is no longer available to you, unless you implicitly readjust your screen position using the browser scrollbar or mouse wheel. While this isn't really that horrible a usability dilemma, it would be a plus if the current form element you were filling out were always in the middle of the screen. Not only would you not have to pick up your mouse, but your eyes could stay focused on one place at all times.

Creating a better form experience

Let's take a look at a Flash solution that addresses all of the issues we discussed in the previous section. Download the `Chapter8_Final.zip` file from the friends of ED website (`www.friendsofed.com`) and export the files within the ZIP file into a directory on your machine. Open the `Chapter8_Final.swf` file, located in the `/source/swf/` subdirectory.

As you can see in Figure 8-4, we've built a basic contact form, which requests the type of information you would expect to see in a typical web form.

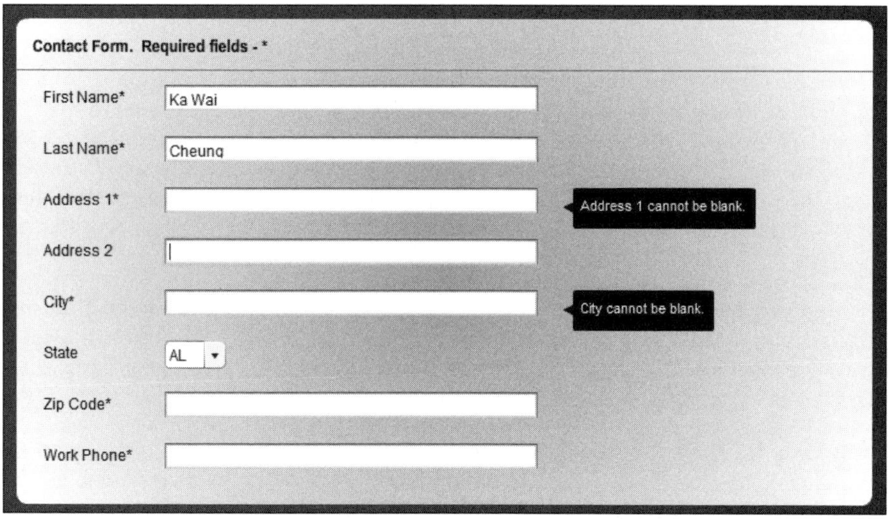

Figure 8-4. The Flash form, with on-the-fly validation and auto-scrolling

Self-scrolling

Go ahead and begin typing your personal information into this form. Use the *TAB* key to move from one field to the next, and press *SHIFT+TAB* to move back to the previous field if you want to correct any typos.

> If you're testing this movie within the Flash environment, make sure you select Control ➤ Disable Keyboard Shortcuts, or else tabbing through the combo box and check box fields will not work.

Now, notice what happens when you reach the City input field. The form should scroll upward! If you continue to tab down the form, you'll notice that each successive field scrolls up to the area just inhabited by the previous form element. If you press *SHIFT+TAB* to move to the previous form element, the form then scrolls back down to the same position. Your eye position stays relatively stable for the entire duration of the form-filling process.

Another benefit is that the self-scrolling form also shows you the next few form elements that lie below the current one. Whatever field you are currently working with, you always see the few elements you've just completed, as well as the next few elements that lie ahead. In a traditional form, you would need to use your mouse wheel or the browser's scrollbar to view the next set of form elements, as tabbing would expose only the very next form element at the bottom of the page. The same scrolling is also achieved if you click a form element with your mouse—the display scrolls up (or down) to it.

As you can see, tabbing, in combination with the automatic scrolling, provides an easier, more fluid user experience when completing the form.

Dynamic and smart validation

At this point, you may have noticed something else. If you tab away from any of the required fields without filling in any information, a red error message pops up to the right of the form element. In fact, whenever you leave one form element to move to another form element (whether you are tabbing or using your mouse to move to a different element), the one that you've just left is validated. Rather than waiting for you to submit everything before doing any validation checks, the example validates each form element as you go.

As we discussed earlier, the validation error messages in this form don't impede the user's progress. They stay on the right side of the form, next to their respective form elements. They don't require you to click an OK button. If you go back and correct your mistake, the validation error disappears.

In this form, we've also implemented smart validation on the two phone input fields: the Work Phone and Cell Phone fields. If you leave the Work Phone field blank, you get the standard "Phone number cannot be blank" error message. But, if you type in something with alphabet characters, or a phone number that doesn't contain ten digits, the message changes to "Unrecognizable format. Try (xxx)xxx-xxxx." (We do realize that a phone number can be written with alphabet characters too, but we'll disallow that for the purposes of this example).

Now, key in a phone number in any sensible format. Formats like *xxx.xxx.xxxx*, *xxx-xxx-xxxx*, *(xxx)xxx-xxxx*, and even *xxxxxxxxxx* are accepted by the phone field because, while they may not be what is specified in the validation message, these are all easily decipherable phone number formats.

An additional piece of smart validation we've added is with the Zip Code field. In the U.S., all zip codes come in the form of five-digit entries (for the purposes of this chapter, let's not consider those nine-digit extended zip codes). Any input that doesn't follow this rule will result in an error message specific to what you did wrong.

Finally, when you click the Submit button at the end of the form, it reveals an alert box much like a JavaScript alert box. If the form still contains errors, you get a message displaying how many errors were found. Here, you do have to click OK before returning to the form to fix your errors. At this point, it's not all that bad that you are forced to acknowledge your errors, because it clearly shows why you can't submit the form, and you have already been warned about the errors.

If there are no errors, you also receive an alert message, "Form Submitted!" Obviously, in a real application, the form would then be submitted to the server. But we'll omit that for the purposes of simplicity here.

You may have realized that this form works well only if all of its elements are added in a linear, vertical fashion. Suppose we moved the Last Name *field to the right of the* First Name *field, and then had the* City, State, *and* Zip *fields all in one line. That would make it harder for us to find real estate to display the validation error for each form element. But we've decided this is an acceptable trade-off. Requiring the form elements to go in one straightforward, linear fashion makes very obvious the intended order of how things should be filled out. You don't have to think twice about where a TAB or SHIFT+TAB will take you.*

Now let's move on to how we've built the various pieces of this form and the code we've written to implement all of its neat functionality!

Building the Flash solution

From your downloaded files folder, open the `Chapter8_Final.fla` file, found in the `/source/fla` directory. We'll start by going over the interface objects we need to construct before showing you how to approach the code development.

Creating the Flash UI components

With the Flash MX release, Macromedia introduced a set of user interface components as part of its standard out-of-the-box components package. All of these components extend the base class `mx.core.UIComponent`. In Flash 8, these UI components can be found in the Components panel (Window ➤ Components), in the User Interface section.

Many of the components found here mimic HTML form elements. Table 8-1 lists the components and their HTML equivalents.

Table 8-1. HTML-based form components and their Flash equivalents

HTML/JavaScript Component	Flash Equivalent
JavaScript alert box	`mx.controls.Alert`
Submit button	`mx.controls.Button`
Check box	`mx.controls.CheckBox`
Drop-down box	`mx.controls.ComboBox`
Multiple select box	`mx.controls.List`
Radio button	`mx.controls.RadioButton`
Text area	`mx.controls.TextArea`
Text input field	`mx.controls.TextInput`

In the solution for this chapter, we will be using the Alert, TextInput, TextArea, ComboBox, CheckBox, and Button components.

When you first view this form, you might think we've simply dragged a bunch of Flash form components onto the screen, and then added some labels to the left side, leaving room for validation controls on the right. You're partially correct. But instead of thinking about the form as one whole piece of functionality, we've broken down each specific type of component we use here into its very own distinct movie clip.

In essence, all the different kinds of form elements we have on the screen have been wrapped inside a movie clip that has self-contained labels and functionality. The general sketch of each of these component-wrapped movie clips looks something like Figure 8-5.

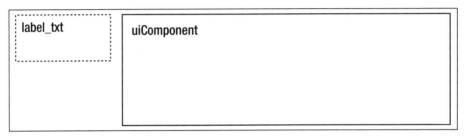

Figure 8-5. A general layout of each of the form component wrapper clips

In addition to these wrappers, we also use a validation control clip and a form container clip. Let's examine each of these elements, beginning with the component wrapper movie clips. Open the library (Window ➤ Library), and we'll begin with the text input wrapper clip.

The text input wrapper clip

Open the MC TextInputWrapper movie clip within the movieclips folder in the library, as shown in Figure 8-6. The bottom layer, label, contains a dynamic text field box named label_txt, sized at 90 height ✕ 40 width and positioned at (0,0) to the registration point of the clip. The font is set to Arial, 10-pt, and we've set the text to Anti-alias for readability, which gives the label font a clean, easy-to-read look.

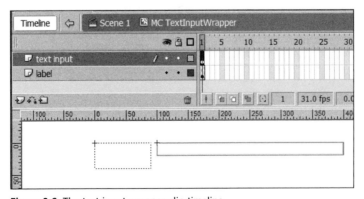

Figure 8-6. The text input wrapper clip timeline

Above the label layer, in the text input layer, we've dropped in a TextInput UI component. We've placed the TextInput component at (100,0), resized it to 300 width × 20 height, and given it an instance name of uiComponent.

> *To add a component, open the* Components *panel (*Window ➤ Components*) and expand the* User Interface *layer. You can then drag-and-drop the component on stage.*

Now, open the linkage properties for this clip (right-click the clip name in the library and click Linkage). We've given this an Identifier name of MC TextInputWrapper and linked it to the ActionScript class TextInputWrapper.

The text area wrapper clip

Now open the MC TextAreaWrapper movie clip, found within the movieclips folder in the library, as shown in Figure 8-7. The bottom layer, label, is the same as in the text input wrapper clip. In the text area layer, we've dropped in a TextArea UI component. We've placed the TextArea component at (100,0), resized it to 300 width × 100 height, and provided it an instance name of uiComponent. The Identifier name is MC TextAreaWrapper, and the linked class is TextAreaWrapper.

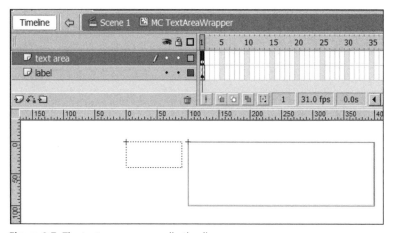

Figure 8-7. The text area wrapper clip timeline

The state combo box wrapper clip

Open the MC StateComboBoxWrapper movie clip found within the movieclips folder in the library. Again, the label layer is the same as in the other wrapper clips. Above this layer is a layer named combo box. Here, we've dropped in a ComboBox UI component. We've placed the ComboBox component at (100,0) and resized it to 50 width × 22 height. Again, the instance name is uiComponent.

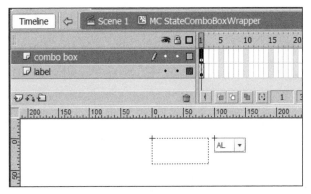

Figure 8-8. The state combo box wrapper clip timeline

Next, open the Properties panel and select the Parameters tab. You'll see that under the data and labels rows, we've added in the initials for the 50 U.S. states.

The Identifier name is MC StateComboBoxWrapper, and the linked class is StateComboBoxWrapper.

The check box wrapper clip

Open the MC CheckBoxWrapper movie clip within the movieclips folder in the library, as shown in Figure 8-9. In this clip, we've swapped the positions of the label and component. The text label will be located to the right of the check box component.

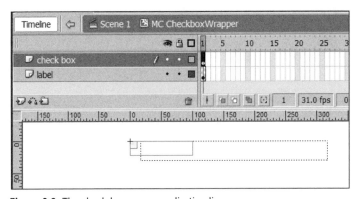

Figure 8-9. The check box wrapper clip timeline

The label layer contains the dynamic text field label_txt, positioned at (18,0) and sized at 300 width × 30 height. In the check box layer, we've dropped in a CheckBox UI component. We've placed the CheckBox component at (0,0).

The CheckBox component comes with a default label already attached to it. For our purposes, we will use the label_txt field to handle the label for consistency's sake. Open the Parameters tab in the Properties panel, and you'll see that the label field is blank, so no text shows by default. Once again, the instance name is uiComponent.

The Identifier name is MC CheckBoxWrapper, and the linked class is CheckBoxWrapper.

Now that we've reviewed the form component wrapper movie clips, let's look at the custom validation control that we will reuse for each form element in our application.

The validation control

While playing with our solution, you may have noticed that the size of the red bubble that surrounds the validation text depends on the amount of text inside it. We'll build this flexibility in as part of the inherent functionality to the clip later on, but from a UI design perspective, we need to provide an equal amount of flexibility.

The ability of the red bubble to resize while maintaining the shape of the rounded corners and left pointer area requires us to cut the bubble into three distinct pieces. See Figure 8-10 for a breakdown of the different pieces.

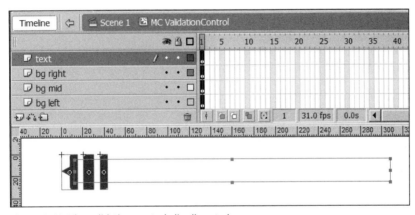

Figure 8-10. The validation control clip dissected

The bottom layer, bg left, contains a movie clip named bgLeft_mc, which represents the left cap of the validation control bubble. The next layer, bg mid, contains a solid red rectangle named bgMid_mc, which represents the middle area of the validation control bubble. The next layer, bg right, contains a movie clip named bgRight_mc, which represents the right cap of the validation control bubble. On the top layer, text, lies a dynamic text field named validation_txt, which we've set to a solid white Arial, 11-pt font, to provide nice contrast against the red background bubble. Also, we've set the text to Anti-alias for readability.

We've set the Identifier name for this clip to MC ValidationControl and linked it to the ValidationControl class that we'll construct in the next section.

Notice that the bgLeft_mc, bgMid_mc, and bgRight_mc clips form a default red bubble (with a pointer on the left end) that has been sliced into three pieces. In code, we'll vary the width of bgMid_mc based on the size of the text label (validation_txt) above it. The bgLeft_mc and bgRight_mc clips "cap" both ends of bgMid_mc to give it the finished look. You can see the individual pieces by viewing the MC ValidationControl clip in the library. Had we not cut the clip into three distinct pieces and just scaled the clip to the appropriate width based on the validation text, we would have gotten stretched corners and a skewed arrow pointer. Taking the extra effort to make the validation control work with a flexible amount of text is well worth it to give our validation controls a consistent look.

If you're building this from scratch, the easiest way to create the control is to start with an overall design of the general validation bubble, and then slice it up three ways, converting each of the slices into movie clips.

The form container

The final piece we need is the form container. In code, we'll attach the form elements within this container. Open the MC FormWrapper movie clip to see how it is constructed.

The bottom layer, background, contains our background clip for the entire form, positioned at (0,0) and scaled to 690 width × 380 height. As in the examples in Chapters 6 and 7, this clip contains a slight radial gradient going from light gray to white. Do you sense a theme here?

The next layer, container, contains an empty movie clip called container_mc. We'll be attaching the form component wrappers to this movie clip in code later. We've positioned this at (20,52).

The next layer, mask, contains a solid rectangular movie clip with an instance name of mask_mc. This will serve as the mask to the form container below it. It is sized to 660 width × 310 height and is positioned at (20,50). Note that we will not set this as a mask in the timeline, but we will dynamically assign it as a mask in code later on.

Next, in the line layer, we've created a solid gray line, which will just be a visual marker for the top edge of the form. We've positioned it at (0,0) and stretched it across the length of the background.

Finally, the top layer, title, contains a simple static text that reads "Contact Form. Required Fields -*."

The Identifier name is set to MC FormWrapper and the linked class is FormWrapper.

Finally, we drag an instance of MC FormWrapper onto the root timeline of Chapter8_Final.fla, positioning it at (50,50). Since all the parts of the form are contained within this clip, there's nothing else we need to worry about on the stage itself.

That's it. All the different clips are in place! Now, it's just a matter of attaching each of these clips to their appropriate linked classes. In the next section, we will show you not only how to build this form functionality, but also ways to make it easy to add in more elements and validation in the future.

Coding the solution

Our approach to the code will follow how we examined the clips in the previous section. We'll first talk about the properties and methods that we need to enable in each of the various form elements, add in the validation control code, and then finish it off with the form container code that will allow you to customize the form to your particular project needs.

Building the form element wrapper code

As you saw earlier, all of the form elements have a common theme, both in terms of how we named the pieces within the clips and how they function. Let's list their shared characteristics:

- A text field label, named label_txt, which describes the form component
- A UI component object named uiComponent, which provides the input area for the particular form element
- A validation control that pops up an error message based on user input
- The ability to scroll the entire form to the element when it has received focus

Because each of these elements shares common characteristics, a good coding approach would be to build a base class that will encapsulate all these common features, and then build the classes that link to the movie clips as subclasses of the base class. This not only lets us avoid duplicating a lot of the same methods and properties in each of the linked classes, but also makes it incredibly easy to add new component wrappers down the line (such as a set of radio buttons or a date field component).

The base class will be called ComponentWrapperBase. Open the ComponentWrapperBase.as class from the /source/classes/ folder and let's dissect this very useful object. Here's how we begin:

```
class ComponentWrapperBase extends MovieClip
{
  private var uiComponent:mx.core.UIComponent;
  private var label_txt:TextField;
  private var label_str:String;
  private var required:Boolean;
  private var errorRaised:Boolean;
  private var validation_mc:MovieClip;

  private var validationStrategy:IValidationStrategy;
```

Because each subclass that extends this class is linked to a movie clip, we'll extend the MovieClip class here. As for the variables, we include the uiComponent and label_txt objects that are common to each form component clip. We've typed the uiComponent as an mx.core.UIComponent object, but will retype it to a specific kind of UIComponent when we define each of the subclasses later. The label_str variable will hold the label name, and the required variable will determine if the particular component wrapper clip is required. These two variables will be set upon instantiation of each of the component clips later on. Next, the errorRaised variable determines the component's current error status. Also, the validation_mc variable will be a placeholder for a validation movie clip, if an error is raised.

The last variable we create will probably make the least sense at this point. The validationStrategy property will be a type of IValidationStrategy. Abstractly speaking, the IValidationStrategy is an interface construct we'll build later that contains a method to define the logic behind how each kind of component validates. If you're unfamiliar with the concept of interfaces in ActionScript 2 (we're not referring to a user interface, but to the object-oriented programming construct called an *interface*), peek back to Chapter 6, where we give a brief overview of it. You'll be hearing a whole lot more about this validationStrategy object later, when we talk about the validation strategy!

Next, we write the constructor, which simply assigns the label_txt text field the label from label_str and also appends an asterisk if the component is required. The tabChildren Boolean (inherited from the MovieClip class) is set to true to allow tabbing to occur inside the wrapper clip (namely, the particular component attached to each wrapper clip).

```
public function ComponentWrapperBase()
{
  this.label_txt.text = label_str;
  if (required)
    this.label_txt.text += "*";

  this.tabChildren = true;
}
```

After this, we define methods that allow public read and write access to some of our private properties. Specifically, we have methods to get and set the validationStrategy property, and methods to return the label_str and required properties.

```
public function getValidationStrategy():IValidationStrategy
{
  return validationStrategy;
}

public function setValidationStrategy(_st:IValidationStrategy):Void
{
  validationStrategy = _st;
}

public function getLabel():String
{
  return label_str;
}

public function getRequired():Boolean
{
  return required;
}
```

Following this, we create a definition for the onLoad() movie clip event handler. When each component wrapper clip loads, we want these clips to listen for the focusIn() and focusOut() events inherent in the uiComponent. As a side note, each mx.core.UIComponent type inherits from the mx.core.UIObject class, which contains an addEventListener() method that allows you to add objects that listen for events, in the same way as the EventBroadcaster class did in our example in Chapter 7. The focusIn() event handler is invoked when the uiComponent receives focus. Similarly, the focusOut() event handler is called when the uiComponent loses focus.

```
public function onLoad():Void
{
  uiComponent.addEventListener("focusIn", this);
  uiComponent.addEventListener("focusOut", this);
}
```

Next, we add in our definitions for the focusIn() and focusOut() definitions for the wrapper clip. Here's where we see the need for listening to these events. When the uiComponent receives focus—whether it's a mouse click or a tab into the component—this clip's job will be to broadcast an event using the EventBroadcaster class described in Chapter 7. You'll notice that we've included the EventBroadcaster class in the /source/classes/ folder in the chapter download files, so it is immediately available for use here. The broadcasted event, elementFocused, will be used by the master form wrapper later on to reposition the entire form to the correct y-position. This is why we also pass the _y parameter of this clip when the message is broadcasted. This code appears next:

```
private function focusIn():Void
{
  EventBroadcaster.getInstance().broadcastEvent("elementFocused",
➥ {y:_y});
}
```

Similarly, when the uiComponent loses focus, which means that the user has either tabbed out of the component or mouse-clicked to some other spot on the form, we call a validateField() method to check the work the user has done. Here are both the focusOut() and validateField() methods, which follow in the class definition.

```
private function focusOut():Void
{
  validateField();
}
public function validateField():Void
{
  // Override this method
}
```

Notice the validateField() method here is empty. We will override this method in each of the subclasses of ComponentWrapperBase, since validation rules will be custom to each form element (this is also where you'll see how the validationStrategy object works).

8

To round out this base class, we provide methods to easily display a validation error and remove that validation error as well. The displayError() method is added next:

```
public function displayError(_message:String):Void
{
  if (!errorRaised)
  {
    EventBroadcaster.getInstance().broadcastEvent("raiseError");
  }

  this.attachMovie("MC ValidationControl", "validation_mc", 1,
➡ {_x:420, mesg_str:_message});
  errorRaised = true;
}
```

The displayError() method accepts a message string and attaches an instance of the MC ValidationControl to this clip, positioning it at (420,0) to the registration point of the clip. Here's where you see the errorRaised Boolean make an appearance. If the previous state of the form wrapper clip validated properly, we broadcast an event called raiseError. The event will be used by the master form wrapper later on to keep track of which form elements did not validate properly.

The clearError() method simply unloads the MC ValidationControl instance, if it exists. In addition, if the previous state of the form wrapper clip did not validate properly, we broadcast an event called removeError. Like raiseError, the master form wrapper will listen to this event to keep track of validated form elements.

```
public function clearError():Void
{
  if (errorRaised)
  {
    EventBroadcaster.getInstance().broadcastEvent("removeError");
  }

  validation_mc.unloadMovie();
  errorRaised = false;
}
}
```

Note that the previous two methods, displayError() and clearError(), are given public access. This is because the validationStrategy object will invoke these methods based on whether each component validates. Therefore, we need these methods to be accessible outside the class itself.

Using a Strategy pattern to create reusable validation logic

In the discussion of the ComponentWrapperBase, you saw how we implemented all the common functionality inherited by each form element clip. Now, let's shift the focus to the subclasses that will extend ComponentWrapperBase to provide whatever custom functionality is necessary for each of the specific component wrappers.

If you think about it, only two differences exist between each of these different subclasses:

- The kind of form element these subclasses implement
- The kind of logic needed to validate the given form element

Let's talk about one way you could go about building these subclasses. Note that this won't be the way we'll use in this chapter, but the discussion will lead up to our method.

First, you could create a subclass of ComponentWrapperBase called, say, TextInputWrapper, that defines the kind of form element it contains (namely, a TextInput component) and a custom implementation of the validation logic (by overriding the validateField() method). In this class, the validation check would be as simple as seeing that a field that is required actually contains some data. This class would be sufficient to link to, say, the First Name, Last Name, and Address fields.

Could TextInputWrapper also be used to create the Work Phone form element? Not in this case, because its validateField() method needs to also check that the element's data represents a kind of phone number. We would need to write a whole new class for the phone field, despite the fact that it wraps the very same TextInput component. Similarly, for the Zip Code form element, we would create yet another subclass to define a third way of validating a TextInput component.

Now, consider a slightly different scenario. If we were to create a subclass for the Comments field, we might create a class called TextAreaWrapper that defines a TextArea component (as opposed to a TextInput component) and implements the validateField() method. But the validation logic would be identical to the validation logic in TextInputWrapper. If Comments is a required field, the method would check whether the data within the Comments field is blank. Here, we couldn't just reuse the validateField() method in TextInputWrapper. We would either copy and paste the method into TextAreaWrapper or extract that method into some other class that both TextInputWrapper and TextAreaWrapper could access.

Notice the dilemma we have here. We need to create a unique subclass of ComponentWrapperBase for each kind of UIComponent type, but we also need to create a unique subclass for each different kind of validation! If we decide to add new kinds of validation methods or add new kinds of form components, the code within these classes would get a bit redundant and bloated. This is a perfect situation to introduce the *Strategy design pattern*.

Don't let the name scare you, because the Strategy design pattern is really very sensible. Instead of creating a new class every time we introduce either a new form component or a new kind of validation logic, we'll just limit it so that each distinct form component (TextInput, TextArea, or ComboBox) is wrapped into one subclass of ComponentWrapperBase. The validation logic will come in the form of different strategy classes. At runtime, we pair a particular form component wrapper class with whatever validation strategy it requires.

Notice the instant benefits we have here. We can easily plug in different validation strategies to different form elements. For instance, if we wanted to create a required Comments field, we would implement it within some class called, say, TextAreaWrapper, and pass it an instance of a strategy class called, say, TextValidationStrategy. A required First Name

8

field would implement, say, TextInputWrapper, but also use the same strategy class TextValidationStrategy. Finally, a phone field would implement TextInputWrapper but use a different strategy class; PhoneValidationStrategy might be an appropriate name for it.

Using the Strategy pattern, we now delegate the validation code into distinct classes so that we can decouple the form component from a particular validation rule. The form elements and the validation logic now work as interchangeable parts, as diagrammed in Figure 8-11. Plus, the added benefit is that if we need to modify a particular validation strategy, we do it in one place, and all components that implement that strategy will be updated automatically!

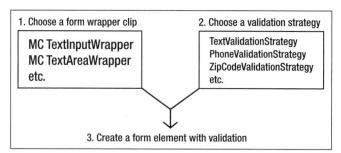

Figure 8-11. Separating validation logic from components to create more versatile form elements

With this new information in mind, let's tackle the subclass construction in this order.

1. Define a generic interface called IValidationStrategy, for all strategy classes.

2. Figure out all the validation strategies we need and implement them individually.

3. Create the form element wrapper classes that will extend ComponentWrapperBase.

Creating the validation strategy interface

We introduced the validationStrategy property in our earlier discussion of the ComponentWrapperBase class (the class that all of our form element wrapper classes will extend). At runtime, we will assign whatever validation strategy class is appropriate for each form element.

```
private var validationStrategy:IValidationStrategy;
```

The IValidationStrategy is an interface for all of the types of validation strategies we'll implement next. The only task required of these validation strategies is to validate data, so the only method signature that we'll need in IValidationStrategy is a validate() method. The validate() method accepts an input (the data to validate), along with a reference to the component wrapper class that requests validation. The IValidationStrategy.as class in the /source/classes/ folder looks like this:

```
    interface IValidationStrategy
    {
      public function validate(_input:Object,
➡   _comp:ComponentWrapperBase): Void;
    }
```

Now, we need to write the logic behind each different kind of validation that exists in our form. Doing a quick audit of the form in this example, we see that we have the following kinds of validation:

- A check that required text has data within it
- A check that an input is set to true (this is the case for the required check box field)
- A check that a phone number validates
- A check that a zip code validates

Validating text

First, let's code the basic text validator strategy class. We've called it TextValidationStrategy so it resides in the TextValidationStrategy.as file.

```
    class TextValidationStrategy implements IValidationStrategy
    {
      public function TextValidationStrategy() {}

      public function validate(_input:Object,
➡   _comp:ComponentWrapperBase): Void
      {
        if (_comp.getRequired())
        {
          if (_input == "")
          {
            _comp.displayError(_comp.getLabel() + " cannot be blank.");
          }
          else
          {
            _comp.clearError();
          }
        }
      }
    }
```

The validate() method first checks if the field in question is required by calling the getRequired() method of the passed-in ComponentWrapperBase class. If it is required and the inputted data is left blank, it then calls ComponentWrapperBase.displayError() to display a validation error message on screen. Otherwise, there is no validation that needs to be done, so it calls ComponentWrapperBase.clearError().

8

Validating a Boolean

Next, let's create the Boolean validator strategy class. It's very similar to the one for text, but instead of checking if a given required input isn't empty, we check that a given required input is set to true. The BoolValidationStrategy.as class looks like this:

```
class BoolValidationStrategy implements IValidationStrategy
{
  public function BoolValidationStrategy() {}

  public function validate(_input:Object,
➥ _comp:ComponentWrapperBase): Void
  {
    if (_comp.getRequired() && !_input)
    {
      _comp.displayError("Must be selected");
    }
    else
    {
      _comp.clearError();
    }
  }
}
```

Validating a phone number

Now, we get into the fun stuff! One of the more interesting validation rules we need to define is whether a phone number is really a phone number. Let's recall our goal from earlier in this chapter. We want to ensure that the user submits a ten-digit phone number, but we also want to give the user the flexibility to type the number in a variety of sensible and easily decipherable ways. To accomplish this, we'll parse each character of the phone text input field one by one. At the completion of the parsing, we want to make sure that the number of digits in the phone number is equal to ten. This allows users the flexibility of typing in delimiters within the phone number, such as (555)555-5555 or 555/555-5555.

The problem here is that an entry like 555a55bd5b555*5 will still validate. What we're assuming here is that anyone typing in such a nonsensical phone number has probably spilled a cup of coffee on the keyboard. In a more common scenario, someone could have typed in 555-555-5r555, given the close proximity of the R key with the 5 key. Here, we should play it safe and not assume the number is correct (despite there being ten digits), but instead display an error message.

The moral here is that we need to be somewhat strict about the kinds of nondigit characters that we should allow a user to key in. We've chosen ., (,), -, and /\ as the allowed set of characters, as these are common delimiters for a phone number. Thus, anytime we find a nondigit character not in this list, we'll display an error message.

As you'll see in the following complete PhoneValidationStrategy class code (and you saw if you played around with the solution SWF earlier), we also vary the error message displayed based on the type of error. Rather than just saying "Phone number invalid," we give users a more meaningful error message to help them know why we couldn't understand what was submitted. Here's the PhoneValidationStrategy class, found in the PhoneValidationStrategy.as file:

```
class PhoneValidationStrategy implements IValidationStrategy
{
  public function PhoneValidationStrategy() {}

  public function validate(_input:Object,
➥ _comp:ComponentWrapperBase) : Void
  {
    if (_comp.getRequired() && _input == "")
    {
      _comp.displayError(_comp.getLabel() + " cannot be blank.");
    }
    else if (_input != "")
    {
      var num_str:String = "0123456789";
      var char_str:String = ".()-/\ ";
      var count_num:Number = 0;

      for (var i:Number=0; i < _input.length; i++)
      {
        if (num_str.indexOf(_input.charAt(i)) > 0)
        {
          count_num++;
        }
        else if (char_str.indexOf(_input.charAt(i)) == -1)
        {
          _comp.displayError("Unrecognizable format.
➥ Try (xxx)xxx-xxxx.");
          return;
        }
      }

      if (count_num != 10)
      {
        _comp.displayError("You must enter a 10-digit number.");
      }
      else
      {
        _comp.clearError();
      }
    }
  }
}
```

Validating a zip code

In the ZipCodeValidationStrategy class, shown here, you'll notice many similarities with the PhoneValidationStrategy class. Again, the check here is that a zip code contains only five digits and nothing else.

```
class ZipCodeValidationStrategy implements IValidationStrategy
{
  public function ZipCodeValidationStrategy() {}

  public function validate(_input:Object,
➥ _comp:ComponentWrapperBase):Void
  {
    if (_comp.getRequired() && _input == "")
    {
      _comp.displayError(_comp.getLabel() + " cannot be blank.");
    }
    else if (_input != "")
    {
      var num_str:String = "0123456789";
      var count_num:Number = 0;

      for (var i:Number=0; i < _input.length; i++)
      {
        if (num_str.indexOf(_input.charAt(i)) > 0)
        {
          count_num++;
        }
        else
        {
          _comp.displayError("Zip code can only contain numbers.");
          return;
        }
      }

      if (count_num != 5)
      {
        _comp.displayError("You must enter a 5-digit zip code.");
      }
      else
      {
        _comp.clearError();
      }
    }
  }
}
```

We've now completed all the different strategy classes for validation! Next up, we need to write the classes for each kind of form component wrapper. Then we'll be ready to put it all together to create the final form.

Creating the component wrapper subclasses

The creation of the subclasses that extend ComponentWrapperBase will be incredibly simple. Remember that most of the functionality for each form component has already been written in the base class. In these subclasses, we just need to assign uiComponent its correct data type, and then implement that validateField() method, using our validation strategy classes.

Let's start off with the easy one. Open the StateComboBoxWrapper.as file within the /source/classes/ folder. This class is the only one that doesn't require any validation. Notice we just define the uiComponent as a type of mx.controls.ComboBox (see Table 8-1, earlier in the chapter), and then create an empty constructor.

```
class StateComboBoxWrapper extends ComponentWrapperBase
{
  public var uiComponent:mx.controls.ComboBox;

  public function StateComboBoxWrapper() {}
}
```

Now, let's get a little more involved. In the CheckBoxWrapper.as file, we'll take the same steps as in StateComboBoxWrapper.as, but also define the validateField() method. For check boxes, the data in question is the value of the selected state. When a box is checked, its selected state will be true. Otherwise, it will return false. In the validateField() method, we tell the validationStrategy object to validate this value, passing along a reference to the class itself to the validation strategy.

```
class CheckBoxWrapper extends ComponentWrapperBase
{
  public var uiComponent:mx.controls.CheckBox;

  public function CheckBoxWrapper() {}

  public function validateField():Void
  {
    validationStrategy.validate(uiComponent.selected, this);
  }
}
```

Next, let's look at how we implement the wrapper class for the two kinds of text fields in our form. Notice that, in this case, we pass the uiComponent.text field to the validationStrategy. The following is in TextInputWrapper.as:

```
class TextInputWrapper extends ComponentWrapperBase
{
  public var uiComponent:mx.controls.TextInput;

  public function TextInputWrapper() {}
```

8

```
public function validateField():Void
{
  validationStrategy.validate(uiComponent.text, this);
}
}
```

Similarly, here's how we create the wrapper class for text area fields, in TextAreaWrapper.as:

```
class TextAreaWrapper extends ComponentWrapperBase
{
  public var uiComponent:mx.controls.TextArea;

  public function TextAreaWrapper() {}

  public function validateField():Void
  {
    validationStrategy.validate(uiComponent.text, this);
  }
}
```

We've now completed both the validation logic and the subclasses that will wrap each form component. We need to discuss just two more classes before we can get all the pieces working. First, we need to write the class that will support the actual MC ValidationControl movie clip. Then we'll write a class that will support the MC FormWrapper clip.

Building the validation control class

The class for the validation control links to the MC ValidationControl movie clip we built a few pages ago. Remember that the ComponentWrapperBase class is in charge of attaching new instances of these validation controls when its displayError() method is called. In that method, we pass a value called mesg_str to the newly created validation clip.

In the following code, we create a setValidationText() method that is called in its constructor. In the setValidationText() method, the validation_txt text field is assigned the value from mesg_str. After this, we resize the width of the bgMid_mc to the length of the text field, and then reposition both the bgMid_mc and bgRight_mc movie clips to new x-positions so the overall red bubble is sized appropriately given the amount of text.

The full class, ValidationControl.as, is shown here.

```
class ValidationControl extends MovieClip
{
  private var bgLeft_mc:MovieClip;
  private var bgMid_mc:MovieClip;
  private var bgRight_mc:MovieClip;

  private var validation_txt:TextField;
  private var mesg_str:String;
```

```
public function ValidationControl()
{
  setValidationText();
}

private function setValidationText():Void
{
  validation_txt.text = mesg_str;
  bgMid_mc._width = validation_txt.textWidth;
  bgMid_mc._x = bgLeft_mc._x + bgLeft_mc._width;
  bgRight_mc._x = bgLeft_mc._width + bgMid_mc._width;
}
}
```

Building the form container class

The last class we need to write is our FormWrapper class, which links directly to the MC FormWrapper movie clip. In this class, we control how the entire form scrolls when you tab or mouse into a particular form element. First, as we've done before with any solution that required dynamic tweening (take Chapter 4's scrolling menus for example), we import a few mx.transitions packages that provide us with an easy way to scroll the form using dynamically assigned tweens.

```
import mx.transitions.easing.*;
import mx.transitions.Tween;
```

We follow this with the class signature, and assign the properties that will help us with correctly positioning the form each time a new element receives focus. In addition, we add in the mask_mc and container_mc movie clip properties.

```
class FormWrapper extends MovieClip
{
  private var focusY:Number;
  private var initContainerY:Number;
  private var yTween:Tween;
  private var level_num:Number;

  private var mask_mc:MovieClip;
  private var container_mc:MovieClip;
  private var elements:Array;
  private var errorCount_num:Number;
```

In this code, the focusY variable is the y-position (with respect to the form wrapper movie clip) that each form element should scroll toward when receiving focus. The initContainerY is the y-position of the container_mc clip with respect to the form wrapper movie clip. We also include a yTween variable that will scroll the clip to its correct position each time a new element receives focus, and a level_num variable that will keep track of levels when we attach the form element wrapper clips to the container. The elements array will store the instance names of each of the form element wrapper clips, and the errorCount_num variable will keep track of the number of total errors in the entire form.

Following our variable declarations, we include the constructor.

```
public function FormWrapper()
{
  level_num = new Number();
  errorCount_num = new Number();
  elements = new Array();

  container_mc.tabChildren = true;
  container_mc.setMask(mask_mc);

  EventBroadcaster.getInstance().addEventListener("elementFocused",
➥ this);
  EventBroadcaster.getInstance().addEventListener("raiseError",
➥ this);
  EventBroadcaster.getInstance().addEventListener("removeError",
➥ this);

  focusY = 230;
  initContainerY = container_mc._y;

  addFormElements();
}
```

In the constructor code, we dynamically set the mask of the container_mc clip to mask_mc. Then we add this clip as an event listener to the elementFocused, raiseError, and removeError events. Next, we set the focusY value to 230 (the amount of pixels roughly halfway between the top and bottom of the container clip) and the initContainerY to the container_mc's _y value.

Finally, we call a method named addFormElements(). This is where all of our hard work finally pays off. This method will be in charge of adding instances of all the form elements to the container clip, while dictating the position, label, and validation rules of each as well. The following code shows this method, along with a new addFormElement() method that's responsible for attaching each *specific* form element wrapper instance to the container clip. Notice that we assign the values of label_str, required, and validationStrategy within a generic object that is passed into addFormElement().

```
private function addFormElements():Void
{
  addFormElement("MC TextInputWrapper", "formFirstName_mc",
➥ {_x:0, _y:0, label_str:"First Name", required:true,
➥ validationStrategy: new TextValidationStrategy()});
  addFormElement("MC TextInputWrapper", "formLastName_mc",
➥ {_x:0, _y:40, label_str:"Last Name", required:true,
➥ validationStrategy: new TextValidationStrategy()});
  addFormElement("MC TextInputWrapper", "formAddress1_mc",
➥ {_x:0, _y:80, label_str:"Address 1", required:true,
➥ validationStrategy: new TextValidationStrategy()});
```

```
   addFormElement("MC TextInputWrapper", "formAddress2_mc",
➡ {_x:0, _y:120, label_str:"Address 2"});
   addFormElement("MC TextInputWrapper", "city_mc",
➡ {_x:0, _y:160, label_str:"City", required:true,
➡ validationStrategy: new TextValidationStrategy()});
   addFormElement("MC StateComboBoxWrapper", "formState_mc",
➡ {_x:0, _y:200, label_str:"State"});
   addFormElement("MC TextInputWrapper", "zipCode_mc",
➡ {_x:0, _y:240, label_str:"Zip Code", required:true,
➡ validationStrategy: new ZipCodeValidationStrategy()});
   addFormElement("MC PhoneInputWrapper", "workPhone_mc",
➡ {_x:0, _y:280, label_str:"Work Phone", required:true,
➡ validationStrategy: new PhoneValidationStrategy()});
   addFormElement("MC PhoneInputWrapper", "cellPhone_mc",
➡ {_x:0, _y:320, label_str:"Cell Phone",
➡ validationStrategy: new PhoneValidationStrategy()});
   addFormElement("MC TextAreaWrapper", "comments_mc",
➡ {_x:0, _y:360, label_str:"Comments"});
   addFormElement("MC CheckBoxWrapper", "receiveUpdates_mc",
➡ {_x:0, _y:480, label_str:"Receive updates from friends of ED"});
   addFormElement("MC CheckBoxWrapper", "agreeToTerms_mc",
➡ {_x:0, _y:500, label_str:"Do you agree to the terms of service?",
➡ required:true, validationStrategy: new BoolValidationStrategy()});

   // Add in a submit button as well
   container_mc.createObject("Button", "submit_btn", ++level_num,
➡ {_x:0, _y:520});
   var submitBtn:mx.controls.Button = container_mc.submit_btn;
   submitBtn.label = "Submit";
   submitBtn.onPress = function() { _parent._parent.doSubmit() };

   private function addFormElement(_linkageName:String,
➡ _instanceName:String, _initObj:Object):Void
   {
     elements.push(_instanceName);
     container_mc.attachMovie(_linkageName, _instanceName, level_num,
➡ _initObj);
     level_num++;
   }
```

8

The addFormElement() method is more or less a glorified version of attachMovie(). Each call to addFormElement() attaches a new movie clip to container_mc, along with a generic object that defines its respective x- and y-positions, label description, a required Boolean, and the validation strategy class to use. The addFormElement() method also keeps track of assigning unique depths to each newly added instance, and pushes the instance name of the clip to the elements array. It so happens that the order of the depths also directly affects the order of the tabbing. By incrementing the depth each time a new element is added, when a user tabs, the focus will go directly to the next added form element.

> *Try it! Replace* level_num++ *with* level_num-- *in the* addFormElement() *method and recompile the code. You'll see the tabbing cycle occur in the opposite direction.*

The other piece of logic in addFormElements() is the attachment of a Button component instance. If you glance back at our library, you'll see we've included a Button component in the components folder. Here, we place it inside the container clip, label it, and also set it to call doSubmit() when pressed. doSubmit() will be added last in this class, so we'll discuss exactly what happens at the end of this section.

Next, we'll include the definitions for each of the methods the form wrapper listens to. Recall the elementFocused() method is invoked each time an individual form element receives focus. Here's the method:

```
public function elementFocused(_event:Event):Void
{
   yTween = new Tween(container_mc, "_y", Regular.easeOut,
➡ container_mc._y, Math.min(initContainerY, focusY - _event.params.y -
➡ initContainerY), .5, true);
}
```

Remember that we pass along the _y position of the form element wrapper clip in the ComponentWrapperBase class as part of the event broadcast. In elementFocused(), we use that value to scroll the entire container clip to the correct new _y value to make the focused clip's y-position equal to focusY (focusY - _event.params.y - initContainerY). But before doing that, we also want to make sure this new y-position is less than the initial y-position of the container clip, or else the container clip would actually scroll in the wrong direction! In the end, we choose the minimum value between this new y-position and the initial y-position. This is why the first four form elements in the solution don't scroll to the new focusY position, but instead move to its original position.

Next, we need to define two more event listener methods. The raiseError() and removeError() methods are broadcasted from each of the form element wrapper clips when validated to a state that's different from its previous one. When the corresponding events are broadcasted, this class just adds to or subtracts from the errorCount_num to keep track of the running total of errors found in the entire form.

```
public function raiseError():Void
{
  errorCount_num++;
}

public function removeError():Void
{
  errorCount_num--;
}
```

And finally (take a deep breath now), we define the doSubmit() method, which gets called when a user clicks the Submit button. Here's where you see the validation come full circle. When a user clicks Submit, this method loops through the instance names of the elements array and calls the validateField() method for each form element wrapper instance to revalidate each field. After validating each field, errorCount_num will now equal the actual number of errors in the entire form. We can then use this number to display an appropriate message in the alert pop-up box.

```
public function doSubmit(_event:Event):Void
{
  var instanceName:String = new String();

  for (var i:Number = 0; i < elements.length; i++)
  {
    instanceName = elements[i];
    container_mc[instanceName].validateField();
  }

  if (errorCount_num == 1)
  {
    mx.controls.Alert.show("There is an error that needs to be
➥ resolved.");
  }
  else if (errorCount_num > 0)
  {
    mx.controls.Alert.show("There are " + errorCount_num +
➥ " errors that need to be resolved.");
  }
  else
  {
    mx.controls.Alert.show("Form submitted!");
  }
}
}
```

The FormWrapper.as class is now completed, as well as all the code we need to write for this solution!

Summary

In this chapter, our goal was to inspire you to change your approach to the design of forms. Functionality that reflects politeness and consideration to your users will make filling out an online form a more pleasant experience for them!

Using the Strategy design pattern, you're able to separate validation logic from the form elements that need to be validated, so that you can more easily mix and match elements to their validation rules. Adding new elements or rules now becomes much easier to do since the parts are interchangeable.

8

As with our other solutions, we suggest that you consider ways that you might extend or improve on our solution:

- Add a traditional scrollbar to the right edge of the form, so that users have the option of scrolling top to bottom. We've omitted it in our implementation not just to emphasize tabbing, but because we feel users might be confused by having a scrollbar available along with the self-scrolling mechanism. But this is certainly a feature you may want to consider adding to give users more options.

- Try adding in some features we've omitted in this solution, such as creating a new validation strategy class to validate e-mail addresses, and then adding an e-mail form element to the solution.

In Chapter 9, we'll continue with this theme of finding ways of being helpful and considerate to the user. Specifically, we're going to discuss using the Flash local shared object to remember your user's previous application settings.

9 STATE MANAGEMENT AND STORAGE

| Foundation Flash 8 |
| Foundation MX Express |
| Foundation MX Studio |
| Foundation MX Upgrade Essentials |
| Foundation MX Video |
| Foundation XML for Flash |
| New Masters of Flash |
| The Flash Usability Guide |
| **Flash Books** ▲ |

Timeline ⇦	🖿 Scene 1
🖿 title
🗋 info text field
🗋 range text fields
🗋 drag handle clips
🗋 slider range bar

Address 1*	
Address 2		
City*	
State	AL ▼
Zip Code*	
Work Phone*	

So far, we've covered many topics related to creating usable interactive functionality within a web application. However, good usability isn't just about what you see or use on the surface.

Another way you can improve usability is to make a web application remember what users have done in the past. Returning users can instantly sense the differences between an application that remembers them as compared to one that treats them as new users every time they come back. An application that remembers you is like an old friend that you're happy to see again.

If you've surfed the Web enough (and we assume you have), you've surely come across many sites that save information about you and remember it when you come back. For instance, Yahoo!'s customizable homepage, My Yahoo!, allows you to choose news feeds that interest you, specify their location for localized news, and keep track of stocks—all from one central page. The best thing about this application is that it remembers these preferences, so you can get to the information that interests you the most without having to set it up more than once.

An even more basic example of remembering the state of a user's session (and more along the lines of this chapter) is the simple concept of a "visited" link that comes standard with most web browsers. By default, in HTML sites, links that you've already clicked appear in purple and unused links are blue. By using CSS, you can style these links as you wish.

Of course, we're here to talk about Flash. In this chapter, we're going to show you some basic ways you can make your Flash applications remember the state of your users' sessions. In particular, we'll employ the sometimes-overlooked local shared object that has been a part of the Flash development library since Flash MX. Here's what we'll cover in this chapter:

- Use cases for remembering the state of a user's sessions
- How to use the local shared object to store data
- A simple "skip intro" function
- How to implement visited link functionality

Remembering state in Flash applications

In Flash applications, remembering state is an enhancement that can go a long way toward good usability engineering. The following are some common scenarios:

- **To skip an intro:** While animated Flash intros are rare these days, they still persist. In some cases, they might be a useful way of introducing a user to a new concept or product on a website the first time a user enters the site. Applications that have such an intro should keep track of returning users and automatically skip the intro page for those users, so they don't need to see the same content again before going to the main page.

- **To store user data during a single session of an application:** Saving information such as a user's shopping cart inventory in an online store minimizes the number of times the application needs to store data on the server. This improves the application, since server access usually involves opening a database connection, executing an INSERT or UPDATE statement, and then closing the connection before sending a notification of completion back to the client.

- **To store specific user settings for a customizable application:** Saving this type of information definitely makes life easier for the user. For instance, your application could save a user's preferred background color or font size so that he doesn't need to modify them again when he returns to the application. Also, the application could fill in the user's login name in a password-protected site, so the returning user needs to fill in only the password.

- **To track where a user has been:** Keeping track of where a user has been on your Flash site will let her more quickly know where it is she has and has not gone yet. As we mentioned at the beginning of the chapter, an HTML page automatically can track visited links through the browser, but this cannot be done by default in Flash. However, it's possible, and you'll see how to implement visited link tracking later in the chapter.

You can implement these types of capabilities in your applications with relative ease using Flash's local shared object, which we'll introduce next.

Introducing the local shared object

When Macromedia released Flash MX in 2002, it also introduced a new kind of object to the Flash ActionScript language: the *shared object*. Shared objects act very much like browser cookies, but offer the following advantages over cookies:

- **Browser-independence:** Local shared objects aren't browser-dependent, as are browser-based cookies. Many web applications employ cookies so you don't need to log in to the site again. However, the first time you use a different browser (say, Mozilla Firefox vs. Microsoft Internet Explorer), you'll be required to log in again. In a Flash-based login, the same bit of locally stored data can be accessed, regardless of which browser the user chooses.

- **Data type retention:** Local shared objects retain the Flash data type of the objects that are stored within it. You can store any common data types—such as strings, Booleans, and arrays—in a local shared object. Browser-based cookies are strictly text-based, so, for data that isn't a string object to start, you're forced to convert the object you have into a string when storing that object, and then translate the string back into the object when accessing the cookie. The local shared object's ability to maintain data types makes it much easier to work with the object in your code.

9

- **Developer control of persistence:** Shared objects aren't as easily removable as cookies. A user can simply clear browser cookies by a few simple clicks in a browser's menu options. Local shared objects aren't taken into account in this cookie-clearing. Of course, whether this is actually a benefit is debatable. The good side is that it does give you, the developer, more options for handling the persistence of a local shared object. You can create a custom clearing option in your application to remove your specific shared object, as you'll see in this chapter's sample application.

> Just as when you use cookies, you should use care with local shared objects in your web applications. Your most important consideration is to respect the user's privacy.
>
> For instance, if you're building a "remember me" login feature that will automatically log in the user to your application, you never want to store a user's nonencrypted password in a local shared object. Otherwise, with a little effort, someone else could access that password from the user's machine.
>
> Many users disable cookies or frequently delete them, because they're often associated with spyware software, where user information is shared among multiple sites for gathering and distributing personal information. Most users probably have not heard of local stored objects, and moreover, local stored objects aren't automatically deleted by clearing cookies in the browser. So, to avoid giving the local shared object the same kind of "cookie stigma," be smart and responsible with the kinds of information you choose to store.

Creating a local shared object

Using the local shared object is incredibly simple. To create a local shared object file named mySharedObject, key in the following code:

```
objSharedObject = SharedObject.getLocal("mySharedObject");
```

This finds a file on the user's machine called mySharedObject.sol, which is stored in a specific directory within your machine (the directory location differs based on the operating system you're using). If the file doesn't exist, Flash will create it the moment the user leaves the application (either by going to another web page or closing the browser). You can implicitly have Flash create the file before a user exits by calling objSharedObject.flush().

> An optional parameter with the objSharedObject.flush() method is the number of bytes of data that the application should allocate for the shared object. By default, Flash allocates 100KB of data for the shared object per domain. While 100KB of data isn't a whole lot to download, it should be more than enough space for your application. If you're creating an application that will store more than this amount, we suggest that you store this data to the server instead. In the examples in this chapter, we store only a precious few bytes of data, which is perfect for the local shared object!

By default, local shared objects are stored in directories that mimic the directory structure of the site (including the Flash filename as a directory) from which the shared object originated. For instance, a local shared object called mySharedObject created in http://www.mydomain.com/swf/myFlashFile.swf will be found in the location .../mydomain.com/swf/myFlashFile.swf/mySharedObject.sol. The directory structure that precedes /mydomain.com/ depends on your operating system, as listed in Table 9-1.

Table 9-1. Default location for local shared objects

Operating System	Location
Windows XP	C:/Documents and Settings/[username]/Application Data/Macromedia/Flash Player/
Mac OSX	/Users/[username]/Library/Preferences/Macromedia/Flash Player/
GNU-Linux	~/.macromedia/

Customizing the location of the shared object

If you're using multiple SWF files in your application (say, you're embedding each one into HTML pages on different directory levels on the server), you can still have them access the same local shared object file by adding an additional parameter to the getLocal() call:

```
objSharedObject = SharedObject.getLocal("mySharedObject", "/");
```

As long as the SWF files that are making the call to access this shared object exist on the same web server (and within the same public root web folder), they will be able to access the same shared object.

Reading and writing data from a local shared object

The shared object contains a built-in object called data that you can use to attach whatever properties you need. For example, if you want to store a user's first name and last name on the user's machine, do the following:

```
objSharedObject.data.firstName = "Craig";
objSharedObject.data.lastName = "Bryant";
```

Now that you've been introduced to the local shared object, let's see how to use it in an application. We'll begin with a simple example: skipping a Flash intro for returning users.

9

Building a skip intro feature

One of the simplest and most straightforward uses for the local shared object is checking if a user has been to a site previously. Technically, we mean if a user on a *particular machine* has been to a site previously, since the object is stored locally on a user's machine rather than on a central database. When users return to the site, you can give them a different experience than they had as first-time users.

The following is a sample implementation of an automatic skip intro feature for a Flash application with an introduction section. You would probably stick this snippet of code onto frame 1 of your application's main timeline, or into whatever initialization code that is executed at the onset of your application:

```
objIntroCheckSO = SharedObject.getLocal("introCheck");

if (objIntroCheckSO.data.isIntroSeen)
{
  // Intro has been seen, so skip to the main section!
}
else
{
  objIntroCheckSO.data.isIntroSeen = true;
  // Intro not seen yet. . .show it!
}
```

Note that we simply check to see if a custom Boolean variable isIntroSeen within the data object of the local shared object is set to true when a user first enters the site. If it is, we allow the user to bypass the intro section. If it isn't (in which case, its return is actually undefined rather than false), we set the variable to true, and then continue playing the one-time-only intro.

That's not too complicated, right? And you should also notice that we don't need to explicitly define the isIntroSeen variable as a boolean. Whatever kind of object we set it to becomes the type for the object. This kind of loose data typing might make object-oriented purists a bit uneasy, but, at the very least, it shows how flexible and easy it is to work with local shared objects in code.

Remembering visited links

At the beginning of this chapter, we mentioned how browsers "remember" the links you click in an HTML website. Visited link functionality comes out-of-the-box when you're working with HTML because browsers work directly with the HTML Document Object Model (DOM) to display text back to you.

With Flash, you don't have this built-in functionality. You need to find your own way of tracking visited links between user sessions. And the local shared object is perfect for the job!

It may seem like a minor detail to track where users have gone on a web application, but the differences between tracking and not tracking visited links can have a great impact for your users. When users come back to a web application that they use frequently, it helps to show where they've gone because that also lets them know where they haven't been (and might want to explore). In some cases, users will continue to come back to the same places they've been to before (such as a links to blogs, news, or other commonly updated information).

According to well-known web usability expert Jakob Nielsen, when you fail to remember where users have been, they tend to run in circles around your application. Displaying links as "visited" helps orient returning users to navigate your application and find where they want to go faster.

Let's employ a simple example of this with our familiar book selection system from Chapter 3. Recall that our book selection system has the capability of tracking links that a user has visited. However, if you close the file and reopen it, all of the links revert back to the normal, unvisited status. Now it's time to enhance the system and add in the ability for it to remember those links you've already visited when you come back to the application.

Follow along with us by downloading the `Chapter9_Final.zip` file from our book's code download files available from the friends of ED website (www.friendsofed.com) and export the files within the ZIP file into a directory on your machine. Open the `Chapter9_Final.swf` file within the `/source/swf/` subdirectory.

You'll see our familiar book item buttons on the left that you can click to retrieve their respective cover images, as shown in Figure 9-1. Go ahead and click a few so that they appear in the faded visited state, and then close the SWF. Next, reopen the SWF, and you should see the items you clicked retain their visited state.

9

Figure 9-1. The book selection system will now retain visited link history.

As you can see in Figure 9-1, we've also included a Clear History button that will clear out all records of visited links for this site. This is a useful addition that you should consider building into your own applications.

All it takes is a few small tweaks to what we built in Chapter 3 to turn this selection system into one that remembers what you did! Let's take a look at what we modified to achieve the extra functionality.

Adding the history functionality to the code

As you would expect, all the work needed for our book application to remember visited links resides in the class that supports each book item button. Open the BookItemButton.as file (the class that links to each of our book item buttons) from the chapter download and let's discuss the additions we've made to add this history functionality. (If you're interested in the other aspects of the code, refer to Chapter 3.)

The first change you'll notice is the inclusion of a private SharedObject property at the beginning of the BookItemButton class:

```
private var so:SharedObject;
```

Next, we've added an init() method that will override the base UIButton class's init() method:

```
public function init(_selectionSystem:SelectionSystem, _id:Number,
➥ _itemData:Object):Void
{
  super.init(_selectionSystem, _id, _itemData);

  so = SharedObject.getLocal("HistoryList", "/");

  if (so.data.history == undefined)
  {
    so.data.history = new Object();
  }

  //check for history in local shared object
  if(so.data.history[id]==id)
  {
    //set history
    visited = true;
    //call method that will set the visited state visually
    handleRollOut();
  }
}
```

Recall that the init() method is called just after the book item button is attached to its selection system parent class. Again, flip back to Chapter 3 if you haven't walked through the way these classes were built initially.

Let's begin by examining the bold code in the init() method. We'll get to the other portion of this method in just a bit.

We first call the UIButton's init() method, passing in the same three parameters that would normally be passed to UIButton.init() if we didn't override this method. Next, we use our so shared object variable to grab the local shared object named HistoryList. It will be in this shared object where we will store the IDs of the links a user has visited in this application.

In the if statement that follows, we check to see if the so.data.history object is defined. This essentially corresponds to whether or not the user has used this application before. If it isn't defined, we create it as a new type of Object. In so.data.history, we set a parameter named with the id of each visited book item equal to the id itself. This will provide us with a way of figuring out which items were clicked. Now, all we need to do is set that parameter when a user clicks a book item button!

If you recall from Chapter 3, the handleRelease() method is called in the base class UIButton after a user has clicked and released the mouse button on an item. Because we're going to want to have additional functionality tied to this method (specifically, tracking this item as having been visited), we override the method in BookItemButton.as. The new handleRelease() method in BookItemButton.as looks like this:

```
private function handleRelease():Void
{
  super.handleRelease();
  so.data.history[id] = id;
}
```

Again, it's really pretty simple! After calling the handleRelease() method on the superclass, UIButton, we then set the ID of the button to a newly created id parameter within the history object.

Now, let's go back to that second half of the code in the init() method:

```
//check for history in local shared object
if(so.data.history[id]==id)
{
  //set history
  visited = true;
  //call method that will set the visited state visually
  handleRollOut();
}
```

Here, we check the history object to see if we've set the attribute given by the book item's id to be equal to the id. If it is, we set the visited status to true. Next, we call handleRollOut(), which is the method called after a user rolls the mouse off an item. Remember that this method handles the non-rollover state for all items (both visited and unvisited). So, once we've set visited=true, calling this method will then apply the visited status to the item visually.

Now, our retrieval of the shared object and check for visited links is complete! It just took modifications to two methods to make this work—now and forever.

Adding a clear history function

One other way we can help our application's users is to give them the option to clear the history of the visited links. Having the option easily available is worthwhile, since clearing the history on their browser won't do the trick.

We've added a Clear History button at the upper-right side of the screen and linked the clip to the ClearHistoryButton class via the Linkage property available when you right-click the MC ClearHistoryButton movie clip in the library.

Open the ClearHistory.as file in the /source/classes/ file to see how we've added a simple history-clearing function. When a user clicks the button, we set the history object to undefined in the HistoryList shared object. This bit is handled in the doHistoryClear() method:

```
class ClearHistoryButton extends MovieClip
{
  public function ClearHistoryButton()
  {
    this.onRelease = doHistoryClear;
  }

  private function doHistoryClear():Void
  {
    var so:SharedObject = SharedObject.getLocal("HistoryList","/");
    so.data.history = undefined;
  }
}
```

With just one small class and a few tweaks to our original book selection system solution, we've now added the ability for Flash to track the history of visited links! Working with the local shared object doesn't take a whole lot of setup, and it provides a great mechanism for accomplishing these types of simple tasks.

Summary

The goal of this chapter was to give you an overview of the local shared object, which offers a quick and easy way to further improve your site users' experience by remembering a bit about what they've done previously. We want you to leave this chapter with a good idea of the kinds of places where storing data on a user's machine makes sense. Here are a few more examples of creative ways of using the local shared object:

- Create user preference options for a Flash application (like choosing a background image or picking a font size) and save these settings automatically.
- Build a search box that remembers what users previously typed in and offers matching words as they type characters into the search box.
- If you're creating a Flash game, offer a save option that saves game settings like level, score, and number of player lives remaining.

You'll find many situations where the use of a local shared object can benefit your application. Just remember to avoid it if you're going to be storing sensitive information or data that should really be stored on the server.

Usability is sometimes about the small accessories you add onto your application that are often forgotten by most developers. Using the local shared object to remember state is a great example of such an accessory. Another nice addition to any web-based application is providing users a way of learning about the application without having to search through long pages of help files. In the next chapter, we'll create a very simple help tip solution that you can integrate into your next great Flash project.

9

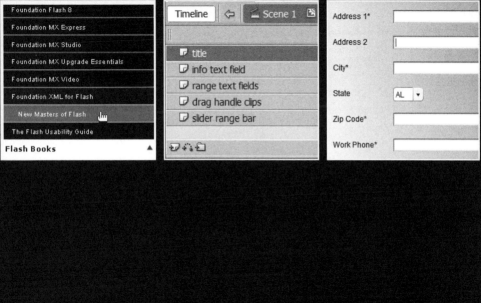

Regardless of what kind of application you're creating, it's always important to give your users quick access to help information. No matter how intuitive your application is to use, some users will not initially understand how to take advantage of all of its great features. That's just the nature of software!

Trying to read how an entire web application works in one gigantic page of directions can be frustrating for a user. Instead, it's better to let users ask for help when a specific part of the application is confusing to them. Giving users instant access to useful help information is one significant way you can keep them coming back and using the software you've spent those long hours building.

In this chapter, we'll explore how to design and build a help tip feature that can easily be plugged into any Flash project. This help tip will be very similar in functionality to the alt or title attribute in HTML.

Here's what we'll cover in this chapter:

- Limitations of the HTML solution for providing help tips
- Features of more user-friendly help tips
- How to build toggleable, mobile help tips that can be used by any objects in your Flash application
- Help tip usability guidelines

Examining the limitations of the HTML title text solution

In HTML, you can supply a title attribute to most any HTML tag to display help text when users roll their mouse over the particular item—such as an image, block of text, text field, and so on—associated with that tag. You've surely seen the distinctive "notes" that pop up when your mouse rolls over and pauses on, say, an image on a website, as shown in Figure 10-1.

> *Veteran HTML coders are probably also familiar with the* alt *attribute of the* <img> *tag. Originally, this attribute was supposed to be used for accessibility purposes (for example, if a browser cannot display an image, or a blind user uses a screen reader to scan elements on a web page). In many browsers, such as Internet Explorer, the* alt *attribute will also render a pop-up note when your mouse rolls over an image. So many designers began refashioning the* alt *attribute as a help tip attribute that the World Wide Web Consortium (W3C) added the* title *attribute as part of the HTML 4.0 specifications to address this need.*

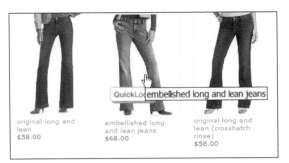

Figure 10-1. The title tag in use in a typical HTML-based web page

Unfortunately, HTML designers have no control over how the title attribute is styled or positioned. As of this writing, CSS doesn't support any stylistic modifications to these help tips. Even if it did, you would most likely expect to see different behaviors among browsers. Here are a few other usability issues that surface when you try to use the title attribute as a help tip:

- **Pop-up lag:** The HTML help tip appears only after you've completely stopped moving your mouse over an item. While this isn't a big deal if only a few help-accessible items are on the page, it becomes a bit onerous when many items require instructions. It's like getting a tour of a new house and having your guide stop you at every piece of furniture, rather than letting you absorb each room on its own.

- **Scope limitations:** Yet another problem is that the title attribute is limited in scope. For example, if you place a title attribute inside a <select /> box, it renders properly in Mozilla Firefox but not in Microsoft Internet Explorer (even in version 6 browsers!).

- **Lack of display options:** Users don't have an easy way to toggle on and off the display of help pop-ups. Wouldn't it be nice if you could turn off the help tips if you already know how everything works? From a development perspective, it would be nice to customize how quickly the help tip appears after the user rolls over an item. On most browsers, you need to wait about three-quarters of a second before the pop-up actually appears, and there's no way in code to change that interval.

- **Immobility:** Once a pop-up appears, it doesn't move around with your mouse arrow. This can be a problem if it covers up a portion of the application that you need to view simultaneously.

> *Developers who have recognized the limitations of the HTML* title *attribute have used a combination of JavaScript and CSS to gain more control. For example, Cooper, an interactive product design consultancy founded by usability guru Alan Cooper, has some innovative help tips at work on its website* (www.cooper.com/content/why_cooper/the_process.asp).

10

If you're starting to believe that Flash can turn these HTML limitations into beneficial features, you just might be on to something!

Improving help tips with Flash

By using Flash, you automatically acquire much greater control over how the help tip is designed. In our Flash version, we will add some usability features that you usually won't find in HTML. Our Flash solution will demonstrate how to achieve the following improvements:

- Build an elegant way to have the help tip follow the mouse cursor as users move it around a particular element.
- Create an easy-to-use toggle feature that can turn the help tips on or off in your application.
- Allow you to easily adjust how the pop-up appears after users roll over an item, so users are not forced to make a complete stop over the item and wait before the pop-up appears.
- Build the help tip so that any object in your Flash application can easily display help information (text, graphics, buttons, and so on).

Let's see this help tip feature in action. Download the Chapter10_Final.zip file from our book's download page at www.friendsofed.com and export the files within the ZIP file into a directory on your machine. Open the Chapter10_Final.swf within the /source/swf/ subdirectory to see the solution we'll build in this chapter.

You'll see a very basic application layout with three friends of ED book graphics similar to those in our earlier chapters. Go ahead and roll your mouse over the book graphics of this application. You should see help tips appear, describing the contents within each book, as shown in Figure 10-2.

Figure 10-2. The Flash help tip solution

Toggle feature

You can easily toggle on and off the help tip feature. Simply click the off option in the upper-right corner of the page, and these help tips will not appear. And, as you might have guessed, when you click on, the help tips will reappear.

Unlike with the anchor tag title implementation in HTML, you get to choose when you want help and when you don't! Now, let's look at some of the subtle behaviors of the help tip itself.

Mobility

Place your arrow somewhere on the right side of the header bar with the help tips toggle set to on. If you keep the arrow on the header while moving it toward the left, the help tip moves, so you can get it out of the way if it's obscuring something that you want to see. However, notice that it doesn't move at the same rate as the arrow itself. Instead, it moves toward the left with a slight bit of lag. If you move the arrow from the right to the left, you should see how it "catches up" to the arrow once you stop moving your mouse.

> We feel that giving the help tip a slight lag in movement creates a more natural feel than if it just follows the mouse at the exact same rate you're moving it. Otherwise, it will start to feel like the tip is stuck to the mouse arrow, and that can get a bit annoying for some users. You may disagree with this approach, and that's perfectly OK. If you don't like how we've created the lag movement, it's very easy to tweak the behavior to the way you or your client prefers to have it! See the "Building the help tip clip class" section later in this chapter for details.

You'll see the same behavior when moving the mouse in the up/down direction as well. However, the help tip always appears below the arrow (unless your mouse arrow is near the very bottom of an application, in which case it will push itself as far as it can go and still be on the page). This is because people have become accustomed to an alt text-like pop-up appearing under the tail of your mouse arrow, and it makes sense to maintain this convention when moving away from HTML.

10

Fade in/snap out

You may have also noticed that when your mouse rolls over a particular item, the help tip fades in rather than appearing immediately on screen. When your mouse arrow rolls off the item, it disappears instantly.

These are simply design aspects that, while not essential to the functionality of the help element, aid in making the entire application feel smoother. And they give it that Flash touch that you simply don't get with most HTML-based applications.

Alright, so now you've seen the end result: a slick help tip component that will enable users to quickly learn the features of an application. Now, let's roll up our sleeves and see how to build this solution!

Building the Flash solution

Creating the solution is fairly straightforward. In order to put it together, we will need to do the following:

- Create an automatically resizing help tip movie clip that can receive a chunk of text and display it regardless of its length.
- Design a movie clip that will have on/off states that can toggle whether the help tip clip appears when users roll over an item.
- Develop a simple way for any item to attach a help tip to it when a user rolls over that item, so that you can reuse the help tip over and over as your application grows.

As we've done in previous chapters, we'll first build the Flash UI assets, and then write the code that will add in the correct functionality we need.

Creating the movie clips

The main Flash UI assets we'll need for the solution are two movie clips: one for the help tip itself and one for the toggle states. Let's start with the help tip clip.

The help tip clip

The help tip movie clip has three different features: the background, the help text field, and the help icon.

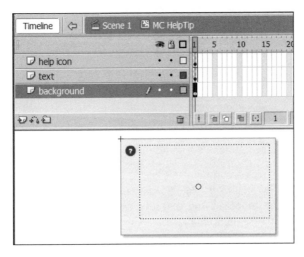

In the Library panel of Chapter10_Final.fla, double-click the MC HelpTip movie clip that resides inside the movieclips folder. You'll see that this clip has three layers, as shown in Figure 10-3.

Figure 10-3. The help tip clip timeline

On the bottom layer, labeled background, we've placed a solid light-gray rectangle (#EFEFEF) positioned at (0,0) and converted it into a movie clip (graph_helpBackground). In addition, we've applied a drop shadow filter to it, to make the help tip stand out from the rest of the application. Open the Filters panel (Window ➤ Properties ➤ Filters) to see the drop shadow settings. The size of this clip is 250 height × 150 width. In code, we'll dynamically change the height of the background to compensate for the amount of text inside it, so the actual height you set your clip to won't matter. We also assigned the clip an instance name of bg_mc using the clip's Properties panel (Window ➤ Properties).

On the next layer, labeled text, we've added in a dynamic text field (Arial, 10-pt font) with an instance name of help_txt. A key here is to set the text to multiline in the Properties panel, so that the help text can wrap within the text field. We positioned the clip at (30,10). Also, notice that the right edge of the text field is 10 pixels from the right edge of the background. This will give equal padding to the text on the top and right sides.

On the top layer, labeled help icon, we've added a help icon graphic (graph_helpIcon). The design is up to you, but we suggest using a question mark in your icon, as it is commonly associated with help tips on many desktop (and web) applications today. We've positioned the clip at (8,10), so that it's located to the left of where the text will display.

Now, open the linkage properties for this clip (right-click MC HelpTip in the library and select Linkage). You'll see that we've set the Identifier name to MC HelpTip (this is the name we can use to reference this clip when we want to attach it to the stage later in the chapter) and the AS 2.0 Class to HelpTip (the name of the class we will create to make this clip function).

The toggle clip

Next, open the MC HelpTipToggle movie clip in the library, and let's go through its layers, as shown in Figure 10-4.

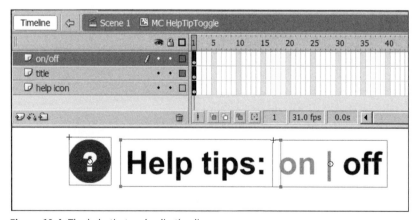

Figure 10-4. The help tip toggle clip timeline

On the bottom layer, labeled help icon, we've placed another instance of graph_HelpIcon at (0,0) so that there is visual continuity between the toggle functionality and the help tips.

Users should more quickly be able to associate the two components with each other given this common iconography.

In the next layer, title, we include a static text field, which just contains the text "Help Tips:" using Arial, 12-pt font.

On the top layer, we include our on/off status clip with an instance name of onOff_mc. If you double-click into this clip, you'll notice that it consists of two frames with stop() actions on each one. Each frame has the same text: "on | off." However, when you click between these two frames, the words alternate in visibility. To do this, we just alternate the color of the two words. In frame 1, "on" is set to #999999 and "off" is set to #000000. These colors are alternated on frame 2. In code, we'll dictate that when this status clip is clicked, the clip just plays the next frame (either 1 or 2), creating the visual toggle effect.

For the clip's linkage properties, we set the Identifier name to MC HelpTipToggle and the AS 2.0 Class to HelpTipToggle. Later in this chapter, we'll create a class named HelpTipToggle to add in the functionality for this movie clip.

This solution uses a few more assets, such as the books and the header bar that have help tips associated to them. We'll get back to these later in the chapter, in the "Putting it all together" section.

Building the code

In coding this solution, the goal, from a developer's point of view, should be to make it incredibly easy to add a help tip to any movie clip, button, or graphic clip you choose. This can be accomplished in just three relatively small classes:

- The HelpTip class, which encapsulates all the functionality inherent to MC HelpTip
- The HelpTipManager class, which will be capable of showing, hiding, enabling, and disabling the help tip
- The HelpTipToggle class, which will use the methods of HelpTipManager to enable and disable the help tip functionality

So, let's get started with the HelpTip class.

Building the help tip clip class

The HelpTip class supports the functionality behind MC HelpTip. Open the HelpTip.as file located in the /source/classes/ folder of the chapter download, and let's take our usual walk-through.

First, we import a few of Flash's out-of-the-box package classes. As we've done in previous solutions that required dynamic tweening (such as the scrolling menu example presented in Chapter 4), we import the following two mx.transitions classes that we'll use to fade in and out the clip when needed.

```
import mx.transitions.easing.*;
import mx.transitions.Tween;
```

Then we add in the class's signature.

```
class HelpTip extends MovieClip {
```

Next, we define the properties for this clip.

```
private var bg_mc:MovieClip;
private var help_txt:TextField;

private var xDest:Number;
private var yDest:Number;

private var alphaTween:Tween;
```

First, we define the variables for the visual elements associated with the clip (the background and help text field) that we just created. Following these properties, we create two number variables called xDest and yDest. These variables will store the (x,y) coordinate that the help tip should position itself to based on the location of the user's mouse. Finally, we include an alphaTween property that will help fade in our clip when it's created.

Now that we have our variables in place, it's time to build our constructor function. As you can see, it's about as functional as a pet rock. But even when the constructor could be omitted, it's generally good practice to always include it.

```
public function HelpTip() {}
```

Next, we create a public method called init(). This is where all the setup for the help tip actually happens. When all is said and done, the help tip manager class we'll build later will be in charge of creating the help tip and then calling this method to initiate the clip.

```
public function init(_helpText:String):Void
{
  help_txt.autoSize = "left";
  help_txt.multiline = true;
  help_txt.wordWrap = true;

  help_txt.text = _helpText;

  bg_mc._height = help_txt._height + 25;

  alphaTween = new Tween(this, "_alpha", Regular.easeInOut, 0, 100,
  5, true);

  _x = _parent._xmouse + 10;
  _y = _parent._ymouse + 10;

  this.onEnterFrame = updateDestination;
}
```

10

217

This init() method accepts a string parameter containing the help text to display. After assigning the help_txt text field's text parameter, it resizes the background clip (bg_mc) to an appropriate height based on the size of the text. We've also given bg_mc an extra 25 pixels of height below the text to allow for a nice bit of padding around the text. Then it gradually fades in the help tip by using the tweening classes. Here, we've set it so that the _alpha property tweens from 0 to 100 in a half second. Lastly, it needs to tell the help tip where to position itself based on the user's mouse. After setting the initial x- and y-positions to 10 pixels below and to the right of the user's mouse arrow, it assigns the onEnterFrame event handler to a new method called updateDestination().

The updateDestination() method's job is to figure out the correct positioning of the help tip at any given point in time.

```
private function updateDestination():Void
{
  //set _x destination
  if (Stage.width - _parent._xmouse < _width)
  {
    xDest = Stage.width - _width;
  }
  else
  {
    xDest = _parent._xmouse + 10;
  }

  //set _y destination
  if (Stage.height - _parent._ymouse < _height)
  {
    yDest = Stage.height - _height;
  }
  else
  {
      yDest = _parent._ymouse + 10;
  }

  doMove();
}
```

Because we've assigned this method to the onEnterFrame event handler, it will be called repeatedly (more correctly, at the frame rate of the movie). Consider that this code will be called whenever a help tip is enabled. For the x-position of the help tip, we need to make sure that the mouse isn't too far to the right of the application. We want to always ensure the help tip is in a position where its entire body is viewable at all times.

The check for the x-position is pretty simple. First, Stage.width - _parent._xmouse retrieves the amount of width that's available to the right of the mouse arrow. (The Stage object contains properties of the entire stage, including its full width and height.) We compare this value to the width of the help tip. If it's less than this width, the help tip's x-position destination (xDest) is set to as far right as the help tip can go without getting cut off. This is given by Stage.width - _width. Otherwise, the xDest value will follow the normal rule: it will just be 10 pixels to the right of the mouse arrow.

The y-position destination is set next, and follows nearly the exact same logic, except that it checks the height of the stage as opposed to the width.

At the very end of updateDestination() is a call to doMove(). The doMove() method will take the new xDest and yDest values and use them to reposition the clip correctly. We add this method next. Here's where we get to create the very slight and subtle lag!

```
private function doMove():Void
{
  _x += (xDest - _x) * .5;
  _y += (yDest - _y) * .5;
}
}
```

In doMove(), we take the current _x and _y values of the help clip and add to it half the difference between where the clip is and where the clip's destination path is. Remember that doMove() will be called repeatedly from updateDestination(), so each time the call happens, the _x and _y positions will get halfway closer to the xDest and yDest values. The overall effect of this is the noticeable little lag you get between the mouse and the help tip when you move your mouse cursor around a particular object. We've separated this functionality into its own method so it's easier to tweak if you want to apply a different set of math equations to how the clip moves.

Building the HelpTipManager class

At this point, MC HelpTip is a fully functional little widget. You can drag an instance onto the stage, call its init() method, pass in some text, and poof—a working help tip! But, in reality, the clip alone won't be effective unless you can easily manage how help tips appear and disappear in the application. Also, you need a way of keeping track of whether the user even wants the help tip to show up in the first place.

These tasks are best delegated to a separate class whose only job will be to manage the showing, hiding, enabling, and disabling of the help tip. We've appropriately named it HelpTipManager, and we'll construct it now.

One notable thing about HelpTipManager is that we are going to make this a singleton class. As we explained in Chapter 7, a singleton class can produce only one instance of itself. We used this technique in Chapter 7 to create our EventBroadcaster class, which managed the dispatching and receiving of events from one object to another. In this chapter, we'll employ the singleton technique again so that we have only one instance of HelpTipManager at all times. We've chosen this approach because if we allowed the possibility of creating two manager instances, we might run into problems like having two help tips visible at once or losing track of which manager controlled which help tip. The singleton approach prevents any of these headaches from ever surfacing.

Open HelpTipManager.as from the /source/classes/ folder of the chapter download, and you'll see how easy this is. The HelpTipManager is a stand-alone class and therefore does not extend any other class.

10

```
class HelpTipManager
{
  private var helpEnabled:Boolean;
  private var targetClip:MovieClip;

  private static var helpTipManager:HelpTipManager;
```

The first two variables are needed to track the help tip. The helpEnabled Boolean variable manages whether the user has elected to turn help on or off. The targetClip movie clip variable will be the clip to which we'll attach an instance of MC HelpTip. Lastly, we include a private static variable called helpTipManager, which will store the lone instance of the HelpTipManager class.

Next up is our constructor. Because it's a singleton class, we make the constructor private so that, even if you tried to create a new HelpTipManager instance using new HelpTipManager(), it would throw an error due to its protection level.

```
  private function HelpTipManager()
  {
    helpEnabled = true;
  }
```

In the constructor, we default the helpEnabled Boolean variable to true. After this, we add a static function called getInstance(), just as we did in Chapter 7's EventBroadcaster. Objects that want to access HelpTipManager will just call getInstance(), which will create a new instance of HelpTipManager or return that instance if getInstance() was already called previously.

```
  public static function getInstance():HelpTipManager
  {
    if ( helpTipManager == undefined )
      helpTipManager = new HelpTipManager();

    return helpTipManager;
  }
```

After this, we build our series of functions that will provide the show, hide, enable, and disable logic for the manager. First up is a method called showHelpTip() which accepts a string of help text and a movie clip to which we can attach an instance of the help tip.

```
  public function showHelpTip(_helpText:String, _clip:MovieClip):Void
  {
    if (helpEnabled)
    {
      var helpTip:HelpTip = HelpTip(_clip.attachMovie("MC HelpTip",
➥ "helpTipClip_mc", _clip.getNextHighestDepth()));
      helpTip.init(_helpText);
      targetClip = _clip;
    }
  }
```

Notice that we check the helpEnabled status before creating the help tip. If helpEnabled is false, this method simply doesn't display the clip. If helpEnabled is true, we create the help tip clip and then call its init() method to pass in the content. Also, we assign the _clip parameter to our private variable targetClip. We do this so that we know from which location to remove the help tip when an object requests the manager to do so.

Next, let's add the hideHelpTip() method. Here, we remove the created help tip from the targetClip location.

```
public function hideHelpTip():Void
{
  targetClip.helpTipClip_mc.removeMovieClip();
}
```

Finally, we finish off the class by creating a toggleHelpTip() method to change the helpEnabled Boolean status.

```
public function toggleHelpTip():Void
{
  helpEnabled = !helpEnabled;

  if(!helpEnabled)
  {
    hideHelpTip();
  }
}
}
```

That's all there is to this class! Now, not only do we have a self-contained help tip, but we also have a manager class that will control the status and implementation of the help tip.

Building the toggle functionality

10

The last class we need to design is the one that links to our MC HelpTipToggle movie clip. Recall from building this clip's assets that it contains an onOff_mc movie clip, which simply toggles between the on and off states (either frame 1 or frame 2). In the class, we will write a method for the onRelease event handler of onOff_mc so that each time a user clicks onOff_mc, the clip plays its next frame (either frame 1 or frame 2) and also calls toggleHelpTip() to toggle the helpEnabled Boolean variable in the help tip manager class. Here's the full HelpTipToggle class (HelpTipToggle.as in the /source/classes/ folder).

```
class HelpTipToggle extends MovieClip
{
  private var onOff_mc:MovieClip;

  public function HelpTipToggle()
  {
    this.init();
  }
```

```
        private function init():Void
        {
          onOff_mc.onRelease = function() {

            HelpTipManager.getInstance().toggleHelpTip();
            this.play();
          }
        }
      }
```

Putting it all together

We've finally reached the part of the chapter where we get to put all the bits of our recipe together! Let's go back to Chapter10_Final.fla and show you how to easily implement help tips. Open the file and look over the root timeline, shown in Figure 10-5.

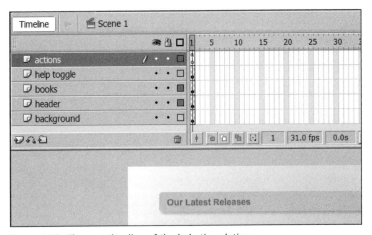

Figure 10-5. The root timeline of the help tip solution

All we've done here is to place four distinct movie clips onto the stage. We have three movie clips that contain images of a few current hot books produced by our fellow friend of ED writers in the books layer. From left to right, these instances are named book1_mc, book2_mc, and book3_mc. In addition, we include the header bar above it with an instance name of header_mc. At the upper right of the stage, we've dropped an instance of the MC HelpTipToggle clip.

Now, click the actions layer at the very top of the root timeline. This is where you can see how simple it is to add help capabilities to our various assets on stage. For example, to add a help tip feature to the header, all we need to do is define its onRollOver and onRollOut states, like so:

```
header_mc.onRollOver = function()
{
  HelpTipManager.getInstance().showHelpTip("This is the header bar,
➥ in case you didn't know.", this._parent);
}

header_mc.onRollOut = function()
{
  HelpTipManager.getInstance().hideHelpTip();
}
```

As you can see, we use the getInstance() method to retrieve the single instance of HelpTipManager, and then call the showHelpTip() and hideHelpTip() methods for the onRollOver and onRollOut states, respectively. The showHelpTip() method is supplied both the help text and the movie clip to which to attach the help clip. In this case, this._parent is just header_mc's parent movie clip, the root timeline. Here's how simple it is to add help to the books on the stage:

```
book1_mc.onRollOver = function()
{
  HelpTipManager.getInstance().showHelpTip("Foundation Flash 8 is
➥ the book you need if you're looking for a solid foundation in
➥ Flash 8 Basic and Flash 8 Professional. Thousands upon thousands of
➥ designers have already learned from its previous editions, and it's
➥ easy to understand why.", this._parent);
}

book1_mc.onRollOut = function()
{
  HelpTipManager.getInstance().hideHelpTip();
}

book2_mc.onRollOver = function()
{
  HelpTipManager.getInstance().showHelpTip("Our original Foundation
➥ PHP for Flash title was rightly regarded as a must-have title when
➥ you wanted to learn just how to have your Flash sites make
➥ use of backend technologies. It was published way back in the
➥ days of Flash 5 and PHP 4, and things move pretty fast in the world
➥ of web design!", this._parent);
}

book2_mc.onRollOut = function()
{
  HelpTipManager.getInstance().hideHelpTip();
}
```

10

```
book3_mc.onRollOver = function()
{
  HelpTipManager.getInstance().showHelpTip("XML is a completely
➡ platform-agnostic data medium. Flash is able to make use of XML
➡ data, which is very useful when you are creating Rich Internet
➡ Applications. It allows you to populate Flash web interfaces with
➡ data from pretty much any source that supports XML as a data
➡ medium - databases, raw XML files, or more excitingly, .NET
➡ applications, web services, and even Microsoft Office applications
➡ such as Excel and Word!", this._parent);
}

book3_mc.onRollOut = function()
{
  HelpTipManager.getInstance().hideHelpTip();
}
```

So, there you have it: a nifty, usable help tip solution that you can easily plug in to any of your applications.

Some help tip usability guidelines

Now that you know how to build the help tip solution, we will round out this chapter with a few usability pointers.

- **Make your help tips short.** Remember that despite the fact that help tips are meant to help the user, long amounts of text are going to be more cumbersome to users than short, succinct descriptions.

- **Make the toggle functionality obvious.** Not only is this just plain good sense, but it is also something that HTML does not provide out-of-the-box. Making the toggle functionality clear and placing it in an obvious spot (like the upper-right corner of your application) will go a long way toward keeping your user base happy.

- **Don't clutter.** Take into account how many items will actually have help tips associated with them. You may want to provide help tips only for links or widgets whose use wouldn't be obvious to your user base. Being selective about your help tips will prevent cluttering up your application.

Summary

Providing direction and help for users is an important part to good usability practice. You've seen a framework that makes it fairly painless to attach help tips to any object you want in Flash. Also, you can modify how the help tip moves and appears at your leisure! Try adjusting the clip's movement or how it fades in and out using the methods provided in the HelpTipManager class.

As you saw in this chapter, we can take many concepts transported from HTML and make them even more functional and usable in Flash. However, there are times when HTML concepts aren't as easily transportable. For instance, how would you go about enabling your browser's back button to click to a prior portion of your Flash application? In Chapter 11, we'll show you how to do just that!

10

| Foundation Flash 8 |
| Foundation MX Express |
| Foundation MX Studio |
| Foundation MX Upgrade Essentials |
| Foundation MX Video |
| Foundation XML for Flash |
| New Masters of Flash |
| The Flash Usability Guide |

Flash Books ▲

Timeline ⇦ Scene 1

- 🏷 title
- 🏷 info text field
- 🏷 range text fields
- 🏷 drag handle clips
- 🏷 slider range bar

Address 1*	
Address 2	
City*	
State	AL ▾
Zip Code*	
Work Phone*	

Up to this point in our usability discussions, we've discussed solutions to improve the usability *within* Flash applications. But, let's not forget that, more than likely, your Flash application will work within the confines of a web browser. You know by now that you can circumvent the usual cross-browser compatibility headaches of HTML websites by employing Flash. However, one of the disadvantages of browser-based Flash sites is that you lose some of the functionalities that are native to the browser, such as the back and forward buttons that track browser history.

If you're reading this book, you probably know that clicking the browser back button on a Flash site may take you back to the previous web page you visited, rather than to a section of that Flash site. But as you may have discovered for yourself, even knowledgeable Internet users occasionally make the mistake of clicking the back button, anticipating it will go back to the previous section of a Flash site. So, for Internet users of any level, enabling the back and forward buttons creates an important safeguard.

Our goal in this chapter is to revive browser history functionality for Flash applications. Here's what we'll cover in this chapter:

- The Flash back/forward-button issue and how it affects users
- What it means to "go back" in Flash
- How browser back/forward buttons work
- How to enable browser history in Flash
- How to add back/forward button functionality to the selection system solution

Reviewing the Flash back button issue

In a usual Flash site, clicking the back button normally doesn't take you back to the last "page" within the Flash application. Instead, it takes you back to the last true web page you visited. The back and forward buttons, taken for granted with normal websites, are usually rendered unusable in Flash.

Depending on the complexity and depth of your Flash creation, a mistaken back button click can be incredibly frustrating to a user. Imagine an online store customer who is ready to check out and purchase his items. After deciding he wants to look for something else, he does something that most users would do naturally—clicks the back button. Unfortunately, not only will he be clicking back to the previous web page, but he will most likely lose all the items he has put into his shopping cart. It's not unreasonable to expect this user won't be returning to this site anytime soon! Now this may be an extreme scenario, as most robust shopping applications will employ some sort of sessions management tool, like local shared objects (see Chapter 9). But without a back button solution in place, users may be confronted with an unexpected interruption in their shopping experience.

Flash applications aren't the only culprits responsible for the loss of browser back and forward button functionality. Most Ajax applications (see Chapter 1) also suffer from this problem. Try any of Google's Ajax-based applications (Google Maps, for example, at `http://maps.google.com`*), and you'll notice similar problems with the back and forward buttons.*

In this chapter, our goal will be to avoid back/forward button clicks giving our users bad experiences. In contrast to our other solutions where we've focused on deficiencies in HTML-based applications, we're going to do a bit of catching up to more traditional HTML-based websites. Let's make sure we keep our users happy by developing a way to re-empower the back and forward buttons in the browser.

Determining where to go

An HTML site has a definitive unit of measurement when it comes to defining what backwards and forwards means: the web page. Each time you navigate to another spot on an HTML website, you are usually moving to a different page. This provides a very natural partition between where you just were and where you are.

But, how do we define what it means to "go back" in Flash? Unfortunately, it's not always cut-and-dried. One of the distinct usability advantages of Flash is its seamless feel and state-management capabilities. But this means that it's sometimes vague when you're deciding exactly what the previous "page" is in a Flash application.

Creating back/forward button functionality in Flash not only involves an added bit of code, as we'll show you in this chapter, but also requires some serious interaction design decisions. You need to determine the level of granularity between different states of your Flash application in order to decide what state the application should fall back to (or forward to) when users click the back (or forward) button. The cool thing is that it's ultimately up to you to decide where the natural partitions of a Flash application exist!

Take, for instance, a robust Flash store with different category links lined up across the top of the screen. Within each category lies an inventory grid similar to what we built in Chapter 6, along with drag-and-drop functionality to place items into a shopping cart. Suppose a user browses to a few different categories, and then goes to one specific category to place five distinct items into a shopping cart. Now, suppose our user then clicks the back button. What happens?

We could either take our user back to the previous category she was on or simply remove the last item she put into the cart. In the first case, we're treating the back button in a more traditional sense by going back to the previous "page." In the second case, we're treating the back button as more of an "undo" button. The second case obviously offers a much more refined level of granularity, but it also requires a comprehensive audit of every possible state in the application.

11

Which option is the more usable implementation of the back button is really up for debate. The second case certainly provides better user control because it tracks the history of your user session more closely. But the first case is a more traditional implementation of the back button. Most users would expect clicking the back button to take them back to the previous category, as in a regular HTML website.

The more seamless your application is (in other words, the less granular your application is), the harder it is to decide where you should send users when they click the back button. However, any amount of browser back/forward button handling is better than none. One method of deciding where to partition your Flash application is to ask yourself the question, "What would a user expect the back button to do if this were a typical HTML site?"

Creating a simple Flash solution

Let's start with a simple implementation of back/forward button functionality just to get your feet wet. Follow along with us by downloading the `Chapter11a_Final.zip` file from this book's website (`www.friendsofed.com`) and export the files within the ZIP file into a directory on your machine. Next, in the `/source/swf/` subdirectory, open the `main.html` file in a new browser window to see the final result of what we'll build in this chapter.

> *This solution does not work if you access it locally on Internet Explorer because of a bug that prevents the browser from recognizing anchor tags as "new pages." So, if you would like to view this example locally, you'll need to use a Mozilla-based browser, like Firefox. Also, because of some new Flash Player 8 security policies, you may need to change your player settings to allow local SWF files to run correctly on your machine (see* `www.macromedia.com/devnet/flashplayer/articles/flash_player_8_security.pdf`*).*

When you view this file, you'll notice nothing more than a rather ordinary-looking blue box in the upper-left corner of the page. Click the box, and you should notice two things. First, the screen changes to show a brown box. Second, and perhaps a bit more exciting, you should see that your browser back button is activated, as shown in Figure 11-1. But

before you get too excited and click the back button, click the brown box instead, and you should see a green box. If you click the green box, you'll return to the blue box. Cycle through the boxes as many times as you please.

Figure 11-1.
A simple back button–enabled Flash movie

Now go ahead and click the back button. You should see the Flash file return to the previous state. In fact, you can click the back button all the way back to the beginning! Also, the forward button works just as you would expect, taking you to the next colored box unless you're at the very end.

We've started with this really simple-looking example to get you acquainted with how to build back/forward button functionality in Flash. Before we dive into the code, let's first quickly review how browser histories (and the back and forward buttons) work.

Understanding how browser histories work

Each time a new page is requested within your browser, the current URL is added to a history queue on your browser. When you click the back button, the browser references the previously indexed URL in the queue. When you click the forward button, the browser references the next index in the queue, if there is one available.

It's important that we also define what a new page request actually is. Clearly, if you're on a page called myPage.html and then click a link to myNewPage.html, myPage.html gets added to your history queue. But changes to the query string or anchor name of a URL also will trigger adding a page to the queue. For instance, if you're browsing a page called myPage.asp?id=1, and then click a link to myPage.asp?id=2, myPage.asp?id=1 will be added to the queue. In addition, if you're currently browsing myPage.html#1, and then click a link to myPage.html#2 (which would lead you to a different part of the web page, via the named anchor tag, 2), myPage.html#1 will be added to the queue. It's this latter case that will play a critical role in executing this chapter's Flash back/forward button workaround.

Tracking history and changing state

Our back/forward button implementation isn't particularly difficult, but you need to understand how and when all the pieces of the puzzle interact with each other. When we dissect exactly what's going on piece by piece, all these interactions should become clear,

First, let's take a look at the key players that will re-create the back/forward button functionality:

- The main HTML page
- The history HTML page
- The SWF file

11

Figure 11-2 shows how all three pieces fit together. The main HTML page (main.html) will embed our SWF file as well as an HTML <iframe>, which will hold the history HTML page (history.html). You may be wondering exactly what an <iframe> is. In a nutshell, it's a fancier way to embed frames in a browser page compared to traditional HTML frames, which require a separate HTML page to hold a frameset of frames. An <iframe> can be embedded into a regular HTML page.

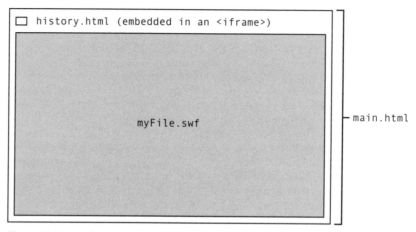

Figure 11-2. How the the main HTML page, history HTML page, and SWF file fit together in the solution

To start the process, you first need to have some sort of defined navigational convention for moving between "pages" of your Flash application. A barebones example would be to have each frame on the root timeline define a new page, and then use the gotoAndStop() method to navigate between states. In fact, this is the strategy that's employed in the colored box example you just played with moments ago.

When a user initiates an event to go to another state in this application (in this case, by clicking the colored box to skip to a new frame), instead of moving to the new state within the movie, the event passes the values necessary to move to this new state to the hidden history.html page via an anchor tag value in the URL. For example, you might choose to pass the frame number of the frame (such as history.html#3).

In the meantime, the history.html page never actually refreshes when you call it with an appended anchor tag value. Calling a named anchor on a page just moves that page to the position of the named anchor within it, rather than refreshing it. So, for the history.html page to know that a new anchor tag value has been passed via the Flash movie, it must store the current value somewhere while making constant checks to see if the URL's anchor tag value has changed. It accomplishes this by storing the current anchor tag value in the main.html page.

When the anchor tag value in the URL differs from the one currently stored in the main page, the history.html page first stores this new value in main.html, and then calls a JavaScript method in main.html that passes the anchor tag value back into Flash. The Flash movie will then use this value to move to its new state.

Notice that we've just passed the original state value from Flash to the history page onto the main page and back into Flash! Why do we pass the state value in this circuitous route? By notifying the history page each time a user navigates to a new state within the Flash application, the browser *updates its history*, adding the page call requested by Flash into its queue. Now, when a user clicks the back button, the history.html page's URL will change to the previous URL in the browser's queue (which contains a different anchor tag value). Figure 11-3 illustrates the process.

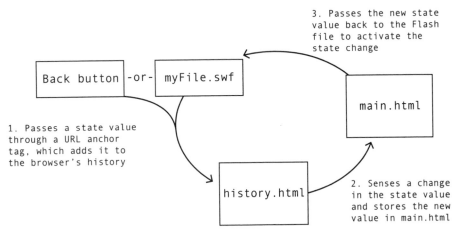

Figure 11-3. How the Flash movie, history page, and main page work together to enable the back button

Again, the history page will detect the difference between the new anchor tag value and the one that's stored in main.html, overwrite the value in the main page, and call the same JavaScript function to pass the previous state value to the Flash movie. The Flash movie will then use this value to move to its previous state. When the dust has settled, you should realize that we just enabled the back button! Since the history.html page is hidden from the users' view, they won't know what's happening behind the scenes.

Think of the history.html page as the history tracker for the Flash movie (hence its name), and the main.html page as the state changer for the Flash movie. Whenever history.html is refreshed, it sends the Flash properties to main.html to change the state of the Flash movie.

This should give you a fairly clear, albeit somewhat abstract, view of how the system works. Now, let's dig into the specifics and explain the code that makes it all happen.

11

Building the SWF file

From the chapter download's /source/fla/ directory, open Chapter11a_Final.fla. Let's see how we built this simple colored box example. In this file, we've just separated our "pages" by keyframes on the root timeline, as you can see in Figure 11-4.

Figure 11-4. Our sample solution partitions Flash pages by frames.

Scripting the page watcher code

In the previous section, we told you that when the history page senses a change in the anchor tag value of its URL, it instructs the main page to pass the new value back to Flash. The Flash movie, in turn, uses the value to change its state with the given value. Now, we'll show you how this is done.

Examine the page watcher layer in the first frame. Here, we define whatever properties are needed to determine to which "page" the Flash file should move. Because we've just separated Flash pages by keyframes, we'll create a variable called page whose value will correspond to the frame number on the root level. The default page will naturally be the first frame, so we set it to 1 initially for clarity's sake.

```
var page:Number = 1;
```

After this line of code, we use the Object.watch method to watch for changes to the page variable. For those of you unfamiliar with Object.watch, it's a method that allows you to "watch" for changes to a property and assign a method to call back to when a change occurs. The method is called, appropriately, a *callback method*.

In the code that follows, we define a callback method for the watch named checkPage(). Remember that this method is called *when the watch method finds that the page value has changed*.

```
checkPage = function(_prop, _oldVal, _newVal)
{
  page = _newVal;
  gotoAndStop(page);
}

this.watch("page", checkPage);
```

The parameters for checkPage() are automatically passed through by the watch method. The _prop value represents the actual property that has changed. The _oldVal represents the value prior to the change, and the _newVal represents the value after the change. For our purposes, we care about the new value of page, _newVal. Here, we set page to the _newVal value, and then move to the frame number given by the value of page. Finally, we actually set the watch method to watch for changes to the variable page and assign checkPage() as the callback method.

Creating the page states

Now that we know how the example accepts changes to the page variable, let's see how it actually passes the values initially. As you saw, when you click the colored box, the box changes colors and also adds the previous state to the history queue.

Click the blue box that lies on the stage at frame 1. Then view the actions tied to this clip by pressing *F9* (or by selecting Window ➤ Development Panels ➤ Actions).

```
on (release)
{
  getURL("history.html#2", "hist");
}
```

When a user clicks and releases the mouse button over the blue box, we pass the page value through to the history page via an anchor tag value (The 2 portion of history.html#2), and set the target of the URL call to hist, which will eventually be the ID of the <iframe> where the history page is referenced. As we explained earlier, the history page will ultimately end up passing this value to the main page and then back to Flash. The watch method will use this value to move to frame 2 of the root timeline.

Frame 2 follows a similar paradigm. Clicking and releasing the mouse button over the brown box passes a value of 3 to the history page. On frame 3, the green box passes a value of 1 to the history page, causing the movie to loop back to the beginning.

Now, let's discuss both the main.html and history.html pages to see how the rest of the chain of events is implemented. First up, let's work on the main page.

Coding the main HTML page

Open the main.html page from the /source/swf/ folder in your favorite text editor so you can view its source code. Our main.html page is an absolute barebones page that includes just the code you need to enable the back/forward button. In a real-life application, this will be the page where your Flash file resides, so you'll probably have a bunch more code decorating this page for whatever non-Flash elements or styles are necessary to make your page visually appealing.

The first bit of code simply sets the page as HTML and then includes an inline CSS style for the unique element in the HTML document called hist. The hist element will be the <iframe> that will include the history.html page. That line of code happens farther down the page. The style we've given the <iframe> is meant to hide it completely from view. While it does an important bit of work to enable the back/forward button, it's something

11

that your users shouldn't even know is there. So, we'll use the visibility:hidden CSS attribute and set the left position, top position, width, and height to 0, tucking the <iframe> away from the user's view.

```
<html>
  <head>
    <style type="text/css">
      #hist { position:absolute; visibility:hidden; left:0; top:0;
➥ width:0; height:0}
    </style>
```

After creating the style, we add in a bit of JavaScript. As mentioned before, this page will be in charge of passing the current state properties to the SWF movie. As you've seen, in this solution, the only property the SWF needs is the page property. So, we first define a corresponding page property in JavaScript, set its value to the initial value of the page property in the SWF, and then write a very simple function (setFlashPage()) that will set the page value within the SWF to the JavaScript page value. Note that both the Flash value and the value used by JavaScript are named exactly the same. This is not a necessity, but rather a recommendation, as it makes for more transparent debugging and readability.

```
<script type="text/javascript">
  var page = 1;

  function setFlashPage()
  {
    window.document.mymovie.SetVariable("page", page);
  }
</script>
</head>
```

Next, we'll create the invisible HTML frame pointing to history.html (we'll build this next) and give the id attribute a value of hist. We need to give it an ID so that our SWF can target this specific frame when reloading the history page. If we couldn't specify a target, the history.html page would reload into the entire window. Also, notice that the target is actually set to history.html#1. Recalling that we pass Flash parameters to the history page via the anchor tag, this URL represents the initial state of the Flash application (the page value set to 1).

```
<!-- Create the hidden iframe with our history page -->
<iframe id="hist" name="hist" src="history.html#1"></iframe>
```

After this, we add in the code to embed the SWF file into the HTML page. Our method is to use the default Flash-generated HTML code you get when you publish your Flash movie. The only addition we'll add is the swLiveConnect=true attribute setter in the <embed> tag. This is needed for Mozilla-based browsers to be able to connect to our JavaScript setFlashPage() method.

In Chapter 13, we'll delve into alternative (and better) ways to embed Flash into a web page. Consider replacing this code after reading Chapter 13!

```
<body>
  <OBJECT classid="clsid:D27CDB6E-AE6D-11cf-96B8-444553540000"
➡ codebase="http://download.macromedia.com/pub/shockwave/cabs/
➡ flash/swflash.cab#version=7,0,0,0" WIDTH=400 HEIGHT=300 id="mymovie">
    <PARAM NAME=movie VALUE="Chapter11a_Final.swf">
    <PARAM NAME=quality VALUE=high>
    <PARAM NAME=bgcolor VALUE=#ffffff>
    <EMBED src="Chapter11a_Final.swf" quality=high bgcolor=#ffffff
➡ WIDTH=400 HEIGHT=300 NAME=mymovie swLiveConnect=true
➡ TYPE="application/x-shockwave-flash"
➡  PLUGINSPAGE="http://www.macromedia.com/shockwave/download/index.cgi
➡ ?P1_Prod_Version=ShockwaveFlash">
    </EMBED>
  </OBJECT>
</body>
```

That does it for main.html. To recap, we've created a hidden <iframe> to hold the history page, written a little JavaScript method to pass state variables to Flash, and then embedded the Flash movie in the page.

Now, let's move on to the history page and see what's going on there.

Coding the history HTML page

Open the history.html page in a text editor and take a look at the source code. Remember that the history page's job is to pass the SWF properties back to the main page, and then tell the main page to update the SWF with the new properties.

All this work can be done with one neatly written JavaScript function, checkURL(). First, we write the necessary html and script tag headers before writing the checkURL() method.

```
<html>
  <head>
   <script language="JavaScript">

     function checkURL()
     {
       var strURL;
       var isMozilla = (navigator.appName == "Netscape");

       if(isMozilla)
       {
         strURL = String(document.location);
       }
       else
       {
         strURL = String(document.URL);
       }
```

```
                var cPage = strURL.split("#")[1];

                if(parent.page!= cPage)
                {
                  parent.page = cPage;
                  parent.setFlashPage();
                }
            }
```

The checkURL() method first checks to see if the browser is Netscape-based. In Netscape-based browsers, the URL of the page can be accessed via document.location. In Internet Explorer–based browsers, the property is called document.url (ah, the beauty of code forking).

Recall that the Flash movie passes parameters from the SWF file to the history page via a page anchor value in the URL. The cPage variable will hold the necessary Flash parameters (in our simple solution, it's just that page value), by storing the data that's past the # character in the URL.

Next, we actually need to call the checkURL() method on this page. However, as we mentioned earlier, since the history page never actually refreshes, we need to make repeated checks on the URL. So, after the checkURL() definition, we use JavaScript's setInterval() method (which acts just like the Flash version) to do the repeated checking.

```
            setInterval(checkURL, 10);
```

To finish off the page, we close out the <script> and <head> tags, and then add a named anchor (for example, <a name="3" />) for every potential page variable.

```
        </script>
      </head>
      <body>
        <a name="3"/>
        <a name="2"/>
        <a name="1"/>
      </body>
    </html>
```

Why do we need to do this? If we don't have named anchors listed on this page, the browser histories in non–Internet Explorer–based browsers won't track these in queue. In other words, if we removed <a name="3" />, calling history.html#3 from Flash won't add this page to the browser's history queue. When we move ahead and then attempt to go back, the back action won't take effect, since history.html#3 is missing from the queue.

That's all there is to the history page. The only thing that ever needs modifying will be the list of named anchors, which will vary based on the list of possible "pages" in your Flash application.

Understandably, writing an anchor tag for all possible state values in your Flash movie can be a bit of a pain depending on the number of possibilities. The task of writing anchor tags into the history frame document could easily be accomplished using any middleware platform, such as PHP or .NET. When the Flash application first loads, it would simply load a server-scripted page into the history frame, passing it the desired values of the anchor tags as a parameter, which it would use to compose the tags on the fly.

Believe it or not, that's all there is to the HTML pages. The implementation takes a bit of getting used to, and like a good book, it's worth reading over the description once more, now that you have the general understanding of the concept.

This first very simple example was intended to give you a good idea of how the technology works. Now, let's try a slightly slicker solution!

The inspiration for our back/forward button implementation comes from the original inventor of the history page concept, Robert Penner.

The original Penner method differs from ours in that it uses a new HTML page for each corresponding Flash "page" with a traditional `<frame>` implementation rather than simply attaching anchor tags within the `history.html` file. The result is that each time you click to a new "page" in Flash, the history frame must actually reload, rather than just skip down to the correct anchor on the page. On initial loads of each HTML page, you'll notice a slight delay (depending on your connection speed) in navigating through each Flash page as the history page reloads. It also uses frames rather than an `<iframe>`, meaning you'll need an additional HTML page with frames that store both the main and history pages. As you saw in our example, by using an `<iframe>`, we just store the history page within the main page.

Penner's solution, while somewhat outdated at this point, provided the original blueprint for this solution, as well as many similar back button implementations. You can find the original Robert Penner back button solution at www.robertpenner.com/ experiments/backbutton/backbutton.html.

11

Enabling browser history in the Flash selection system solution

The simple solution we just walked through demonstrated the concepts and mechanics of adding back/forward button functionality to a Flash application. However, we doubt if you'll want to use it to cycle through colored boxes! So, let's see how to apply it a more real-life example. We'll expand on the simple book selection system we created in Chapter 3—one that displays book cover images when you click a specific title, as shown in Figure 11-5. You'll see that with just a few small tweaks to the code, we can turn this solution into a back button–enabled solution!

Figure 11-5. We will add back button functionality to the book selection system solution (created in Chapter 3).

Deciding which page states to track

What is a natural way to enable the back/forward button functionality for this solution? To us, there's an obvious way: each different cover image should represent a distinct page. In other words, if you clicked the Foundation Flash 8 link, the resulting event (a picture of the *Foundation Flash 8* book) should be considered a single, unique page. Since we think you'll agree, that's the approach we'll take here. We will enable the back button so that users can click any number of items in any sequence and use the back button to trace back through the link history.

You can view the back button–enabled book selection system movie by downloading `Chapter11b_Final.zip` from www.friendsofed.com and opening `main.html` in a browser.

> *Like the previous solution in this chapter, this example does not work if you access it locally on Internet Explorer. To view this example locally, use a Mozilla-based browser, like Firefox. Also, with Flash Player 8, you may need to change your player settings to allow local SWF files to run correctly on your machine (see www.macromedia.com/devnet/flashplayer/articles/flash_player_8_security.pdf).*

Modifying the book selection system code

Remember that the doAction() method in the book selection system class (BookSelectionSystem) is where we define what happens when a user clicks a book item. Because we're now defining each distinct Flash "page" as the display of a different cover image, we just need to find which parameters to pass along to the history.html page that can then be interpreted back into Flash to display the correct cover image. Conveniently, we have the id of each book item at our disposal! All we need to do is pass this value (the currentSelection value in the BookSelectionSystem class) to the history.html page.

Here is the modified doAction() method in BookSelectionSystem.as, which now includes a getURL() call to the history.html page, passing along the id of the currently selected item (currentSelection).

```
private function doAction():Void
{
  getURL("history.html#" + currentSelection, "hist");

  _parent.createEmptyMovieClip("image_mc", 100);
  _parent.image_mc._x = 315;
  _parent.image_mc._y = 52;
  _parent.image_mc.loadMovie(systemData[currentSelection].image);
}
```

Just as in our first example, calling the history page will set up the chain reaction of events that will add the new page anchor to the browser's history queue and then pass the new page parameter back to Flash.

One other change we need to make is in the BookItemButton class, which controls the functionality behind each button. Here, we'll override the setSelected() method to include the handleRollOver() call, as follows. This is needed so that when the user clicks the back button, the handleRollOver() method is called. In the original implementation, handleRollover() was called only as a result of clicking the button item.

```
public function setSelected():Void
{
  super.setSelected();
  handleRollOver();
}
```

11

Adding the watch method in Flash

Next, open the Chapter11b_Final.fla file. Notice nothing has changed since Chapter 3 except an additional keyframe on the root timeline. Click into the second frame of the actions layer and press *F9* (or choose Window ➤ Development Panels ➤ Actions) to see the code we've put on this frame. Just as we did in our initial example, we use the watch method and implement a checkPage() callback function. When we sense a property change to a defined variable, we'll again call page.

```
var page:Number = 0;

checkPage = function(_prop, _oldVal, _newVal)
{
  page = _newVal;
  bookSelectionSystem_mc.setSelection(_newVal);
}

this.watch("page", checkPage);

stop();
```

In this case, when the watch method senses a change to the page variable initiated by the browser back button, the callback function calls bookSelectionSystem_mc. setSelection(newVal) with the previous book item id value, which will set the corresponding previous book item button to its selected state and call the doAction() method to display the previous cover image.

With that, the modifications to our Flash file are finished. We'll now need to make a few minor changes to the history.html and main.html pages.

Modifying the history and main pages

The history and main pages in this solution are nearly identical to the first solution in this chapter, with just a few changes. In the history.html page, you'll need to add all the possible values of pages as named anchors. Since the range of values goes from 0 to 6 (the id values of the button items), and we've set our default page value to 0, you'll need to add these anchors to the history.html page:

```
<a name="0"/>
<a name="1"/>
<a name="2"/>
<a name="3"/>
<a name="4"/>
<a name="5"/>
<a name="6"/>
```

Also, since our default page value is 0, we need to change the initial call to history.html from main.html.

```
<iframe id="hist" name="hist" src="history.html#0"></iframe>
```

With those minor adjustments to the HTML files, the solution is complete!

Examining Flash's named anchors

Our back button–enabling solution isn't the only one you can use. In fact, Flash came out with an integrated method to enable the back button from within the development environment itself as part of its MX release. You may have heard of Flash's *named anchors*, and even used them in the past. If you are contemplating whether or not to use them in the future, we would like to suggest reasons why you shouldn't. First, let's see how they work.

Flash named anchors allow you to create divisions within Flash by labeling keyframes on the root timeline of your movie. Just as you would name keyframes to reference in your Flash code, you can label keyframes as anchors to respond to the browser's back button and to bookmark from your browser, as shown in Figure 11-6.

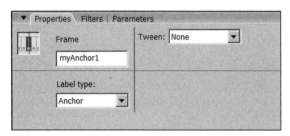

Figure 11-6. Adding named anchors to your Flash movie

The general idea is that you structure your Flash document to have a number of named anchors spaced across your root timeline. When the user has accessed a particular keyframe, he can then use the browser back button to go "back" to the nearest frame with a named anchor on it. In Figure 11-7, if the currently displayed keyframe is the one labeled myAnchor3, clicking the back button will cause the Flash movie to move back to myAnchor2 because it is the named anchor nearest and to the left of myAnchor3 in the timeline.

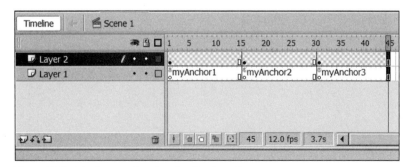

Figure 11-7. A basic named anchor timeline layout

11

You may notice a problem here already. If you create a movie that allows users to access different parts of the root timeline in a random order (rather than sequentially), the browser back button won't take them to the last named anchor frame they were on, but rather to the named anchor frame that is closest to and behind the current named anchor. This forces you to use a linear flow for the application, which makes creating complex applications difficult. By complex, we mean any Flash application that uses something other than the main timeline to navigate from state to state. In this day and age, that eliminates just about every robust Flash application out there!

> *In order for the named anchors to work in a browser, you'll need to change your publish settings for HTML by selecting* File ➤ Publish Settings ➤ HTML *and changing the* Template *option to* Flash with Named Anchors.

Additionally, named anchors don't work in all browsers (Mozilla Firefox, for example) and require some additional JavaScript code forking on your parent HTML page.

If there is one benefit of the named anchor paradigm, it is that you can bookmark each different "page" of your Flash site because each named anchor frame actually modifies the URL associated with the main HTML page.

Summary

You should now have a good grasp of how to enable the browser back and forward buttons! Although defining the concept of a "page" in Flash is not always clear-cut, providing some level of partitioning of your Flash application will enhance its usability. It's your job as a developer to define the sections (pages) in a way that makes sense to your users.

In the next chapter, we'll show you how to provide flexible layouts to maximize the screen real estate of your Flash projects!

12 **LIQUID LAYOUTS**

In most of the previous chapters in this book, we've covered usability topics from the standpoint of specific components. Navigation menus, help tips, data selection, filtering, and forms are all particulars of a Flash application.

In this chapter, we'll take a more general look at Flash from the macroscopic level. Once you've completed building all the components within your Flash application, how can you best lay out your content for variable screen resolutions and browser window sizes? This chapter will try to answer this question.

It may come as a surprise even to some veteran Flash developers that you can very easily create liquid layout applications in Flash. No, we aren't talking about simply setting your movie to 100% width and 100% height when you publish it to a browser. Instead, we're talking about providing your application with the ability to reposition and resize the elements in your Flash application to fit any screen resolution. In addition, you can modify layouts in Flash on-the-fly when the browser or Flash Player is resized. To demonstrate the ins and outs of liquid layout design in Flash, this chapter will lead you through the creation of a basic two-column liquid layout, including a navigation bar at the top, that adjusts to the size of your screen.

In the design process, you should also consider how your application "stretches" to conform to the available screen real estate. We'll discuss appropriate boundaries and size restrictions, specifically as they pertain to columns of text.

Here's what we'll cover in this chapter:

- Fixed-width vs. liquid-width layouts
- Guidelines for usable liquid layouts
- Common headaches of HTML-based liquid layouts
- How to use the Stage object to create liquid layouts with Flash movies
- How to build a two-column, flexible navigation liquid-layout solution

Exploring the fixed-width vs. liquid-width layout dilemma

One of the great debates in web design is whether the website or application should have a fixed-width layout or a flexible one that adjusts to the size of your Flash Player or to the browser window that contains your Flash Player. You may have heard the term *liquid layout* before, or something similar, such as *fluid*, *adjustable*, or *dynamic* layout. The fact that the viewable area of a browser can vary based on screen resolution and browser resizing gives web designers and developers a unique challenge.

No other visual media compares to the highly variant nature of web browsers. Imagine if your daily newspaper came in a different shape every day, or if movie theater screens didn't adhere to a 16:9 aspect ratio. Other media have adopted strict standards for the viewable area of their respective medium because it ensures that designers can lay out their media to best suit the consumer.

In the world of web design, we're largely left to come up with our own rules. The general consensus in today's web design landscape is that . . . there is no consensus! Some designers prefer a fixed layout because it gives them more control of the overall look of the application. Others prefer a liquid design because it takes better advantage of all of the real estate available in the browser window.

However, one of the real benefits of creating liquid-layout applications is that they will remain usable even as screen size standards get larger. A significant percentage of computer users today (roughly two-thirds according to some metrics) has at least a 1024×768 screen resolution. In the mid-1990s, the standard resolution was 640×480. Fixed-width sites that were built in that era now look incredibly tiny on today's standard screen resolutions. If the designers of those sites had built a liquid layout and adjusted the content to the size of the browser window, the sites might still be as readable today as they were back then.

Even so, many designers still favor fixed-width layouts. Ultimately, the decision should depend on what most benefits your user.

Something that most designers *have* agreed on is that, when used, a liquid layout should follow a few rules.

Designing a usable liquid layout

If you are going with a liquid layout, the following are some basic guidelines to consider in your design:

- **Maximum text column width:** You should have a maximum boundary set for the width of a text column. The readability of a block of text decreases as line length increases, as in the example in Figure 12-1. When you've completed reading a line of text, it's more difficult to find your spot if your eyes must move a long visual distance to get back to the beginning to find the next line. This is why newspapers, in particular, employ such narrow-width columns in their layouts. Almost universally, designers agree that text should have a maximum width set.

Figure 12-1. Liquid layouts without boundaries on widths of text columns can render content unreadable.

12

- **Liquid vs. fixed elements:** In addition, when designing a liquid layout, you should consider whether elements should grow in size proportional to the size of the browser window or stay fixed. For example, some designers employ "elastic text" techniques (see www.alistapart.com/articles/elastic/ as an example) to make text readable on all screen resolutions. However, most leave images a fixed size, because dynamically changing their sizes based on screen resolution will cause unwanted resolution reduction and pixelation.

- **Element repositioning:** Finally, if you go with a liquid-based layout, it's essential to consider how elements will reposition themselves when a user resizes his browser window. Some elements of a page might work best if they are aligned to the right or left edge of the browser window, as shown in the example in Figure 12-2. Other elements might "float" proportionally with the size of the browser window.

Figure 12-2. On Amazon.com, the Amazon Search box stays aligned to the left, while the A9 Web Search box stays aligned to the far right.

Building liquid layouts in HTML: The CSS problem

Historically, HTML applications designed with a liquid layout were usually constructed with a table using 100% width. Back in the day, using nested tables and transparent spacer images were some of the tricks of the trade for laying out content on a browser. This method of coding, while effective, had its flaws. Adding in empty table cells with clear images to provide padding between content areas kills the purity of your HTML code. Also, it quickly becomes difficult to update, even if you wrote the original code.

Today, with most HTML sites moving toward separating all presentational markup into CSS and structural markup into XHTML, using tables for layout has become a sin for web standards purists. Instead of tables, the suggested method of implementation is with labeled <div> tags and the use of the float property in CSS to position, say, two columns side by side. However, because the defining bounding box of a particular <div> can differ based on which browser you are using, unwanted overlapping of columns can occur when you're trying to create liquid layout with CSS. We won't go into too much detail about this (if you would like to learn more, we suggest reading Chapter 12 of Jeffrey Zeldman's book, *Designing with Web Standards*), but it's worth knowing that liquid layouts in HTML are still somewhat of a pain to create, even with the movement toward better markup code.

As we mentioned earlier, one key to usable liquid-layout design is to ensure that text does not run too long across the screen, as that makes it hard to read. In CSS, the max-width property allows you to do just that. By setting a max-width property in a <div> layer to

500px, for example, the <div> will never expand to more than 500 pixels, even when the browser window is resized. However, Internet Explorer versions up to and including 7 do not support the max-width (and min-width) properties in CSS.

HTML has its share of problems with creating liquid layouts because of how different browsers interpret CSS. Again, the browser-compatibility bug bites HTML when it comes to producing liquid layouts that work well universally across all browsers.

In Flash, you can build liquid-layout designs without the headaches of dealing with browser-compatibility issues. You have a lot of flexibility when it comes to how elements on a page should reposition or reconfigure themselves based on different screen sizes or the resizing of a browser window.

Using the Flash Stage object to create liquid layouts

By and large, Flash applications on the Web are viewed at fixed dimensions, regardless of the size of your screen. Many Flash designers either aren't aware of this option or simply don't have a compelling enough reason to create a liquid-layout design with Flash. There's no getting around the fact that designing a true liquid layout in Flash adds another dimension of difficulty.

For one, the Flash development environment doesn't really reflect how a Flash application will look on a web browser unless you intentionally hard-code the width and height of the application when you export the movie to HTML. Naturally, this is what most Flash designers end up doing. For the same general reason that many HTML designers adopt fixed-width design, it's just *easier* to design to a fixed width and height in Flash, rather than attempt to scale it to the size of the browser window.

If you simply scale the application by changing the height and width parameters of the <object> and <embed> tags to, say, 100%, the entire movie will scale to the size of the browser window. The main problem with this method is that any imported graphics may appear pixelated because they are being scaled to larger than their default size. Also, text will likewise scale proportionally, meaning you'll get content that's probably larger than necessary.

Fortunately, there is a way to create flexible liquid-layout designs in Flash much like the ones you see in HTML! Using the Stage object, you can automatically adjust the different objects in a Flash movie to create applications that look great on any screen resolution.

The Stage object is a class of static methods and properties that allow developers to access information about the Flash stage. Here are the key methods and properties you'll need to be familiar with to create liquid layouts:

- Stage.height: The height property returns the height of the viewable stage area.
- Stage.width: The width property returns the width of the viewable stage area.

12

- Stage.align: The align property determines how the movie clip aligns within the Flash Player or the browser in which it is embedded. Setting this value to T aligns the stage to the top. Setting it to B aligns it to the bottom. Similarly, setting it to L or R aligns the stage to the left or right. You can use these letters in combination as well. In the example in this chapter, we will set the align property to TL, which will position our movie clip on the top-left corner of the Flash Player.

- Stage.scaleMode: The scaleMode property specifies how the movie clip will scale within the Flash Player. You can assign the scaleMode property to one of the following: showAll, noBorder, exactFit, noScale, or autoSize. In this chapter's example, we will set this property to noScale, so that the objects within the application do not change in size, even as the stage expands.

- Stage.onResize(),Stage.addListener(): The onResize() method is an event handler that is invoked only when Stage.scaleMode is set to noScale and the Flash Player (or browser that holds the Flash Player) is resized. The method can be defined within a generic object. You can then add this object as a listener for the stage via the Stage.addListener() method and define how objects within the stage reposition or resize themselves when the browser window is resized.

Designing a liquid layout in Flash

Now that you have a basic familiarity with the Stage object, let's create a fairly basic application that contains two text columns along with a navigation header. To see how this works, download the Chapter12_Final.zip file from this book's download page at the friends of ED website (www.friendsofed.com) and export the files within the ZIP file into a directory on your machine. Open the Chapter12_Final.swf in a browser, or simply use your Flash Player, and experiment with resizing the Flash application.

The first thing you should notice is how the two columns resize instantly in response to the size of the available screen real estate. Also, the text within each column readjusts to the amount of available space within each column, while maintaining the same amount of padding between itself and the background at all times.

If the given amount of space is too small to fit the entire text, a scrollbar automatically appears in each column, as you can see in the example in Figure 12-3. This allows users to scroll through a particular content area without needing to use the browser's scrollbar. The entire layout remains intact, and scrolling through one content area does not affect the state of another content area.

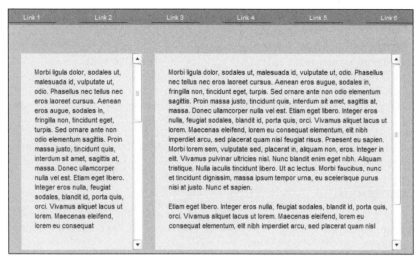

Figure 12-3. A basic two-column liquid layout that resizes the text area when the browser window is resized

Now, try resizing the Flash Player to a very small width. You should see that the columns don't just collapse to the available stage size. Instead, a minimum width is set for both the right and left columns, maintaining the overall readability of the text. Similarly, we've set a maximum width for the text columns, so that when expanded on wider monitors, they are still easy to read.

Let's move on to the header. Notice how the navigation items move as you increase the width of the Flash Player. We've included some navigation items that don't actually take you anywhere; they are here to illustrate the effects of resizing. The items within the header spread out at equal distances across the length of the header. If you decrease the width of the player, the navigation items won't just collapse on each other, but will stop repositioning when they are all stacked laterally along the header.

While, in reality, most people won't be constantly adjusting the size of their browser window when they are using your application, screen resolutions will vary. And, whether you view this application on an 800×600 pixel resolution or a 1280×1024 resolution, the overall layout should look natural. This is the distinct advantage a liquid layout has over a fixed-width layout, and it will go a long way to benefiting the user experience!

Now that you've seen the final application, let's open the hood and see how we've built it.

12

Building the Flash solution

From the chapter download, open `Chapter12_Final.fla`. First, let's walk through the different UI pieces for this application. Then we'll take a look at the code.

Designing the UI components

To put together our application, we need to create essentially three different pieces: the content area movie clips, the header bar, and the navigation items that lie on top of the header bar.

The content area movie clips

Within the Library of `Chapter12_Final.fla`, double-click the movie clip labeled MC ContentArea inside the Content Control folder. This is the clip used to create both of the text columns within the final SWF file.

As you can see in Figure 12-4, the bottommost layer, labeled background, contains a solid-colored background movie clip positioned at (0,0) with an instance name of background_mc. We make this background its own symbol so that we can reference and resize it in response to a stage resize event.

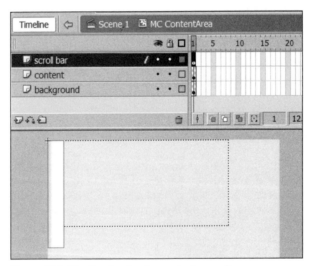

Figure 12-4. The timeline for the content area clip

Above this layer, in the content layer, lies a dynamic text field with an instance name of content_txt. The exact positioning and size of the text field do not matter. Instead of worrying about it here, we will establish the position and size parameters in code later. However, it is important that the text field is set to Multiline within the Properties panel (Window ➤ Properties ➤ Properties), so that text will wrap from within the text field. Also, our text field font is set to Arial, 14-pt. Here, we are once again taking advantage of Flash 8's

Anti-alias for readability option for font rendering and have also set the font to full-justified.

The top layer for this clip, scroll bar, contains a UIScrollBar component that you can add to your library from the Components panel (Window ➤ Components). Again, the position of this scrollbar doesn't matter, because it will be established in code. We've given this an instance name of scroller and set the _targetInstanceName parameter to content_txt. This latter parameter can be set in the Parameters panel. The _targetInstanceName defines the text field to which our scrollbar is registered.

The MC ContentArea clip now essentially has become a stand-alone text column compo-nent. As you can see, the position and size of each of the different elements will vary. We will do all this work in a class file that links to MC ContentArea. If you open the linkage properties (right-click the clip in the library and selecting Linkage), you'll see we've linked it to an AS2 class named `ContentArea.as`. We'll dig into the code for this in the "Building the content area class" section later in this chapter.

Returning to the root timeline, you can see that we've placed two instances of MC ContentArea onto the stage, within the Content Areas layer. The left column has been given an instance name of leftColumn_mc and is positioned at (20, 70), and the right col-umn (rightColumn_mc) is positioned at (250, 70). Once again, where you actually position these on stage doesn't matter, since we will be setting the x- and y-positions in code. We've placed them on stage here just to get a sense of their general positions while we develop the solution.

The header bar clip

Staying on the root timeline, the layer above the Content Areas layer holds the header background clip. We're fairly certain even your pet dog could build this one! The header background clip is simply a solid rectangular movie clip that spans the top portion of the stage. We've given this an instance name of headerbg_mc.

As the application resizes, we'll just need to set the width of the header bar to the width of the stage. The header bar's darker color will make it easier for users to differentiate the navigation items from the rest of the application.

The navigation items

And, where are those navigation items? As we've done throughout this book, any time we're faced with building a set of state controlled items, we revert back to our Chapter 3 solution code. We'll do the same here. If you haven't read Chapter 3, or forgotten what we did there (after all, that was nine chapters ago!), don't fret. We'll explain the bits you need to know for this particular solution.

For the purposes of this solution, you just need to know that each navigation item is an instance of MC NavItemButton and that the clip containing all of the navigation items is an empty movie clip, MC SelectionSystem. The MC NavItemButton clip links to the `NavItemButton.as` file in the /source/classes/ folder. We will create the actual instances of the navigation items using an array of data passed in to the selection system. You'll see this in the code coming up shortly.

12

Setting up component data

Usually, at this point of the chapter, we move on to the AS2 files that control the clips we've just built. However, in this particular solution, we've stuck a fair bit of setup code on the first frame of the root timeline to fill the various elements with data. Let's run through this code first.

In the actions layer of the root timeline, view the Actions panel for frame 1. The beginning code follows the standard way we've created a set of navigation buttons in previous chapters. We begin by setting up an array of data that will help produce our navigation items. We won't do anything fancy with the items in this chapter. All we've done is provided each item with its own title.

```
var selectionData:Array = [
  {title:"Link 1"},
  {title:"Link 2"},
  {title:"Link 3"},
  {title:"Link 4"},
  {title:"Link 5"},
  {title:"Link 6"}
];
```

We then attach an instance of MC SelectionSystem to the stage, and set it with a y-position of 5. It's not necessary to set the x-position, as each navigation item's x-position will be reset initially, and then reset any time the application is resized. The work for this will be handled by each of the navigation buttons in code later.

Next, we call the doInit() method, found within the SelectionSystem class, which will take the array of data we created and churn out the navigation items we've defined within the array.

```
this.attachMovie("MC SelectionSystem", "SelectionSystem_mc",
➥ getNextHighestDepth(),{_y:5});

SelectionSystem_mc.doInit(selectionData, "SelectionItem");
```

After this, we define the text that will go into each of our columns. In the actual source code, we've used dummy text (a whole lot of it) to showcase how text flows when you resize the application. We'll shorten what we wrote in code here to save some trees:

```
leftColumn_mc.content_txt.htmlText = "A whole lot of text";
rightColumn_mc.content_txt.htmlText = "A whole lot more text";
```

Lastly, we'll call an initializeStageLayout() method, which is part of a StageManager class that will handle the repositioning and resizing of most of our components. We call this immediately from the start, so that the components within it will automatically adjust, regardless of what the initial dimensions of the stage happen to be.

```
StageManager.getInstance().initializeStageLayout();
```

Notice we've hit on an entirely new class! In fact, the StageManager class acts as—you guessed it—the manager of the stage. It will be in charge of making sure all our components readjust to a resizing of the application, and, as shown in the previous line of code, to the initial size of the application.

Delegating layout responsibilities

Building flexible layouts in Flash requires a few things. First, it requires a good deal of arithmetic. Second, it requires an even better understanding of how each element's position and size affect the position and size of other elements within the application. Third, it requires you to seriously consider where to delegate these responsibilities. The construction of a liquid layout is by no means trivial, and the correct approach to take really depends on the complexity of the position and size logic of each of the elements.

You can go about programming this chapter's application layout functionality in a variety of ways. Our goal is to make this work as maintainable as possible in the future. It's quite tempting to just create a big global function that will simply look up the parameters of the Stage object, and then resize and reposition everything in the application right then and there. But, if we wanted to later add, say, a third column of text or three more navigation links, this big function would begin to get larger and more unwieldy!

The general approach we suggest is to, as much as possible, delegate the responsibilities of resizing and repositioning the flexible elements in your application to the elements themselves. However, when these properties of an element depend on the properties of another element (for example, the x-position of the right text column depends on the x-position and width of the left text column), you'll need to consider creating a manager that will oversee all of this work. In our solution, we'll delegate this layout work as follows:

- Create the ContentArea class that links to the MC ContentArea movie clips. This class will provide a method to set the minimum and maximum width and height requirements (to keep text from becoming too lengthy) and a method to resize and reposition itself given new width, height, and x- and y-positions.
- Create a StageManager class that listens for changes in the Stage object to send repositioning and resizing information to the ContentArea classes and to the header clip as well.
- Create the NavItemButton class and override UIButton's base setPosition() method to set the position of the navigation items based on the Stage object.

12

Let's step through how each of these different classes is created.

Building the content area class

The ContentArea class will provide an API that will allow us to define a few parameters about the MC ContentArea clips:

- minWidth: The minimum width that the column can collapse
- maxWidth: The maximum width that the column can expand

- minHeight: The minimum height that the column can collapse

- maxHeight: The maximum height that the column can expand

- padding: The amount of padding between the background of the column and the text

By defining these parameters, we can leave the work of correctly resizing the content area to the content area itself. Open ContentArea.as in the /source/classes/ folder to see how we begin. First, since we have a UIScrollBar instance in this clip, we'll import the UIScrollBar class. Next, we'll build the class signature and include the properties this class will own.

```
import mx.controls.UIScrollBar;

class ContentArea extends MovieClip
{
  private var background_mc:MovieClip;
  private var content_txt:TextField;
  private var scroller:UIScrollBar;

  private var minWidth:Number;
  private var maxWidth:Number;
  private var minHeight:Number;
  private var maxHeight:Number;
  private var padding:Number;

  public function ContentArea()
  {
  }
```

Next, we create a method called setParams(), which will allow us to define these boundary and padding numbers for the content area. In this method, we also go ahead and set the text field's _x and _y values to the value of _padding. Since the background clip's registration point is (0,0), the content_txt's x-position and y-position are just equal to whatever the padding is.

```
  public function setParams(_minWidth:Number, _maxWidth:Number,
➡ _minHeight:Number, _maxHeight:Number, _padding:Number):Void
  {
    minWidth = _minWidth;
    maxWidth = _maxWidth;
    minHeight = _minHeight;
    maxHeight = _maxHeight;
    padding = _padding;

    content_txt._x = content_txt._y = padding;
  }
```

The method that follows is where the resizing and repositioning work gets done. In the doResize() method, we pass the content area clip the new width, height, and x- and y-positions, and the method will then readjust the elements within the clip accordingly. Let's break down this method into smaller chunks to make it easier to explain.

The first part is pretty easy. After defining the method signature, we assign the clip's _x and _y values to the passed-in values _newX and _newY. We want to leave these parameters optional, so if they don't get passed in, we don't try to assign them.

```
public function doResize(_newWidth:Number, _newHeight:Number,
➥ _newX:Number, _newY:Number):Void
{
  if (_newX)
    _x = _newX;

  if (_newY)
    _y = _newY;
```

Next, we'll adjust the area of the background clip. Here, we compare the passed-in _newWidth and _newHeight parameters to the boundary widths and heights, and then determine the correct new width and height to assign the background. We take advantage of the Math object's min() and max() methods, which compare two numbers and return the smaller or larger of the two, respectively.

```
background_mc._width = Math.min(maxWidth, Math.max(minWidth,
➥ _newWidth));
        background_mc._height = Math.min(maxHeight, Math.max(minHeight,
➥ _newHeight));
```

In this code, _newWidth is first compared to minWidth, and the higher value is returned, to ensure that the width is no less than minWidth. That value is then checked against maxWidth, and the lower number is returned to ensure that the width is no greater than maxWidth. The resulting width is assigned to the background's _width property. The _height calculation is accomplished in a similar fashion.

After this, we concern ourselves with the new size of the content_txt text field. Remember that we already set the x-position and y-position of the text field in the setParams() method. Now, we set the height.

```
content_txt._height = Math.max(0, background_mc._height - (2 *
➥ padding));
```

12

259

Figure 12-5 shows how we calculate the new height. As you can see, we need to take the height of the background and subtract twice the size of the padding.

Figure 12-5. Correctly sizing the height of the text field

Next, we see whether the current height of the text field is less than the height created by the text within it. If it is, that means we need to activate our scrollbar by setting its visibility to true, and set its height x- and y-positions so that it sits flush against the right side of the background clip. Staying inside the if statement, we now reset the width of the text field. Just as illustrated for the height in Figure 12-5, the width of the text field can be deduced from taking the background clip's width and subtracting twice the padding. Also, because the scrollbar is activated and sits on the right edge of the background clip, we'll subtract its width from the overall width of the text field. The following code achieves all of this.

```
if (content_txt._height < content_txt.textHeight)
{
  scroller._visible = true;
  scroller._x = background_mc._width - scroller._width;
  scroller._y = background_mc._y;
  scroller.setSize( "", background_mc._height);
  content_txt._width = Math.max(0, background_mc._width - (2 *
➥ padding) - scroller._width);
}
```

If the text within the text field is not longer than the currently available height of the clip, then we'll hide the scrollbar. The width of the text field is handled in nearly the same way, except that we no longer need to subtract the width of the scrollbar.

```
      else
      {
        scroller._visible = false;
        content_txt._width = Math.max(0, background_mc._width - (2 *
➥ padding));
      }
    }
  }
```

That completes the code for the `ContentArea` class. In summary, we've created two methods. One, `setParams()`, allows you to set the boundaries and padding of the clip, and the other, `doResize()`, will readjust all the elements inside a content area based on new size and position values. We will now move on to the `StageManager` class to see how we use these methods.

Building the stage manager class

The `StageManager` class's main responsibility is to respond to changes to the size of the stage by passing along this information to the various elements on the stage. Open the `StageManager.as` file from the `/source/classes/` folder of the chapter download.

Because there needs to be only one instance of this class at any time, we will once again make this a *singleton class* (as we first discussed in Chapter 7) by including a static private instance of StageManager as a property, and then creating a `getInstance()` method to retrieve this static instance when we want to access anything within StageManager.

```
class StageManager
{
  private static var stageManager:StageManager;

  private function StageManager()
  {
  }

  public static function getInstance():StageManager
  {
    if ( stageManager == undefined )
      stageManager = new StageManager();

    return stageManager;
  }
```

12

Next, we create the initializeStageLayout() method. As you saw earlier, we call this method on the root timeline to do all the initial work in laying out the elements on the stage. The following method first sets the Stage object's align property to TL to make sure the movie is always aligned to the top-left side of the player. Then it sets the scaleMode property to noScale. Finally, it adds the StageManager object as a listener of the Stage object. In the "Creating the resize event handler" section later in this chapter, you'll see how this class reacts to changes in the size of the stage.

```
public function initializeStageLayout():Void
{
  Stage.align = "TL";
  Stage.scaleMode = "noScale";
  Stage.addListener(this);
```

The method isn't finished just yet! Next, we'll initialize those boundary and padding values for the two content areas that are on the stage using setParams(). Here, we set the leftColumn_mc clip so that its width values can vary from only 100 to 300 pixels, and its height values can vary from only 300 to 900 pixels. Then we give the text inside it a padding of 20 pixels with respect to the background. For the rightColumn_mc clip, the width values can vary from 200 to 600 pixels, while everything else remains the same.

Then we will call an updateLayout() method:

```
  _root.leftColumn_mc.setParams(100, 300, 300, 900, 20);
  _root.rightColumn_mc.setParams(200, 600, 300, 900, 20);

  updateLayout();
}
```

This updateLayout() method will contain all the logic to pass down the correct sizing information to the different elements that StageManager will manage. Namely, it will do the following:

- Resize the width of the headerbg_mc clip to stretch to the size of the stage.
- Call the doResize() method on both content areas, passing along the new width, height, x, and y values.

Let's look at the updateLayout() method in full, and then break down what we've done.

```
private function updateLayout():Void
{
  _root.headerbg_mc._width = Stage.width;
  _root.leftColumn_mc.doResize((Stage.width - 60) * .33,
Stage.height - _root.leftColumn_mc._y - 20, 20, 70);
  _root.rightColumn_mc.doResize((Stage.width - 60) * .67,
Stage.height - _root.leftColumn_mc._y - 20, _root.leftColumn_mc._x +
  _root.leftColumn_mc._width + 20, 70);
}
```

After setting the headerbg_mc clip's width to stretch to the size of the stage, we want to figure out the correct values to pass to the content areas' doResize() methods to give them their new size and position values based on the stage size.

Setting the size of the content areas

Examine Figure 12-6 to see a diagram of how we want both the left and right column widths to flow at any given stage size.

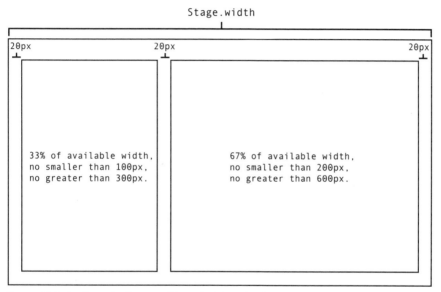

Stage.width

| 20px | 20px | 20px |

33% of available width, no smaller than 100px, no greater than 300px.

67% of available width, no smaller than 200px, no greater than 600px.

Figure 12-6. A schematic diagram of how the left and right column widths relate to the overall width of the stage

First, we put a 20-pixel margin between the content areas and between the edges of the screen. After that, we want to have the left column take up one-third of the remaining width of the screen, and the right column should take up the other two-thirds. So, doing a little math here tells us that the new width of leftColumn_mc should be (Stage.width - 20 - 20 - 20) * .33, or (Stage.width - 60) * .33. Similarly, the rightColumn_mc width will be (Stage.width - 60) * .67. Note that we don't need to worry about the boundary widths of either content area clip because they will be taken care of in the content area's doResize() method. Now, let's move on to the height values.

12

Examine Figure 12-7 to see a diagram of how we want both the left and right column heights to flow at any given stage size.

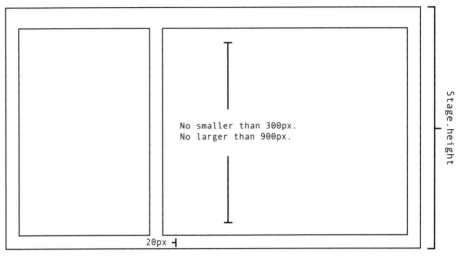

No smaller than 300px.
No larger than 900px.

20px

Stage.height

Figure 12-7. A schematic diagram of how the column heights relate to the overall height of the stage

Figure 12-7 shows that we can find the height of the both columns by subtracting the y-position of the columns from the height of the stage and another 20 pixels to give it a bottom-edge buffer. The equation for the column heights is then just Stage.height - _root.leftColumn_mc._y - 20 and Stage.height - _root.rightColumn_mc._y - 20.

Now that we've figured out the equations that dictate the content area size, let's work on positioning.

Setting the positions of the content areas

The leftColumn_mc clip will have a static x-position and y-position. We're going to set the clip to always be at (20,70) with respect to the stage. As for the rightColumn_mc clip, we set the y-position to be 70 pixels again, but the x-position must change in response to the state of leftColumn_mc. Referring back to Figure 12-6, you'll see that the _x value of rightColumn_mc can be given by _root.leftColumn_mc._x + _root.leftColumn_mc._width + 20.

So, that sums up how we figure out the parameters for resizing and repositioning the content area clips. Refer back to the updateLayout() method to see the entire code in one spot.

Creating the resize event handler

The last thing we need to create for StageManager is the onResize() event handler method. Remember that this method will be called each time the stage is resized by the user because we've added StageManager as a listener to the Stage object. All onResize() needs to do is call updateLayout().

```
private function onResize():Void
{
    updateLayout();
}
}
```

That does it for the StageManager class. We've created a class that takes care of almost all the readjustments to the elements in our application. The key word here is *almost*. There's still the matter of the navigation items.

Modifying the navigation item positions

Because the position of each navigation item is controlled by its own class (NavItemButton.as), we'll modify this class to handle resize changes.

Open NavItemButton.as in the /source/classes/ folder. NavItemButton extends the UIButton class that we described in Chapter 3. As you may recall, this class controls how each navigation item in the header behaves. Let's focus solely on the code that specifically relates to the resizing of the stage.

The first thing we've done is added the NavItemButton class as a listener of the Stage object in our constructor.

```
public function NavItemButton()
{
    super();
    Stage.addListener(this);
}
```

By adding NavItemButton as a listener, we can now define the onResize() method that will be invoked each time the stage resizes, just as we did for StageManager.

```
public function onResize():Void
{
    setPosition();
}
```

Note that, in onResize(), we just need to call setPosition(), the method used to define where the item lies within our set of navigation items. There's an added bit of niftiness here. The setPosition() method now serves a dual purpose. Where it once was responsible for just the initial position of each navigation item, it is now also responsible for the position of each navigation item when the stage resizes.

12

Figure 12-8 illustrates how we need to reposition each navigation item correctly. Notice that the position of each item depends not only on the width of the stage, but also on the width of each item. With the lone exception of the rightmost item, the calculation of the x-position of each item is the same.

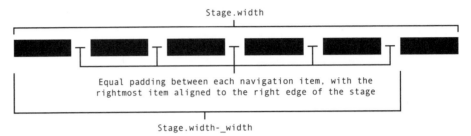

Figure 12-8. A schematic diagram of how the navigation items reposition themselves with respect to the stage

Take the width of the stage and subtract the width of the end navigation item (which is the same as the width of any navigation item). From the resulting width (Stage.width - _width), divide equally among the remaining items (total items − 1). This gives you the amount of width and padding required to fit one navigation item. Multiply this by the index of the item, and the result will give you the correct x-position of the item.

The calculation of the x-position for the rightmost navigation item is simple. It is nothing more than the width of the entire stage minus the width of the item.

The only other exception we need to take into account is when the stage is sized to a very small width. Certainly, we wouldn't want the navigation items to overlap each other. So, our logic in setPosition() will check that the available stage width is greater than the combined widths of all our items. If it isn't, then we'll just reposition the items to stack horizontally across the header bar without any padding in between, regardless of the width of the stage.

With this in mind, the resulting logic for setPosition() method in NavItemButton.as can be achieved as follows:

```
private function setPosition():Void
{
  //total number of selection items
  var totalItems:Number = selectionSystem.getTotalItems();

  var minWidth = totalItems * _width;
  var sWidth:Number = Stage.width;
```

```
    if(sWidth > minWidth)
    {
      if(id == totalItems - 1)
      {
        _x = sWidth - _width;
      }
      else
      {
        var xSpace = sWidth - _width;
        _x = (xSpace/(totalItems - 1)) * id;
      }
    }
    else
    {
      _x = id * _width;
    }
  }
```

Notice the getTotalItems() method (highlighted in the preceding code) from the SelectionSystem.as base class. We've added this method for this chapter's solution only (we didn't use it in our implementation of the selection system in Chapter 3), because the button needs to know how many other buttons are in the navigation header to determine where to place itself. All this method does is return the number of button items that have been attached to the selection system.

> Another way we could have solved the problem of getting the total number of navigation items would be to consider refactoring our code from Chapter 3 to move the work of setPosition() from the UIButton base class to the SelectionSystem base class. As you know, programming is an iterative process that often involves some reconsideration of how you first implemented your solution. Here's one case where such a reconsideration might be beneficial.

Summary

There you have it. We've taken advantage of the Stage object to create an application that flows to the size of the Flash Player! We hope that you've gotten a grasp of not only some of the features of the Stage object, but also the techniques and thought processes that go into building a liquid layout. Empowering the application to adjust itself to a user's size preferences goes a long way towards creating a more user-friendly application.

12

Certainly, you can go many more places with liquid layouts than what we've shown you here. However, whatever new ideas you may have, always keep in mind potential usability hazards that might await users. Constraining the width of your content areas to minimum and maximum values will help keep the text readable, but also consider adjusting the size of the text based on how much screen real estate is available. A 12-pixel font on a 1240-pixel width screen will look tiny in comparison to how it appears on an 800-pixel width screen. You may want to consider changing (or allowing users) to change font sizes based on screen resolution, for example.

Of course, the most common place you'll see your Flash movie is inside of a web page on a browser. In our next, and very sadly, final usability solution, we'll discuss common techniques for embedding Flash into an HTML page. Some bright minds have done a lot of great work to improve the user-friendliness of Flash as a browser-based application. Let's take a look, shall we?

13 **EMBEDDING FLASH**

| Foundation Flash 8 |
| Foundation MX Express |
| Foundation MX Studio |
| Foundation MX Upgrade Essentials |
| Foundation MX Video |
| Foundation XML for Flash |
| New Masters of Flash |
| The Flash Usability Guide |
| **Flash Books** |

Timeline ⇦ Scene 1

- title
- info text field
- range text fields
- drag handle clips
- slider range bar

Address 1*	
Address 2	
City*	
State	AL ▼
Zip Code*	
Work Phone*	

So, you've just put the finishing touches on your latest Flash masterpiece. Everything looks perfect, and you're ready to deploy your project to the Web. You'll take the HTML file that publishes with your Flash project and throw it up on a web server, and that's that, right? Not quite—if you're thinking in terms of usability, using the default HTML created by Flash may not be your best option.

Many Flash developers pay little attention to the HTML code that's produced by the Flash development environment. But this is a part of the development process that you should consider with great care. After all, it would be a shame to have all the hard work you put into your Flash project go to waste because it looks different on certain browsers or because you didn't provide a way to check that users have the Flash Player version needed to view your application.

In this chapter, we'll make sure that you don't fall into the traps that can be found in poorly built HTML embedding methods. We'll also get you up to speed on today's current methods for embedding Flash into the browser. Here's what we'll cover in this chapter:

- Key usability criteria for embedding Flash movies into HTML pages
- The Flash Express Install feature
- The default Flash embedding method
- The Flash Satay embedding method
- The nested object embedding method
- The Macromedia Flash Player Detection Kit
- The FlashObject method
- How to use FlashObject with Express Install

Optimizing usability when embedding Flash movies

Your most important goal should be to minimize the amount of work users need to do to get your Flash movie up and running, regardless of the browser or Flash Player version installed on their machine. Ideally, a user should be able to just open an HTML page and begin enjoying your creation, but we know that's not always the case. The better you can eliminate any hiccups in the loading of a Flash movie in a user's browser, the better the user's experience will be.

Browser compatibility

One of the main advantages of Flash is that it looks about the same in any browser and on any platform. When we're talking about embedding Flash into an HTML page, naturally, this requires some HTML to be written to the page. Different browsers support different HTML tags for embedding Flash content.

You should also take into account whether the HTML used is valid XHTML, or standards-compliant. Web standards look like they are here to stay, so it's crucial that the HTML code validates against XHTML standards to ensure compatibility with future versions of browsers. Certain methods of embedding use HTML that doesn't work in all browsers or isn't valid XHTML.

Flash sniffing

It's also critical that you consider users that either don't have the Flash Player installed on their machine or don't have the version of the Flash Player needed to render your application properly. As of the time of writing this book, more than 97% of Internet users have a version of Flash Player installed on their computers, but they could have an older version that won't fully support all the functionality you have in your movie. In addition, the 3% of remaining users without Flash Player shouldn't be ignored.

A good embedding method should include some way to "sniff" your browser for the currently installed version of Flash. If the installed player is a lower version than required (or a player does not exist at all), you have a couple options:

- Display an alternative block of HTML content to tell the user to download the latest version of Flash.
- Download and update the user's Flash plug-in automatically. Although this is more intuitive, it's also more invasive; downloading the plug-in automatically without requesting permission from the user is not ideal.

You'll want to give users the option to download the new version of the Flash Player. However, instead of forcing users to go to Macromedia's website and download the player from there, you can ease the process by allowing them to install the player without having to go to a new page. Flash offers a component called *Express Install* that does just this, provided the user has at least Flash Player 6.0.65 or later installed on the machine.

Express Install is a new feature for the Flash Player that allows users to install the player from within Flash, as shown in Figure 13-1. The installer isn't controlled by the browser, but rather by the Flash movie itself. After installation, the application refreshes your Flash page automatically to the state at which the user was prompted to update his software.

Figure 13-1. The Flash Express Install feature handles on-the-spot installation of the latest version of the Flash Player.

13

Express Install comes in the form of a modifiable HTML page and SWF file that handles the installation. For more information about Express Install, visit www.macromedia.com/software/flashplayer/download/detection_kit/.

In this chapter's example, we will show you a very easy way to integrate Express Install into your Flash movie in conjunction with FlashObject, one of the Flash embedding techniques we'll cover in this chapter.

Choosing an embedding method

Now that we've covered some considerations for optimizing usability when embedding Flash, let's take a look at the most common forms of Flash embedding and evaluate each one individually.

The default Flash-generated HTML method

The most common method for embedding Flash into HTML is through the HTML page that the Flash environment generates when you publish your movie. While there aren't any metrics available out there to tell us what percentage of Flash movies are embedded in this way, it's safe to say that it is by far the most common method, since it requires the least amount of setup.

Since the HTML code is created automatically, you can simply copy and paste the snippet into the HTML page that will contain your Flash movie. If you've embedded Flash movies into HTML before, you've probably used this technique, and the following code will look very familiar!

```
<object classid="clsid:d27cdb6e-ae6d-11cf-96b8-444553540000"
➡ codebase="http://fpdownload.macromedia.com/pub/shockwave/cabs/
➡ flash/swflash.cab#version=7,0,0,0" width="100%" height="100%"
➡ id="Chapter13_Final" align="middle">
  <param name="allowScriptAccess" value="sameDomain" />
  <param name="movie" value="Chapter13_Final.swf" />
  <param name="quality" value="high" />
  <param name="bgcolor" value="#cccccc" />
  <embed src="Chapter13_Final.swf" quality="high" bgcolor="#cccccc"
➡ width="100%" height="100%" name="Chapter13_Final" align="middle"
➡ allowScriptAccess="sameDomain" type="application/x-shockwave-flash"
➡ pluginspage="http://www.macromedia.com/go/getflashplayer" />
</object>
```

The default HTML code uses a dual approach for displaying your Flash movie in a browser. As it turns out, Internet Explorer (and browsers that primarily follow Internet Explorer standards) use the <object /> tag to display Flash, and a series of <params /> tags to specify properties within your Flash movie. Netscape, on the other hand (and browsers that primarily follow Netscape standards), uses the <embed /> tag. So, the HTML needs to describe the properties within Flash twice for it to handle the major browsers, which adds some undesirable bulk to the download of your page.

Another drawback is that the code itself doesn't validate with HTML or XHTML web standards. In fact, the <embed /> tag is not part of the current XHTML or HTML specification. You may be wondering what valid HTML code has to do with usability. Well, as newer browsers comply with web standards, they will also become stricter about "invalid" code. Ensuring your HTML code is valid today will reduce your browser-compatibility headaches for years to come.

There must be a way to write standards-compliant HTML code without duplicating your parameters, and have your Flash movie play correctly in all browsers, right? In fact, there are several ways.

The Flash Satay method

The Flash Satay method is a technique developed by Drew McLellan of the Web Standards Project. His idea was to get rid of the unsupported <embed /> tag, while still rendering the Flash movie in browsers that relied on <embed /> to attach Flash movies. After some bit of work, McLellan figured out that you could get rid of the <embed /> tag and reduce the embedding code to this:

```
<object type="application/x-shockwave-flash" data="movie.swf"
➥ width="400" height="300">
  <param name="movie" value="movie.swf" />
</object>
```

However, as it turns out, manipulating the code in this way prevents Flash movies in some browsers (older versions of Internet Explorer, for example) from streaming. The workaround for this is to embed an empty container SWF file with the same dimensions as the actual SWF file, and then load the actual SWF file on the first frame of the container movie. This allows for near instantaneous loading of the movie, because the base SWF will be on the order of a few bytes, and it still lets you load the actual movie you wanted to originally embed in HTML. To do this, you pass the name of the real SWF file you want to embed as a parameter to the empty container SWF, like this:

```
<object type="application/x-shockwave-flash"
➥ data="c.swf?path=movie.swf" width="400" height="300">
  <param name="movie" value="c.swf?path=movie.swf" />
</object>
```

In this code, you pass the name of the actual SWF file in as a path query string parameter. On the first frame of the container SWF, the following line of ActionScript code will then load the desired movie:

```
_root.loadMovie(_root.path,0);
```

Since Internet Explorer needs to load only a very light, hollow container movie, there is no noticeable lag due to the lack of streaming.

13

The Satay method omits the codebase attribute of the object tag because, this, in combination with the removal of the <embed /> tag, prevents movies from playing in some Netscape-based browsers. However, the value provided within the codebase attribute contains the version of the Flash Player necessary to render the movie. Without it, Internet Explorer browsers won't prompt users with older versions of Flash Player to download an update.

The workaround is to include another empty movie clip somewhere on the page that does nothing else but include the codebase tag. This way, like the default published HTML method, the Flash Satay method will launch an ActiveX pop-up box for Internet Explorer users to download a newer version of the plug-in, or a similar dialog box in Netscape-based browsers.

A drawback to the Satay method is that it is not as accessible as other methods. For instance, the screen reader JAWS can't interpret the code properly.

You can find Drew McLellan's description of the Flash Satay method at www.alistapart.com/articles/flashsatay/.

The nested object method

Similar to the Flash Satay method, the nested object method, developed by Ian Hickson, takes the two-object technique of Flash Satay and nests the objects, so that the outer object renders in Internet Explorer-based browsers and the inner object renders in other browsers. The code looks like this:

```
<object classid="clsid:D27CDB6E-AE6D-11cf-96B8-444553540000"
➥ codebase="http://download.macromedia.com/pub/shockwave/cabs/flash/
➥ swflash.cab#version=6,0,40,0" width="300" height="120">
   <param name="movie" value="http://www.macromedia.com/shockwave
➥ /download/triggerpages_mmcom/flash.swf">
   <param name="quality" value="high">
   <param name="bgcolor" value="#FFFFFF">
   <!--[if !IE]> <-->
   <object data="http://www.macromedia.com/shockwave/download/
➥ triggerpages_mmcom/flash.swf" width="300" height="120" type=
➥ "application/x-shockwave-flash">
   <param name="quality" value="high">
   <param name="bgcolor" value="#FFFFFF">
   <param name="pluginurl" value="http://www.macromedia.com/go/
➥   getflashplayer">
   FAIL (the browser should render some flash content, not this).
</object>
<!--> <![endif]-->
</object>
```

The Flash Player Detection Kit

With Flash Player 8, Macromedia has released its own Flash Player Detection Kit, which you can download from www.macromedia.com/software/flashplayer/download/ detection_kit/. The Detection Kit offers three examples of how to check for Flash Player versions on your user's browser. Each method allows you to indicate the lowest version of Flash Player that will successfully run your movie. Which method you use depends on some general assumptions you'll need to make about your user base:

- **Client-side scripting method:** This method uses a mixture of JavaScript and VBScript to handle detection on Netscape and Internet Explorer-based browsers, respectively. It won't work if scripting is disabled on the browser.

- **ActionScript-based method:** This method won't work if no version of the Flash Player is initially installed.

- **Server-side script method:** This method won't work for users with an installed version of Flash Player earlier than the 6.0.65 release.

Of the three methods, the client-side scripting version is probably the most commonly used and least onerous, since the number of Internet users with client-side scripting disabled is probably far less than those without Flash Player or with a relatively old version of it. As a community, web developers today can assume, with fair confidence, that web users will have client-side scripting enabled, as JavaScript-based functionality like image rollovers and form validation are commonplace in most commercial websites.

If you view the sample client-side scripting method from the Detection Kit, you'll notice it's a rather big mess. The intertwining of JavaScript, VBScript, and HTML makes modifications a bit of a pain. You'll also notice that the outputted HTML code for embedding Flash still uses the noncompliant <embed /> tag. If you use this method, you should modify the outputted code to fit a standards-compliant HTML output like Flash Satay, for example.

While we certainly anticipate Macromedia will support the Detection Kit code and update it as necessary, we have found another option to be easier to use and more effective: the FlashObject method.

The FlashObject method

The method we prefer to accomplish embedding and Flash sniffing is a JavaScript-based solution written by Geoff Stearns of www.deconcept.com called *FlashObject*. You can view a very detailed and well-updated description of FlashObject at http://blog.deconcept. com/flashobject/. Here is an overview of what FlashObject does, straight from that site:

"FlashObject is a small JavaScript file used for embedding Macromedia Flash content. The script can detect the Flash plugin in all major web browsers (on Mac and PC) and is designed to make embedding Flash movies as easy as possible. It is also very search engine friendly, degrades gracefully, can be used in valid HTML and XHTML 1.0 documents,* and is forward compatible, so it should work for years to come.

* Pages sent as text/html, *not* application/xhtml+xml."

13

An implementation of FlashObject is incredibly simple. After you've downloaded the `flashobject.js` file (as of this writing, you could download a ZIP file including FlashObject version 1.2.3 from http://blog.deconcept.com/flashobject/flashobject1-2.zip), you simply need to reference it in the <head /> portion of your HTML page, just as you make any external JavaScript file reference. Then you create a <div /> layer on your page and give it an id attribute. Within it, you can specify content that will either be replaced by the Flash movie or be shown to those without the proper version of the Flash Player. Just after the <div /> layer, you include an easy-to-manage snippet of JavaScript code that instantiates a new FlashObject and writes the embedding into the <div /> layer. The entire code will look something like this:

```
<html>
  <head>
    <script type="text/javascript" src="flashobject.js"></script>
  </head>
  <body>
    <!-- Create the div layer -->
    <div id="flashcontent">
      Alternate content for users without the Flash version required.
    </div>
    <!-- Embed the Flash movie with FlashObject -->
    <script type="text/javascript">
      var fo = new FlashObject("movie.swf", "mymovie", "200", "100",
➥ "8.0.22", "#336699", true);
      fo.write("flashcontent");
    </script>
  </body>
</html>
```

In this code, after creating the <div /> layer, you then create an instance of FlashObject (in this example, named fo), passing in the essential information needed to load the movie. Specifically, you pass in the following information:

- The name of the SWF file to embed
- The ID of the object (which can be referenced in HTML just as you would reference any HTML tag that supports IDs)
- The width of your movie
- The height of your movie
- The version of Flash Player required for your movie
- The background color for your movie
- A Boolean value indicating whether to use Express Install (you'll see exactly how this is done in the next section)

The fo.write("flashcontent") then replaces the <div /> with the id of flashcontent with the movie itself. If your user does not have the correct player version installed, it will then leave the HTML content inside the <div />.

FlashObject also supports easy integration of Flash parameters to your player plug-in, as well as variables to pass into the Flash movie. Adding these requires a minimal amount of code, and the parameters and variables are passed using JavaScript methods, rather than through tag attributes or a query string. The following could be added in between the creation of the FlashObject variable and the call to the `write` method to add three Flash player parameters and one variable into the embedding movie.

```
fo.addParam("quality", "low");
fo.addParam("wmode", "transparent");
fo.addParam("salign", "t");
fo.addVariable("myVariable", "myValue");
```

FlashObject also can integrate with Flash Express Install to even further enhance usability by allowing users to update older versions of Flash Player without needing to go to another page. You can find more information about this technique at http://blog. deconcept.com/2005/08/13/using-flash-player-express-install-with-flashobject/. We'll show you how to use Express Install with FlashObject in the very next section.

You'll notice that the HTML required for FlashObject is minimal, and better yet, you can use it in XHTML code, and it will still validate! Actually embedding the Flash movie is handled entirely within the downloadable JavaScript class, which makes it even easier to manage as future updates of FlashObject are released.

> *Another embedding method inspired by FlashObject is UFO (Unobtrusive Flash Object) created by Bobby van der Sluis. You can find more information about UFO and download it from* www.bobbyvandersluis.com/ufo/.

Using FlashObject with Express Install

Let's see just how easy it is to use FlashObject, along with Macromedia's new Express Install feature. Begin by downloading `Chapter13_Final.zip` from the friends of ED website (www.friendsofed.com) and export the files within the ZIP file into a directory on your machine.

This example uses the liquid-layout solution from Chapter 12. Our goals here are the following:

- Embed the SWF file into HTML using FlashObject.
- Let the SWF file take up the full area of the browser.
- Implement Express Install to allow Flash Player upgrades (for versions 6.0.65 and later) to be done within the movie.

Begin by opening `Chapter13_Final.html` in the /source/swf/ folder in the browser of your choice. If you happen to have a version of Flash that is older than 8.0.22 (but later than version 6.0.65), you should see an alert box pop up inside the movie (similar to the one shown earlier in Figure 13-1), asking permission to download the newer version.

13

Because you are running this on your machine locally, you may first be prompted to change your security settings to allow the Macromedia website to interact with the movie on your machine. Either allow access to it or upload and run these pages from a remote web server instead.

After you have downloaded the latest version of Flash (or you already have it), you should be taken to the same liquid-layout solution example we dissected in Chapter 12. Now, let's see what it took to embed the movie.

> *We will not be going through the* `flashobject.js` *and* `ExpressInstall.as` *files included in this solution, for two reasons. First, we did not have a hand in the development of either of these files and would not want to misrepresent how the original authors created them in any way. Second, you really shouldn't need to know how they work; the point is to see how easy it is to implement them.*

Writing the HTML code

Open the `Chapter13_Final.html` page in a text editor. Here, we start out by setting this page's DOCTYPE to XHTML 1.0 Strict. One of the benefits of FlashObject is that all the HTML code we need to write will validate as strict XHTML.

```
<!DOCTYPE html PUBLIC "-//W3C//DTD XHTML 1.0 Strict//EN"
➡ "http://www.w3.org/TR/xhtml1/DTD/xhtml1-strict.dtd">
```

Then we write the following HTML code. You'll notice everything looks the same as the HTML code we initially wrote for FlashObject, aside from a few CSS styles we've created to allow the Flash movie to expand to the full width and height of the browser. Also, notice that the `flashobject.js` page has been included in the same folder as this HTML page, which we reference in the `<script />` tag.

```
<html xmlns="http://www.w3.org/1999/xhtml" xml:lang="en" lang="en">
  <head>
    <script type="text/javascript" src="flashobject.js"></script>
    <style type="text/css">
      html {
        height: 100%;
        overflow: hidden;
      }

      #flashcontent {
        height: 100%;
      }
      body {
        height: 100%;
        margin: 0;
        padding: 0;
        background-color: #f60;
```

```
        }
      </style>
    </head>
    <body>
      <div id="flashcontent">
        Alternate content for users without the Flash version required,
        and lower than version 6.0.65.
      </div>
      <script type="text/javascript">
      // <![CDATA[

        var fo = new FlashObject("Chapter13_Final.swf",
➡ "Chapter13_Final", "100%", "100%", "8.0.22", "#666666", true);
        fo.write("flashcontent");

      // ]]>
      </script>
    </body>
  </html>
```

Notice that when we create the FlashObject, we now set the width and height properties to 100%, rather than to a fixed pixel width and height. The version we require is Flash 8.0.22 (the latest version available on Macromedia's website as of this writing). We've also set the background to dark gray and set the Express Install Boolean variable to true. By setting the Boolean value to true, the FlashObject instance will do the setup required to test whether the Flash Player version can be updated via Express Install.

Next, we'll show you how simple it is to add the Express Install check to the Flash movie.

Checking for the ExpressInstall component

Open the /source/classes/ folder, and you will discover that all the class files here are identical to the ones in Chapter 12 except for a new ExpressInstall.as file. Geoff Stearns has kindly included this as a part of the download package for FlashObject, and we've included it in this chapter's solution.

Now, open Chapter12_Final.fla in the /source/fla/ folder. To ensure that the movie stops playing if the Express Install dialog box appears, all you need to do is call a static method in this class on frame 1 of the root timeline of your Flash movie. Because the ExpressInstall class sits inside one of the paths in our movie's classpath (see Chapter 2), we can just reference the object as follows:

```
  if (ExpressInstall.init()) {
      stop();
  }
```

This simple code just tells the current movie to stop if Express Install has started on your machine by returning a Boolean value. You can see that we've added this in frame 1 of the root timeline of the movie and then moved the actions and movie clips that were

13

originally on frame 1 over to frame 2. It is suggested that you leave frame 1 completely for this task alone to ensure that someone running Flash Player 6.0.65 can view the first frame of the movie, and thus will see the upgrade dialog box.

Amazingly, those are all the changes needed to embed our previous chapter's solution into an HTML page that handles browsers with any (or no) versions of Flash gracefully!

Summary

As you've seen, you have several alternatives for embedding your Flash application into a web page. The automatically published HTML code coming from your Flash development environment is not the optimal choice. (In all fairness, the others were all developed to enhance the limitations of the default HTML method, so naturally it would be the least capable.)

This and the previous ten chapters have covered an assortment of web usability topics and shown you ways to design very usable Flash applications. Our hope is that you've gained some new insight and ideas about how to tackle usability given the current capabilities of Flash and ActionScript 2.0. We've said that programming is an iterative process that often involves some reconsiderations of code after you've built the underlying functionality. This concept applies to usability as well.

In a few years, when the Flash version number has hit double digits and the latest enhancements to ActionScript surface, some of the solutions and implementations you've seen here may seem fairly outdated. However, we hope that what stays fresh and everlasting is the usability thought process. How you approach application design and development is often just as important as how you implement it.

In Part 3, we'll step away from covering the specifics of building solutions to talk a bit more about the Flash usability thought process, and then show you a full-featured application that harnesses many of the concepts we've explored so far!

PART THREE **PUTTING THE PIECES TOGETHER**

14 PLANNING FOR USABILITY

In Part 2, we described ways to create viable solutions to common usability problems in Flash. In each chapter, we described a particular issue, designed a solution, and then implemented the solution. What was left out of the equation is how any of these design decisions are made in the first place.

In this chapter, we'll discuss how and where usability fits within the design process. Think of this as a primer for how to organize and prepare for creating a usable Flash application. This chapter will cover how you and your team members should implement a process for usability. Here's what we'll cover in this chapter:

- Your goals for Flash usability
- The new usability paradigm for rich Internet applications
- Members of a crack usability team
- Preparation for the development phase
- Guidelines for usability testing

Setting the bar for Flash usability

Recall our definition of usability in Chapter 1 of this book:

> *Usability measures how intuitive, efficient, and pleasurable the experience of using a Flash application is, as well as how effective the application is in achieving a user's end goals.*

The goal of any web application is to provide a service to an interested user. The user has come looking for that service, and it's in your best interest to deliver it by the most efficient means possible. However, as you've seen throughout this book, that doesn't mean you should stop designing with innovation in mind.

If innovative design played no part in a consumer's experience, you would have no outlet to improve existing techniques or methodologies. Think of a world without sports cars or Xboxes; the Model-T Ford and Atari 2600 console would still be doing a dandy job! That's what we view as the differentiator between rich Internet applications (RIAs) and traditional websites: RIAs provide a richer, more pleasurable online experience than traditional applications, while still being usable for the consumer.

Conversely, if traditional expectations and predictability had no part in design, it's possible that the modern day sports car wouldn't even have a steering wheel, if the designer decided at some point it no longer fit visually with the design of the interior! The point is you should observe certain standards when developing new web applications. For example, a clearly defined navigation menu is essential for the average website. Moreover, using familiar iconography, such as a shopping cart icon or an envelope icon indicating an e-mail contact, enhances usability.

Knowing where and when you should feel free to explore and take liberties in design becomes paramount to *innovative usability*. As they say, there's no reason to reinvent the wheel, but feel free to make it faster! The solutions you saw in Part 2 try to balance familiarity with innovation.

The past few years in Internet development have seen RIAs explode on the scene. These applications have both extended and challenged the bounds of web usability. From the Ford Motor Company's online car configuration application (www.fordvehicles.com), shown in Figure 14-1, to Google Maps (http://maps.google.com), to more experimental applications like the NewsMap news aggregator (www.marumushi.com/apps/newsmap/newsmap.cfm), shown in Figure 14-2, the boundaries between innovative design and usable functionality have gotten increasingly fuzzy.

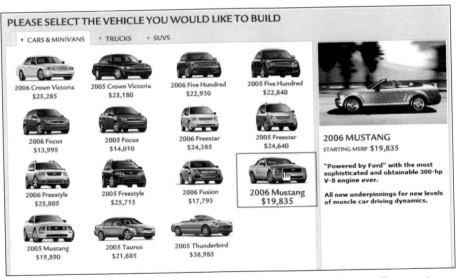

Figure 14-1. The Ford Motor Company's Flash-based car configuration application allows you to customize and purchase a car online.

14

Figure 14-2. An experimental Flash news aggregator correlating the importance of news items to their size

So what can you do to ensure that a user can quickly grasp the use of an application, while at the same time continue to make advancements with the user experience?

The answer lies in the phases of planning and discussion that occur before you ever even open Flash and start developing your application. So let's explore the challenges that Flash and RIAs in general have introduced to the usability world and the new usability standards evolving as we speak.

RIA usability: a new paradigm

Since the dawn of the Internet, HTML has been the primary method of delivering web applications. Most web usability methods are naturally based on what we will call the *page paradigm*. The page paradigm is nothing more than the process of explaining a user's experience in terms of the pages he must view before accomplishing his task.

For example, imagine an HTML application that allows you to configure and order a car (an HTML version of Ford's car configuration application, for example). To accomplish your task, you must first visit the homepage, click through to the models page, select a model, then proceed to the configuration page, where you will be led through a series of subpages to put together the car of your dreams.

But as Flash applications and other RIA technologies like Ajax gain popularity, it's becoming more difficult to describe a user's workflow in terms of the page views necessary to accomplish a task. It's far more relevant to describe RIA experiences in terms of interactions and states. We call this the *interaction paradigm*, a more applicable approach to describing a user's experience in terms of interactions made to accomplish a task. We don't mean to imply that the slate has been wiped clean of pages, only that there is a lot more activity that can happen on one page that just doesn't fit with the old way we thought of web applications.

Consider the drag-and-drop solution in Chapter 6 if it were integrated into a real bookstore application. To explain how a user views and orders a book, you would need to describe how the user has interacted with the book thumbnail items and the resulting state changes to the application. For instance, you might say, "Jane drags and releases a book item over the shopping cart, which initiates a change to the state of the cart," rather than, "Jane clicks on a book item, which leads to the shopping cart page." Another interaction might be similar but with a very different result: "Jane drags and releases a book item over an empty space, which causes the book item to fade back to its original position and no other state change to occur." There wouldn't even be a comparative interaction in a normal HTML application.

Another good way to think about RIAs is to compare them to different types of desktop applications. HTML is like a "widget" or "wizard" application—a page-based application providing a limited set of tools and a linear workflow. An RIA, on the other hand, is more like Adobe Photoshop—an application with a complex user interface and many controls to allow for the richer, customizable interactions that certain tasks require.

Recognizing the challenges that RIAs have posed to traditional usability and understanding the need to describe their interactions in a different manner, when and how does usability planning happen? Let's take a peek into what it takes to successfully design for usability and optimize the user experience, beginning with the usability team members.

The usability team members

Key players compose a good usability team. Each team member requires not just expertise in the specific tasks related to the job, but also a good understanding of the roles and assignments of the other team members.

14

Here are the usability team members:

- **Experience planners:** These are usually the first ones to get their hands on a project after thorough market analysis, financial expectations, and the like are solidified by the management team. Their primary role is information architecture—determining and organizing all of the use cases of an application into an efficient flow of states and pages. Over the past few years, this job has grown more into an application mastermind who interfaces with clients and addresses their marketing concerns and goals in terms of application experience (thus the title!). They translate their findings into documents (for example, interaction models, wireframes, and application maps), which the visual designers can use to begin to make art and the technical architect can use to begin structuring the application. We discuss these various documents in the following section.

- **Technical architects:** These translate the experience planner's documents into technical objectives (logic diagrams, UML, and so on), so that developers have a road map to guide them through the coding process. They manage the development team and address clients during the development phase. They're integral in deciding which software platforms will be used to best fit the needs of the application and generally have a broad knowledge of most web technologies.

- **Visual designers:** Often divided into *art directors* and *screen designers*, visual designers turn the experience objectives into an engaging and intuitive user interface design. Visual designers need to design for each state of an application, while considering the marketing and identity goals of the project. The successful designer will foresee and accommodate certain scenarios unrecognized by the experience planner, and often will work as a production artist with the development team to break out the design into visual assets that can be incorporated into the final application.

- **Flash developers:** Before development even starts, Flash developers have their hands full! While architects lead the development from a high level, developers are the ones actually doing the coding. The successful developer shouldn't just be able to write code, but have the ability to write code that's scalable and reusable within the application, as well as document it in a manner that other developers can easily understand. Flash developers also often find themselves playing the role of interaction designers.

- **Interaction designers:** Somewhere in between the experience planners, visual designers, and Flash developers lies a handyman who ensures that the solution is well designed purely from the viewpoint of the interactions between the user and the application. They often will start where the visual designer leaves off and complete tasks such as state transitions and rollovers. The need for this middleman has grown exponentially over the past few years because planning for RIA development has many more caveats than planning for traditional web applications.

Of course, if you're doing a project by yourself or with just a few people, you may not have the resources to fill all of these positions. It's a situation you've probably been in before. As an independent contractor, you'll often fill more than one, if not all, of these roles!

Preparing for development

Whether you're working as part of a team or taking on the task all by yourself, preparing for development is almost as critical as the development itself. We find that rushing into projects without clearly defined objectives leads to poorer usability. Before you even begin delegating the work (or doing the work yourself), consider the following preparatory steps. Usability thinking plays an integral role in each of them.

Defining the application's purpose

First, you must define the purpose your Flash application serves for its future users. Is it a shopping tool to help a buyer find the best price, or an online help desk for software support? If this definition doesn't make crystal-clear sense in a couple of sentences, consider refining it by chopping out the extra noise that clutters the perceived goal of the application. Think of this as defining a thesis for your web project. In the end, if a visitor can spend a few moments on the site and state something similar to this thesis, then you've succeeded!

Creating an application map

When you've firmly defined what you will be building, begin creating an *application map*. This is a chart that lists all of the project's sections and subsections. This map should be the grounds for you to define your primary navigation items, as well as the secondary, tertiary, and so forth sections. An application that is clearly organized in such "buckets" makes it easier for the user to navigate. This stage also helps you define a budget for the project, by giving you a road map to just how many things will be a part of the application and how long each portion will take to develop.

Figure 14-3 shows a generic map for an application. Notice how each major step is documented as a column and how it creates an organized navigational workflow.

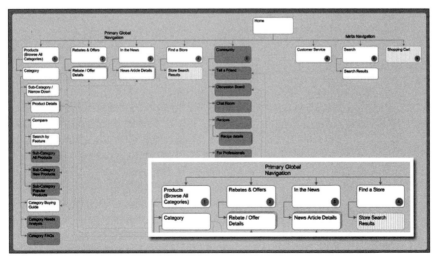

Figure 14-3. A sample application map with inset

14

Exploring interactions through interaction models

When you've defined the goals and the different sections of your application, it's time to explore all of the ways a user will be able to accomplish her goals by sketching out *interaction models*. An interaction model describes all of the states of an application and what results occur when a user "does something." Models typically consist of several logic flowcharts showing which routes users may take and what logic leads them down each path.

An example of an interaction model is shown in Figure 14-4. In the flowchart, the rectangles represent an application's state or result of a user decision, and the diamonds indicate a user decision.

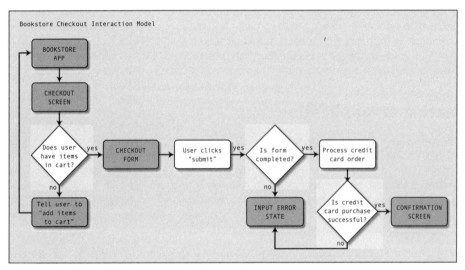

Figure 14-4. A sample interaction model for a bookstore application checkout scenario

Designing wireframes for the application states

After defining the interaction models, it's time to get into the real specifics of what sorts of interface elements will be in the application. Based on the application map and interaction models, design a *wireframe* for each state of the application. Each wireframe defines the elements that need to be present to allow the user to accomplish her goals for that portion of the application. These are the blueprints a visual designer must work from, so all the important elements should be documented thoroughly here.

Figure 14-5 shows an example of a wireframe for a hypothetical website.

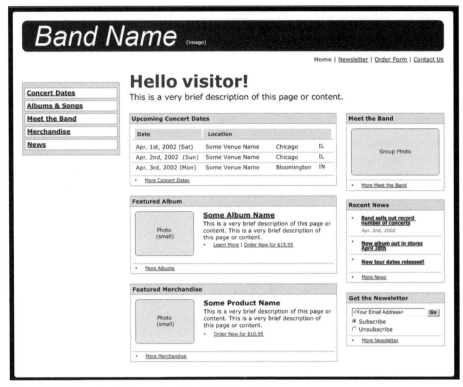

Figure 14-5. A sample wireframe for a hypothetical website

When you have these phases completed, you will automatically be steps ahead of the game. Issues that you may not have foreseen expose themselves before you encounter them during development.

Another important process that should begin during the preparation phase and continue throughout development (and beyond!) is usability testing. Let's take a look at just what this involves.

Usability testing

Usability testing is the process of observing and evaluating the ability of a user to accomplish specific tasks with a web application. It's often the most useful reality check in each phase of a project, as it gives insightful, firsthand evidence of whether things are in good shape or in need of rethinking based on feedback from users.

14

While a formal usability testing phase performed by usability experts is a great complement to a project, it's often more feasible (and easier on smaller budgets) to make smaller, more ad hoc tests at specific points in a project to ensure that no major roadblocks pass under the radar.

> A fantastic resource for usability testing (and much inspiration for this chapter) is a book called Don't Make Me Think: A Common Sense Approach to Web Usability (New Riders Press, ISBN: 0-32134-475-8), by a very well-spoken author named Steven Krug. It's a very insightful primer for web usability in general and offers some smart guidelines for usability testing.

Testing is meant to help your application become more usable, not to be a giant pat on your shoulder. Take criticism as an invitation to make your application more successful. Bear in mind that it's not yet public. This is your chance to iron out those kinks before the masses notice them.

The phases of usability testing

It's important to test early, and test often, so that your project is always closely aligned to the expectations and desires of the user. Let's look at the phases of the project where you'll find it most useful to test with users.

Concept/experience design

As you are defining the goals of the application, this is also the time when you should try out the concept on some test subjects. Give them some conceptual text to read describing the application's purpose. Then devise a series of questions to ask them about the proposed experience. What do they like about it? What's useful or would be useful in addition to your concept? After all, usability isn't just about how the application works, but whether it's a useful one in the first place!

You may find that users will come up with ideas that your team hasn't thought of yet. The concept may trigger users to reference experiences with similar applications and potential pitfalls of your idea. The goal of this test is to refine your statement of purpose and objectives for the application.

Screenshot design

Show printed designs of a few major states of the application to your testers once the design is underway. Show them what the application's initial state and a few top-level navigation links will look like. Ask them to describe how certain elements on the page make them feel. What is good or bad about the page hierarchy and color schemes? Is the copy readable? Provide them with some tasks that would take place on a screen. Would they be able to guess how these tasks are accomplished?

The objectives here are to settle on the overall look and feel of the application and decide whether the general interaction design decisions you've made are headed in the right direction. Addressing the major problem spots now will save dozens of hours of design changes later.

Prototyping

Build a simple prototype of the application—no frills, no whistles. Simple screens with hard-coded data and canned responses for certain tasks will do the trick. The objective here is to have the users follow specific paths in hopes of them reaching a goal. Unless animation is integral to the usability, you can leave out these types of details.

The prototyping phase of usability testing will guide further design decisions, as well as give interactive designers a good start. Along with the information you've obtained from screenshot design testing, you can now complete the predevelopment documentation phase and begin actually building your application!

In theory, a well-executed series of usability testing should provide enough information to complete the application. But, if you've ever worked on any complex project, you know bumps in the road will occur along the way. From unforeseen issues with code development to design problems that went under the radar in the prototyping phase, diverging slightly off track from your timeline and end deliverables is all part of the game. That's why it's just as important to provide usability testing during and after development, as discussed next.

Beta release

This version of the application is close to final and works on most levels with a few known bugs or functional deficiencies. The application should now be about 90 percent programmed and functional, albeit not optimized for public release.

The previous three usability tests should have provided you the input necessary to be fairly certain that your application is ready for prime time. Still, some problems may arise, and it's worth the extra effort of a beta release to be sure that you launch a stable product to the market. Test the beta version of the site with users to see if they can still accomplish the tasks outlined in the previous usability tests.

Public release

Launching your application to the public is always a satisfying step in the development process. But, even though the project has launched and hopefully gained some momentum in the public, your job isn't over yet. Keep an eye on everyone you see using the site, and if the budget allows, do one more complete phase of testing. If your client is happy with the end product, you'll likely be doing facelifts and new versions of the application in the future, so keep documenting usability issues for that second round of fun!

14

Testing materials

Getting together a usability testing environment is pretty simple and requires only a few common resources.

Of course, you'll need testing subjects for your tests. For each iteration of the testing you're planning on doing, we suggest having three or four people test your materials. Whether it's commenting on color schemes or clicking through your beta release, you'll need fresh eyes each step of the way. These people will ideally represent the entire spectrum of your target user base.

For example, a car configuration application should be tested on users of all driving ages, young and old. A more specific application, say a patient-tracking system in a hospital, should be tested on doctors, nurses, and staff members who are familiar with the process and potential problem areas of tracking the status of patients. Having a computer engineer, or someone unfamiliar with the goals of the application, test the system might lead to feedback that could actually hurt the usability of the application.

For more general applications that you typically find on the Web, these test subjects can be friends, family, or a random group of willing participants, as long as they have no prior knowledge or preconceptions of the project.

Along with your subjects, here are the ingredients you need for the perfect usability recipe each time you do a round of testing:

- **Documented task scripts:** The experience planner should write a document containing detailed lists of tasks that the test users should perform. These tasks will give you a much better understanding of whether your application is satisfying the end goals of your target audience. This document will take different shapes over the different phases of testing, but each item will contain a description of the task, an area to give a grade (alpha-based, A through F) based on the ease of the user to accomplish the task, and plenty of room for comments.

- **Supervisor:** The supervisor's job is to go through the documented tasks with each of the testing subjects. This person should be someone who has no emotional attachment or bias toward the project (despite being on the budget!) and can write detailed notes and comments regarding how the users approached each task.

- **Video camera:** The only person in the room with the test subject should be the supervisor. All others will be able to view the usability tests either live or via a recorded session. If you can, set up a video camera facing the monitor so you have a record of how the user interacts with the application. This is helpful not only to document the testing process for later review on other projects, but also to give the rest of your team insight into how a typical user actually reacts when using the application.

- **Office space:** Finally, you should have a spare office or space set up with a desk, comfortable chair, computer, and Internet connection. This space should be somewhat quarantined from the surrounding activities of a typical workplace to keep the test subject focused on the task at hand and not distracted by other people in your office.

Summary

Usability planning is one of the most valuable tools for a project. This is where the important decisions are made regarding what the user experience will be and how it can be fine-tuned into a veritable racehorse of usability and efficiency.

In the real world, you might often find that usability planning is reduced (or even worse, omitted) from a project due to time constraints or unexpected shifts in the functional specifications of an application. When it comes down to it, things first must function before they can function well, and sometimes there's only time given for things to just function! That's why we believe it's critical to plan for usability from the outset of the project.

Needless to say, the revising of an application never really ends, which is why we're already on the eighth version of Macromedia Flash! No application can ever be perfect. The goals of usability planning are to get as close as you can.

In our next chapter, we will put together all of the solutions in Part 2 to create one integrated solution! Let's see how well we planned for creating that perfectly usable application.

14

Alas, we've come to the very last chapter of our little book about Flash usability. We hope that the past 14 chapters have made you think about developing Flash applications with a new perspective. We also anticipate that you haven't agreed with everything we've said. If you have an objection to a coding approach, a line of thought, or any other subjective statement we've made in this book, that's good! It means you've thought of a better way to solve a particular usability problem. Usability design needs this kind of constant argument from all angles of development to be both progressive and innovative.

However, that's not to say we won't put up a good fight and defend what we've written in the previous chapters! In this final chapter, we will synthesize many of the solutions discussed previously into a complete, usable Flash application. Think of this chapter as a final exam for our solutions—an exam we hope we'll pass with flying colors before graduating from Flash University (and prove that we're not just a party school).

You may have noticed a theme with many of the solutions in Part 2. A whole bunch of them revolved around the concept of an online bookstore using some friends of ED book titles. It shouldn't come as a huge surprise then that our final project will be to create a friends of ED bookstore with the kinds of usability enhancements you saw earlier.

Our Book Shopper application can be found at www.userenabled.com. First, let us assure you that this is a demo only—feel at ease to use the demo as often as you wish, with the knowledge that you aren't really going to be purchasing 500 copies of *Podcast Solutions* and absolutely no information you share will be stored anywhere on the server! Second, we recommend that you give the application a few trial runs before you continue with this chapter, so that you develop your own unbiased opinions of it.

We'll spend the bulk of this chapter analyzing the bookstore from the user's perspective, stepping through a typical user's workflow, so you can see how all the usability enhancements combine to aid the user experience. At the end, we'll summarize the solutions used in the application.

Here's what we'll cover in this chapter:

- Navigation through the bookstore application
- Where each solution fits into the usable bookstore application

Navigating through the application

When you first arrive at www.userenabled.com, you are presented with a clean interface with a clear objective: to browse and potentially purchase (OK, pretend to purchase) some informative books by friends of ED publishers. Our statement of purpose for the application is clear and simple.

> *The purpose of this application is to make the experience of browsing and potentially purchasing books an efficient and enjoyable process.*

Arriving at the Book Shopper

Before you even begin your book shopping experience, we've done a few things to optimize the delivery of the application. First, we've made accommodations for users who do not have the version of Flash Player this application requires (Flash Player 8). For those of you with Flash Player version 6.0.65 or higher, you should see a prompt within the player that will let you install Flash Player 8 without having to leave our site. Otherwise, you will see some HTML directions that will lead you to the Flash Player download site.

In addition, we've built the application to be flexible on all browser sizes. Whether you are using an 800×600 screen or one of those monster 1920×1200 screens, the bookstore should take full advantage of your screen real estate. Notice how the application adjusts as you expand or contract your browser. Figure 15-1 shows the opening screen.

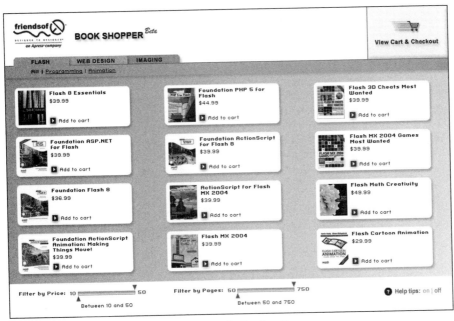

Figure 15-1. Our completed Flash bookstore application in action

Finding help

If you begin using the bookstore and find an area of the application that looks unfamiliar to you, you can use the help tip feature by clicking the on button in the lower-right corner of the application. In designing this application, we assumed that its average users are more technically advanced than average Internet users (given that they are here to buy a book on a particular technical subject), so we've defaulted the help to off, with the anticipation that it won't be used frequently.

15

If you have turned the help on, you can use the mouse cursor to roll over and get additional information about each different element of the application. For instance, roll over the shopping cart area on the upper-right side of the screen with the help turned on to reveal its help tip, as shown in Figure 15-2.

Figure 15-2. Using help tips to provide better support for newer users

Selecting a category of books

The first thing you probably want to do when looking for books is head to a category of interest. Technical book consumers know a good deal about the kinds of books they are interested in before they even step through the door. As Flash-o-philes, we head right for the Flash section on the computer book shelves at the local bookshop. Likewise, HTML enthusiasts will be looking for books on web standards, CSS, and so forth.

As shown in Figure 15-3, we section off the entire friends of ED catalog into major categories, represented as selection tabs across the top of the application (Flash, naturally, is the default section!). Within these categories are more specific subcategory links that allow a more refined level of categorization for our expansive book catalog.

Figure 15-3. Using sensible categories to help customers find the topics they are seeking

When you first click a tab, the catalog displays all of the books within the category, and if necessary, a scrollbar on the right side (based on the height of your browser). You can then sort your selection even further by clicking the text links underneath the tabs.

By the way, as you navigate through the various categories and subcategories, you may want to click your browser's back button to go to the previous section of books. We've enabled the browser back button to do just that.

Filtering the book catalog

The book's topic is essential but probably not the only criterion you'll use to buy a book. Another key consideration about book purchases is the price of the book. Even the most successful web professionals still hunt down the good deals!

The application includes a slider, as shown in Figure 15-4, which allows you to filter the book results to just those that meet your price range. Those book items that no longer match the price range fade out instantly, so you know which items just missed your price range. In addition, we've included another slider that filters books by their page counts, for those of you who want to know how much reading you're getting yourselves into!

Figure 15-4. Using sliders to filter prices and page counts

Learning about books in a category

You can learn about each book in several ways. When you click a book item, the application will load and display a description, product information, and a larger cover image in a pop-up window, as shown in Figure 15-5.

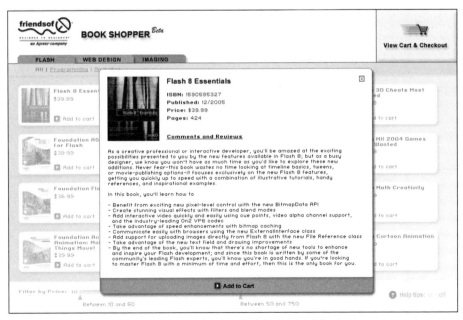

Figure 15-5. The description window provides great insight into each book.

15

An additional, unique feature we've added to the application is a comments and reviews pop-up window. Because books are often purchased based on recommendation, we felt that including this information would be an asset to users.

Click the Comments and Reviews text link within the description panel to pop open a window that includes other people's opinions on the books in your category, as shown in Figure 15-6. You can then filter through the most recent entries by rolling your mouse toward the bottom or top of the listing using mouse-position-based scrolling.

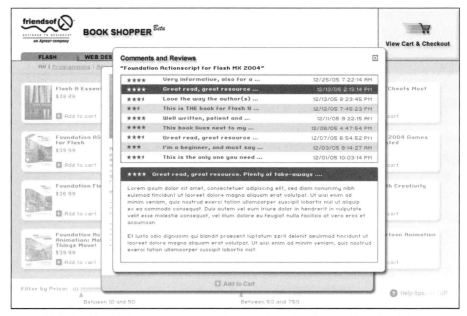

Figure 15-6. The blog window uses mouse-position–based scrolling to cycle through entries.

Adding and modifying items in your cart

Relying on drag-and-drop, the application includes a shopping cart drop area in the upper-left corner. Adding an item to the cart is simply a matter of dropping the item over the panel, or clicking the Add to cart link within a book item.

You can then click the cart itself to bring up a window that shows detailed information about your current purchases, as shown in Figure 15-7. Here, you can use a numeric stepper component to buy multiple copies of the books you've placed in your cart. In addition, you can remove items from the cart by dragging an item from the listing over to the garbage can icon displayed within the pop-up window.

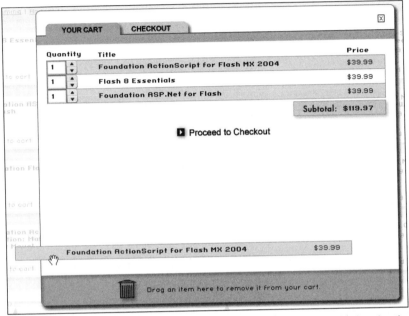

Figure 15-7. The shopping cart detail window allows you to remove items by dragging them over a garbage can icon.

If you accidentally close your browser after adding items to your cart, don't fret—your cart information will be stored automatically for you when you return! This is helpful not just if you closed your browser, but also if you want to take your time searching for the perfect set of books and decide to come back later.

Submitting your billing and shipping information

When you're ready to check out, simply click the Proceed to Checkout button on the bottom of the shopping cart window or the Checkout tab, and you'll be presented with a form, as shown in Figure 15-8. This form provides a quick way to fill in your billing and shipping information by taking advantage of tabbing, auto-scrolling, and on-the-fly validation.

15

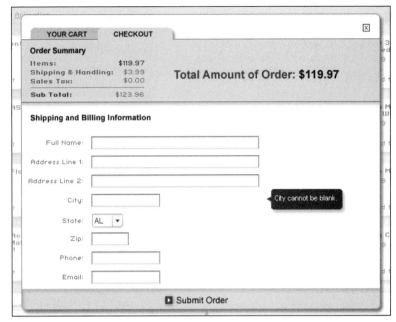

Figure 15-8. The billing and shipping form uses on-the-fly validation for increased efficiency.

Submit the form, and you've just completed your fictitious book purchase!

Synthesizing the usability solutions

Having played around with the bookstore, you've probably found some elements that look all too familiar to you now. That's because we've done our best to incorporate all the different chapter solutions into this final application. It's like a geeky game of Where's Waldo. Can you find all of them? In Table 15-1, we list the different usability solutions that are incorporated into the final solution.

Table 15-1. How the usablity solutions fit into the completed bookstore

Solution	Implementation
Mouse-position–based scrolling	Allows gesture-driven scrolling for book comments and recommendations
Loading progress bar	Used to load the individual book thumbnail images
Drag-and-drop selection	Allows you to drag a book into the shopping cart or into a trash can from within your shopping cart

Solution	Implementation
Data-filtering slider	Lets you filter books in a category by price and page count
Scrolling forms with on-the-fly validation	Allows you to efficiently submit billing and shipping information
State management	Maintains the state of your shopping cart the next time you return
Help tips	Provides easily accessible pop-up tips for the major sections of the application
Enabled browser back/forward button	Allows you to go back and forth between previously selected book categories
Liquid layout	Adjusts the application's interface to any browser size
Embedding Flash using FlashObject	Displays alternative content for users without Flash Player 8, and also includes an implementation of Flash Express Install for users with a player version higher than 6.0.65

Summary

While the sun has set on our little book, it should just be rising for you in your exploration through this boundless medium we call Flash. We sincerely hope you've enjoyed your time reading this book and that it finds a nice spot on your office desk or nightstand. That being said, we would be remiss if we didn't point out some other great pieces of literature.

In Chapter 1, we said that this is neither a book on ActionScript programming nor a book on usability theory; rather, it sits somewhere comfortably in between. The appendix that follows contains our recommendations for reading material that focuses more on one or the other. Just as pairing a great wine with your dinner makes the experience that much better, pairing this book with one (or more) of the books that follow will also give you a much richer experience! So, check out those books and have another great read.

Until then, happy Flashing everyone!

15

APPENDIX **RECOMMENDED READING**

Foundation Flash 8	
Foundation MX Express	
Foundation MX Studio	
Foundation MX Upgrade Essentials	
Foundation MX Video	
Foundation XML for Flash	
New Masters of Flash	
The Flash Usability Guide	
Flash Books	▲

Timeline ⇦ ◣ Scene 1 🖼

- ▣ title
- ▱ info text field
- ▱ range text fields
- ▱ drag handle clips
- ▱ slider range bar

Address 1*	
Address 2	
City*	
State	AL ▼
Zip Code*	
Work Phone*	

As we mention in the introduction, this book is neither a doctrine for usability nor a primer for learning Flash—it's somewhere in between. We hope that in reading our chapters, you are both invigorated to consider how to make your Flash projects more usable and eager to harness the true power of ActionScript 2.0 (AS2) code.

That being said, we wanted to use this appendix to provide you with a summer reading list of sorts. Many great books and websites help you focus in on usability, Flash, and the mix of the two. Here some of our own personal favorites.

ActionScript 2.0 (and OOP) programming

This book is not just about how to make pleasurable web interfaces. A whole lot of code goes into making these solutions work. Sprinkled with our discussions on usability are some helpful tips on making your code reusable and scalable through using object-oriented programming (OOP) techniques.

The truly advanced Flash developer needs a thorough knowledge of OOP to really benefit from (and enjoy) the advantages AS2 programming has to offer. The following are some books we consider to be absolutely essential reference guides to have near your computer.

- *ActionScript 2.0 Language Reference for Macromedia Flash 8* by Francis Cheng, Jen deHaan, Robert C. Dixon, Shimul Rahim (Macromedia Press, 2006): This book provides the most thorough print documentation we've seen on the AS2 language, with understandable explanations of pretty much every Flash method, object, and property. You'll find it an invaluable resource when you need that refresher on a particular object. Coming in at over 1,000 pages and 2 inches thick, it also makes a great paperweight or seat booster!

- *Essential ActionScript 2.0* by Colin Moock (O'Reilly, 2004): This book is broken into three parts: an overview of AS2, application development strategies, and how to use design patterns with Flash. Even if you're a well-seasoned Flash developer, the introduction to design patterns is a must-read! It will give you a real flavor of the incredible power and flexibility of AS2 and OOP.

- *The Object-Oriented Thought Process (2nd Edition)* by Matt Weisfeld (Sams, 2003): This is a very solid, easy-to-read book on basic object-oriented concepts. If you're new to OOP and haven't yet taken advantage of AS2, this book will get you up to speed on key concepts and methodologies. It's also a great refresher and reference guide if you've forgotten anything along the way. As the book title suggests, this book makes you see the world in an object-oriented way.

In addition, watch for the following friends of ED books coming out in the very near future. These make great companions to the code discussions we have in this book!

- *Foundation ActionScript for Flash 8* by Kris Besley, Eric Dolecki, and Sham Bhangal: The ultimate beginner's book for learning how to use ActionScript in Flash 8, this book explores all the fundamentals you'll need, as well as the new features Flash 8 has to offer. It expands on some of the new Flash 8 features we discuss in this book (such as filters and new font-rendering capabilities).

- *Object-Oriented ActionScript for Flash 8* by Peter Elst, Sas Jacobs, and Todd Yard: This book is all you'll need if you want an up-to-date guide to coding object-oriented applications in Flash 8. It covers OOP basics, design patterns, custom component frameworks, and more.

Usability design

We recommend the following books for information about usability design:

- *About Face 2.0: The Essentials of Interaction Design* by Alan Cooper and Robert M. Reimann (Wiley, 2003): Cooper, author of *The Inmates Are Running the Asylum,* is the founder and chairman of Cooper, an interaction design company, as well as the "father" of Visual Basic. This book takes a very refreshing look at software design (both on the Internet and the desktop) and introduces you to goal-directed design. If you're looking for a serious study in usability and interaction design, this is the book for you!

- *Don't Make Me Think: A Common Sense Approach to Web Usability (2nd Edition)* by Steve Krug (New Riders, 2005): Usability is often discussed in a dry, deliberate, plodding manner. It doesn't have to be this way! Case in point: Steve Krug's second edition in the *Don't Make Me Think* series of usability books. Krug approaches usability in a humorous way, uncovering the myths and facts about how people use the Web.

- *Homepage Usability: 50 Websites Deconstructed* by Jakob Nielsen and Marie Tahir (New Riders, 2001): This book specifically examines the usability of website home-pages. It offers a number of specific tips on improving a homepage, and then deconstructs 50 different website homepages. One interesting approach they use is to break down the screen real estate of each home page to determine how much of your page is dedicated to different user tasks. This book will give you a very visual lesson in homepage, and website, usability.

- *Making the Web Work: Designing Effective Web Applications* by Bob Baxley (New Riders, 2002): If you're looking for a comprehensive discussion on web application design, this book is a great place to begin. It has a good mix of material on information architecture, usability engineering, and web design.

Flash usability (historical)

One of the reasons we felt compelled to write a book on Flash usability is that there hasn't been one on the market in the past few years (at least not since AS2 was released). Why this came to be is anyone's guess. Perhaps the initial interest in discussing Flash usability has lost some momentum in recent years. We hope we'll be the ones to revive it!

The following are a few "historical" books on Flash usability that gave us great inspiration for the book you hold in your hands right now. While some of the technical approaches and feature discussions are somewhat outdated, they are still worth reading, as they provide a ton of useful information on usability best practices that are just as relevant today as they were a few years ago.

- *Flash 99% Good: A Guide to Macromedia Flash Usability* by Kevin Airgid and Stephanie Reindel (Osborne/McGraw-Hill, 2002): The title of this book is a bit tongue-in-cheek. In 2000, usability guru Jakob Nielsen proclaimed Flash to be "99% bad" based on the prevalence of unusable Flash sites. This book seeks to repudiate Nielsen's claims by offering sage advice on Flash usability. Included are interviews with Flash developers and designers, as well as several real-world case studies.

- *Skip Intro: Flash Usability and Interface Design* by Duncan McAlester and Michelangelo Capraro (New Riders, 2002): This book was probably the first true code-heavy Flash usability book to hit the market. McAlester and Capraro approach usability without sacrificing innovation. Some of the solutions found in the book your holding (such as help tips and gesture-driven scrolling) are also found in *Skip Intro*, though the implementation there is geared toward Flash MX.

- *The Flash Usability Guide: Interacting with Flash MX* by Chris MacGregor, Crystal Waters, David Doull, Bob Regan, Andrew Kirkpatrick, and Peter Pinch (friends of ED, 2003): This guide talks about design principles, conventions, and methods that are critical to successful usability projects in Flash. This book goes more into the thought process of usability engineering rather than specific solutions.

Web resources

The following are some Web resources we recommend:

- www.actionscript.org: Actionscript.org is a good site for Flash tutorials, job postings, and news.

- www.digital-web.com: If you're into reading articles on a wide range of web design issues (or even want to contribute your own), *Digital Web Magazine* is a great site to keep up-to-date on the state of the Web.

- http://blog.deconcept.com/flashobject: *Deconcept: FlashObject* contains a full explanation of the FlashObject embed method that we discuss (and highly recommend) in Chapter 13 of this book.

- http://livedocs.macromedia.com/flash/8/index.html: Flash 8 LiveDocs is a great resource for AS2 language reference, samples, and tutorials

- www.flash99good.com: Flash 99% Good is Kevin Airgid's (coauthor of *Flash 99% Good*) website, which was revamped in the fall of 2005. It provides great links and ideas about Flash usability.

- www.useit.com/papers: Jakob Nielsen, perhaps the most well-known web usability supporter, writes a host of articles worth reading at Useit.com.

INDEX

A

About Face 2.0 (Cooper and Reimann), 111
ActionScript
  directory structure, 15
  features, 4
  Flash Player and, 8
  navigation menus, 51–62
  recommended reading, 310
  shopping cart solution, 121
  usability benefits, 4
ActionScript Settings window, 15
addDropArea method, 130, 135
addEventListener method, 179
addFormElement method, 190–192
addListener method, 100
adjustable layouts. *See* liquid layouts
Ajax, 8, 229
alert boxes (JavaScript), 166, 170–171
Alert component (Flash), 171
alpha property
  content loading and, 79, 91, 102
  data filtering example, 160
  movie clips, 50
  shopping cart solution, 119, 133
  Tween object and, 34–35
alphaTween property, 217
alt attribute (HTML), 210
Amazon.com, 112, 250
anchor tags
  browser history solution, 238, 243–244
  hyperlinks and, 20
  Internet Explorer and, 230
Anti-alias for readability option, 254
APIs, 83
application maps, 291
applications
  Book Shopper, 300–307
  building skip intro feature, 202
  defining purpose, 291
  form validation, 165–167
  liquid layout, 248, 252–267

remembering state, 198, 203
RIAs, 10–11, 286–289
usability testing, 294–295
wireframes for states, 292–293
asynchronous processing, 6, 8, 69
attachButtonItems method, 123, 126
attachDragItem method, 128–129
attachMovie method, 33, 191
audio clip loader
  building audio player, 77–82
  laying out features, 75–76
  Model-View design pattern, 82–96
audio players, 77–82
AudioFileLoader.as class
  building loader model, 84–89
  building loader view, 89–95

B

back button
  browsers, 228
  Flash history solution, 230–242
  Flash issues, 228–230
bandwidth, content loading and, 68
beta releases of applications, 295
billing and shipping information, Book
    Shopper, 305
Blur X property, 49
Blur Y property, 49
book item button clip, 23, 30–32, 34
book item buttons, 203–204
book selection system
  browser history solution, 241
  creating movie clip, 32
  linking classes to movie clip, 23
  state management example, 203
Book Shopper application, 300–307
BookItemButton class
  browser history solution, 241
  creating, 23, 33–36
  state management example, 204
BookSelectionSystem class, 23, 37–38

friendsofed.com/forums

Join the friends of ED forums to find out more about our books, discover useful technology tips and tricks, or get a helping hand on a challenging project. *Designer to Designer*™ is what it's all about—our community sharing ideas and inspiring each other. In the friends of ED forums, you'll find a wide range of topics to discuss, so look around, find a forum, and dive right in!

■ **Books and Information**

Chat about friends of ED books, gossip about the community, or even tell us some bad jokes!

■ **Flash**

Discuss design issues, ActionScript, dynamic content, and video and sound.

■ **Web Design**

From front-end frustrations to back-end blight, share your problems and your knowledge here.

■ **Site Check**

Show off your work or get new ideas.

■ **Digital Imagery**

Create eye candy with Photoshop, Fireworks, Illustrator, and FreeHand.

■ **ArchivED**

Browse through an archive of old questions and answers.

HOW TO PARTICIPATE

Go to the friends of ED forums at **www.friendsofed.com/forums**.

1-59059-543-2 $39.99 [US]

1-59059-518-1 $49.99 [US]

1-59059-542-4 $36.99 [US]

1-59059-517-3 $39.99 [US]

1-59059-533-5 $34.9

EXPERIENCE THE
DESIGNER TO DESIGNER™
DIFFERENCE

1-59059-306-5 $34.99 [US]

1-59059-238-7 $24.99 [US]

1-59059-149-6 $24.9

1-59059-262-X $49.99 [US]

1-59059-224-7 $39.99 [US]

1-59059-221-2 $39.99 [US]

1-59059-236-0 $39.99 [US]

1-59059-372-3 $39.99

1-59059-304-9 $49.99 [US]

1-59059-355-3 $39.99 [US]

1-59059-409-6 $39.99 [US]

1-59059-314-6 $59.99 [US]

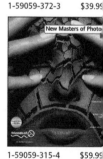

1-59059-315-4 $59.9

1-59059-231-X $39.99 [US]

1-59059-408-8 $34.99 [US]

1-59059-428-2 $39.99 [US]

1-59059-381-2 $29.99 [US]

1-59059-554-8 $xx.99